A Garland Series

RENAISSANCE DRAMA

A COLLECTION OF
CRITICAL EDITIONS

edited by
STEPHEN ORGEL
The Johns Hopkins University

The Valiant Scot
by J.W.
A Critical Edition

GEORGE F. BYERS

GARLAND PUBLISHING, INC.
NEW YORK & LONDON • 1980

All volumes in this series are printed on
acid-free, 250-year-life paper.

Library of Congress Cataloging in Publication Data

Main entry under title:

The Valiant Scot, by J. W.

(Renaissance drama)
Bibliography: p.
Includes index.
I. W., J., gent.   II. Byers, George F., 1937–
III. Series.
PR2411.V3   1980   822'.3   79-54332
ISBN 0-8240-4451-7

TABLE OF CONTENTS

INTRODUCTION

I. THE TEXT OF 1637

The <u>Valiant</u> <u>Scot</u> was entered in the Stationers'
Register on April 26, 1637 to "Master Waterson." The form
of the entry is as follows:

> Entred for his Copie vnder the hands of Master
> Thomas Herbert deputy to Sir Henry Herbert and
> Master Downes warden a Tragedy called <u>the</u>
> <u>Valiant</u> <u>Scott</u> . . . vj^d.[1]

The quarto appeared in the same year, printed by Thomas
Harper, published and sold by John Waterson. The authorship was credited on the title page to J. W., Gent/leman7.

Very few references to the play in its own century are
recorded. It is listed in the 1640 drama collection
compiled by Humphrey Moseley[2] and in the drama catalogues
of Rogers and Ley (<u>c</u>. 1655 or 1656),[3] Edward Archer (1656),[4]
and Francis Kirkman (1661).[5] Five quotations from the play
appear in John Cotgrave's <u>English</u> <u>Treasury</u> <u>of</u> <u>Wit</u> <u>and</u>
<u>Language</u>, a collection of commonplaces from notable dramas

---

[1]Edward Arber, ed., <u>A</u> <u>Transcript</u> <u>of</u> <u>the</u> <u>Registers</u> <u>of</u>
<u>the</u> <u>Company</u> <u>of</u> <u>Stationers</u> <u>of</u> <u>London</u>: <u>1554-1640</u> (London:
Priv. Printed, 1877), IV, 356.

[2]W. W. Greg, <u>A</u> <u>Bibliography</u> <u>of</u> <u>the</u> <u>English</u> <u>Printed</u>
<u>Drama</u> <u>to</u> <u>the</u> <u>Restoration</u>, Illustrated Monographs of the
Bibliographical Society, No. 24 (London: The Bibliographical
Society, 1957), III, 1318.

[3]Greg, III, 1326.

[4]Greg, III, 1337.

[5]Greg, III, 1352.

of the seventeenth century.[6] The only mention of a
performance of the play is the five-day run recorded in a
puritan pamphlet, <u>Vox</u> <u>Borealis</u>, <u>or</u> <u>the</u> <u>Northern</u> <u>Discoverie</u>
(1641) and reprinted the following year in <u>A</u> <u>Second</u>
<u>Discoverie</u> <u>by</u> <u>the</u> <u>Northern</u> <u>Scout</u>.[7]

Numerous copies of the 1637 edition of <u>The</u> <u>Valiant</u>
<u>Scot</u> are extant. Using the Trinity College, Cambridge,
copy as copy-text, I have collated twenty copies. Below
are listed the locations of the copies, the abbreviations
by which they will be referred to in the "List of Accidentals," and the nature of the collation, whether by eye or
by Hinman collator:

Ashley Collection (British Museum)	Ash	Hin
Bodleian Library, Oxford	Bod	Hin
Boston Public Library	Bos	Hin
British Museum (162 e. 17)	BM^a	Hin
British Museum (643 c. 44)	BM^b	Hin
Chapin Library (Williams College)	Cha	Hin
Columbia University Library	Col	Eye
Dyce Collection (Victoria and Albert Museum, London)	Dyce	Hin
Folger Library	Fol^a	Hin
Folger Library	Fol^b	Eye
Houghton Library, Harvard University	Hou	Hin
Henry E. Huntington Library	Hunt	Hin
University of Illinois Library	Ill	Eye-Hin
Library of Congress	LC	Hin
Newberry Library	New	Hin
University of Pennsylvania Library	Pa	Eye
University of Texas Library	Tex	Hin
Trinity College Library, Cambridge	Q	Hin
Worcester College Library, Oxford	Wor	Hin
Yale University Library	Yale	Hin

[6]Gerald E. Bentley, "John Cotgrave's 'English
Treasury of Wit and Language,' <u>SP</u>, 40 (1943), 198.

[7]Gerald E. Bentley, <u>The</u> <u>Jacobean</u> <u>and</u> <u>Caroline</u> <u>Stage</u>
(Oxford: Clarendon Press, 1941-1968), V, 1235.

Most of the collation was done with reproductions, either Xerox copies or "xerographic prints" made from microfilms. However, original copies were consulted in the cases of those at the University of Pennsylvania and the University of Illinois. The Illinois copy was collated once in reproduction on the Hinman collator, but as a final check the original text was collated again by eye against the completed edition. Besides the twenty copies of the play compared for this edition, five other copies were located but not examined. These are at the University of Arizona (Tucson), Eton College, Chetham Library (Manchester), Glasgow University, and the Norwich Public Library.

The collation of The Valiant Scot is as follows: Quarto, A-K^4 (eight full sheets).

[A 1] Title page: THE / VALIANT / SCOT. / By J. W. Gent. / [Ornament] / [rule] / L O N D O N, / Printed by Thomas Harper for John Waterson, and are / to be sold at his shop in Pauls Church-yard, / at the signe of the Crown. / 1 6 3 7.

[A 1^v] Blank

A 2   Dedication: [Ornament] / "To the right Honorable James, Mar- / quesse Hamilton, Earle of Cambridge / Arran, Lord of Even, Emner- / dale and Arbroth, Master of the / Horse to his Majesty, Steward of the Ho- / nour of Hampton Court, Gentleman of / the Kings Bed-chamber, and Knight of / the most noble Order of

6

the Garter, / and one of his Majesties Privie /

Councell in both King- / domes." (seven lines of text

following the salutation: "Right Honorable").

/A 2V/ Conclusion of dedicatory epistle signed

"Your Lordships most humble / servant and Souldier, /

William Bowyer."

A 3 Ornament / Beginning of the text of the play (five

acts in verse and prose).

/K 4/ Conclusion of the text of the play ending with

"F I N I S."

/K 4V/ Blank

The Valiant Scot contains forty leaves. In the A

gathering, as was customary, the title-page is not signed;

otherwise, each gathering is signed on the first three

recto pages, the fourth being left blank (B, B2, B3), which

conforms to the standard practice of signing one over half.

The gatherings are regularly signed through K, J being

omitted as was normal practice.[8]

A running-title, "The Valiant Scot.", appears through-

out the text (A 3^V through K 4). The various sets of

running-titles were initially identified by eye through

distinguishable variations of broken and bent letters and

through the interchanging of regular and swash italic

capital letters. A further examination on the Hinman

---

[8] Ronald B. McKerrow, An Introduction to Bibliography
for Literary Students (1927; Oxford: Clarendon Press,
1967), p. 80.

collator positively identified minute differences in the
spacing and shape of the letters of the separate titles.
An analysis of the arrangement of the running-titles
indicates that three skeletons were used in the printing
process as there are three distinct sets of running-titles
that were transferred from forme to forme. In normal two-
skeleton printing two groups of running-titles appear
alternately in a predictable position--one group of titles
transferred from inner forme to inner forme, and the other
group correspondingly transferred from outer to outer forme.
This is not the case in <u>The</u> <u>Valiant</u> <u>Scot</u>, where we find
remarkable variety in the patterns of recurrence. I
tabulate below the running-titles as they occur in the ten
gatherings of the quarto. Upper-case letters indicate the
gathering; lower-case letters distinguish the different
individual settings. The asterisk indicates a page without
a title. Also indicated are the groups into which the
running-titles fall: Group I (edab-deba); Group II (gfhc-
fgch); and Group III (ijkl).

	Inner Forme (1^V, 2, 3^V, 4)	Outer Forme (1, 2^V, 3, 4^V)
A	* * a b ⎤	* * * c ⎤ anomalous version of -Group II
B	e d a b ⎬ -Group I	d e b a ⎤
C	e d a b ⎦	d e b a ⎦ -Group I
D	g f h c ⎦ -Group II	f g c h ⎤
E	e d a b ⎤	f g c h ⎬ -Group II
F	e d a b ⎦ -Group I	f g c h ⎦

8

	Inner Forme (1^v, 2, 3^v, 4)		Outer Forme (1, 2^v, 3, 4^v)	
G	g f h c	-Group II	i j k l	-Group III
H	g f h c		i j k l	
I	e d a b	-Group I	i j k l	
K	e d a b		f g c *	-Group II

From this table it can be seen that gatherings B, C, and D were set by the inefficient process of stripping and recomposing the same skeleton, which presumably would have forced the compositor to seek work on other projects while the skeleton was in the press. Gatherings E and F were then printed by regular alternation between two skeletons. The process slowed again as the outer forme of F was stripped and recomposed to the inner forme of G, which then alternated regularly through H with another skeleton revealed by a third set of running-titles. In the I gathering the second skeleton (f g c h) is replaced by the first (d e b a), which had been kept intact through the intervening printings. In gathering K, the third skeleton (i j k l) was replaced by the second in the outer forme.

This arrangement must have been inefficient in terms of both the compositor's time and the equipment involved. Not only was the compositor unemployed much of the time as mentioned above, but an extra skeleton was standing idle throughout much of the process. It will be noted that running-title "c", used in the outer forme of gathering A, appears in a different position in the inner forme of

gathering D. The forme, broken down except for the single
usable running-title, had been standing idle while skeleton
No. 1 (d e b a) was used to set both formes of gatherings
E and C. This latter skeleton was then set aside through
gathering D, to be employed again in gatherings E and F.
Once more, it was set aside through G and H, to be re-
employed in I and K.

We may trust Thomas Harper's printing shop to arrange
its printing operations as productively as possible; therefore, perhaps, an outside cause may account for this unusual
printing procedure. Fleay points out that 1637 was a
plague year in which the theaters were closed, with the
exception of one week, until October.[9] The number of items
listed for Thomas Harper in the Short-Title Catalogue
shrank from the twenty-one of 1634 and 1635 to sixteen in
1637. Death, disease, or the common flight from the city
in plague time may have decreased the number of workmen
available to operate the Harper printshop. If the compositor were forced occasionally to help operate the press to
run off his own settings, the single-skeleton printing of
many of the gatherings could be explained. If this were
the case, the compositor would naturally strip down and
reset the skeleton at hand, turning to another skeleton

---

[9]Frederick G. Fleay, A Chronological History of the
London Stage, Burt Franklin Bibliography and Reference
Series, No. 51 (1890; New York: Burt Franklin, 1965), p. 340.
See also Bentley, Jacobean and Caroline Stage, II, 661-665.

only when not needed at the press. In the event that there
was no one to help him in the shop (the presswork was
normally a two-man job), the compositor would go on to a
third skeleton lying idle because of the lack of workmen.
At times when the regular press crew could be made up, he
could proceed in normal two-skeleton order. Thus the
exigencies of a plague-decimated printshop may account for
the awkward pattern of composition as the workmen switched
off at the various tasks to keep the work flowing steadily.

An examination of the spelling of common words ("do,
go, here") indicates no evidence that more than one compositor worked on The Valiant Scot. There is some variation
in the abbreviations of the speech-headings; for example,
pages $F2^V$-F4 abbreviate "Ieffrey" as "Ie." instead of the
"Ief." that is usual elsewhere. However, "Ie." occurs in
the midst of an extended dialogue between Sir Jeffrey and
Bolt. "Bolt is normally abbreviated "Bo." throughout the
quarto; thus the anomalous abbreviation "Ie." may be
explained as conforming to the pattern of "Bo." Other
anomalies in abbreviations are not so explainable; but they
do not appear by gatherings, or even by pages, and spelling
evidence fails to substantiate a division of the play into
the settings of different compositors.

Catchwords appear at the foot of every page of the
play, except for $\lfloor G \ 1^V \rfloor$ and $\lfloor H \ 1^V \rfloor$, where there is a chance
of confusion since one page ends and the next begins with

11

stage directions. An obviously misspelled catchword on
⟦C 1ᵛ⟧, "Blwon," indicates the probability that proofreading was perfunctory or nonexistent.

The text is fairly clearly printed for the period.
Misprints are not common and there are few cases of slipped,
twisted, or turned type. There are a number of cases of
blotted letters and, perhaps the most serious problem,
there are numerous instances of lightly or unevenly inked
letters. Many letters, however, that are only partly
visible in some copies of the play may be verified by comparison with other copies in which they are clear.

My collation has turned up no significant variation in
any of the twenty copies examined. There appears to have
been no correction of proof during the printing of these
copies. Printing errors that did emerge during the working
off of the book, such as the twisting of a letter on ⟦F 1ᵛ⟧
or the dropping of two pieces of type on ⟦K 3⟧, were
permitted to remain through the end of the run. The
presence of a few very obvious errors, such as the above-
mentioned misspelling of the catchword "Blown," indicate
the lack of attention to proofreading at any stage in the
printing. This being the case, the general accuracy and
clarity of the text is remarkable.

There remain a few instances of confusion or error
which appear to derive from the parent text. This seems to
be the case with the improperly assigned speech heading of

12

I.ii.52. As I argue in the commentary on that line, it is
doubtful if a compositor would give to both Coming and
Mentith a line which belongs to one or to both of the
Gallants. A compositor might drop a speech heading, as in
V.iv.8 and V.iv.42, but he would hardly attribute a speech
to _two_ characters, especially as there are few other cases
of a double speech heading in the play. Likewise, a couple
of speeches which seem out of place in the sequence of
ideas may be blamed on a defective text. This may be the
case with I.iv.100-101 where Grimsby would appear to
represent "messengers" of the previous line. There is also
at least one case of an incomplete line (IV.ii.69) which is
cut off after two words of address.

I have relined substantial portions of the verse in
the present edition. All individual speeches are set as
separate lines in Q, even when short speeches clearly form
segments of an iambic pentameter verse. For example,

Have ye yet spoke?

<u>Mountford</u>.   We have.

<u>Wallace</u>.   Then we begin,
                                        (II.iii.70)

is set in Q as three separate lines of prose. Although
lines have been adjusted when the verse seems to call for
it, no attempt has been made to force all the speeches into
a regular pattern. Particularly in moments of extreme
activity the metric regularity gives way to swift exchanges
of prose discourse. Q includes a number of passages in

13

which verse is treated as prose and _vice versa_. Such
passages are especially prevalent in scenes in which the
comic characters Sir Jeffrey and Bolt come into contact
with figures from the main plot. The two modes of speech
are confused despite the clear distinction of rhythm, tone,
and subject matter.

The Valiant Scot was printed by Thomas Harper for the
stationer John Waterson.[10] It was presumably Waterson who
received the manuscript from William Bowyer, arranged with
Harper for the printing, and then sold the copies "at his
shop in Pauls Church-yard, at the signe of the Crowne."
Waterson, from the third generation of a prominent family
of stationers, became something of a specialist in the
publication of drama. He published twelve plays, including
four printed by Thomas Harper: Sir William Davenant's The
Just Italian (1630), Philip Massinger's The Emperor of the
East (1632), The Valiant Scot, and John Fletcher's Monsieur
Thomas (1639). J. W., the author of our play, was in
exalted company, for among the other playwrights published
by Waterson are Ben Jonson (The Staple of News, 1626) and
William Shakespeare and John Fletcher (The Two Noble Kins-
men, 1634). Plomer reports that Waterson is thought to

----

[10]See the biographical sketch on Harper and Waterson
in John Linton Carver, "The Valiant Scot by J. W.," Studies
in English Drama, 1st series, ed. Allison Gaw, Univ. of
Pennsylvania Series in Philology and Literature, 14
(Philadelphia: Univ. of Pennsylvania, 1917), pp. 87-92.

have abandoned his business in 1641.[11] The timing may be
significant as showing Waterson's unwillingness or in-
ability to maintain "business as usual" under Parliamentary
rule during the Civil War. His great interest in the publication of drama or, possibly, his connections with the
theater may have influenced his retirement when the
theaters closed.

The printer Thomas Harper definitely had his troubles
with the Puritan authorities. "For printing pamphlets
against the Parliament," he found himself in trouble early
in the War.[12] Harper was a leading stationer and printer
from 1614 until his death in 1656. Unlike John Waterson,
he was concerned only marginally with the printing of plays,
religious works making up his largest category by far.
However, he was involved, both as printer and as publisher,
in many works important to dramatic history. Beside those
items mentioned above printed for John Waterson, Harper
printed Thomas Middleton's Michaelmas Terme (1630), and The
Phoenix (1630), Shakespeare's The Merry Wives of Windsor
(1630), George Chapman's The Warres of Pompey and Caesar
(1631) and Ben Jonson's The New Inne (1631), to mention
some of the more important. Harper's interest in the

---

[11]Henry R. Plomer, A Dictionary of the Booksellers and
Printers Who Were at Work in England, Scotland, and Ireland
from 1641 to 1667 (London: The Bibliographical Society,
1907), p. 187.

[12]Plomer, p. 91.

theater continued into his old age, for he contributed a
large sum, £275, to a project of Sir William Davenant's to
build a "New Theater" in 1656. The scheme soon fell
through, and the stockholders took the matter to court in
an effort to recover their investment, but Harper must have
been represented by his heir, for his death took place less
than a month after the project had been initiated. It
could not have been Harper himself who was amusingly represented as the "city Dun" in one stanza of a contemporary
ballad on the affair:

> But city Dun disturb'd him then,
>   And cries, Discharge your debt sir,
> But he reply'd with cap in hand,
>   I beg your patience yet sir.[13]

There is no external evidence as to the nature of the
manuscript from which the play was printed. William Bowyer,
in his Dedication, describes the play as "what I have"--the
vaguest of clues in the search for details of provenance or
the attempt to learn the state of the manuscript. It is
from internal evidence alone that we must deduce the nature
of the document which the compositor set. I have already
indicated that the compositor seems to have produced a text
that is fairly accurate typographically. Beside the errors
I have already ascribed to the manuscript itself, there are
a few readings that require emendation, and a still larger
number that are questionable. At least one extended

---

[13]Leslie Hotson, The Commonwealth and Restoration
Stage (1928; New York: Russell & Russell, 1962), p. 142.

16

passage is so confused that it has defied absolute reconstruction (V.iv.42-46). It is hard to imagine any competent compositor setting such a text from a "fair copy." Whatever the nature of the manuscript, whether "foul papers" (the author's rough draft before an acting copy could be taken from it) or prompt copy designed for direct use in the theater, the manuscript which the compositor had before him must have presented difficulties of interpretation.

To penetrate further into the actual nature of the manuscript, we must examine such features as the stage directions and the speech headings, which would probably reflect theatrical use of the manuscript, if any. However, it is possible that much of the evidence may already be excised from the text as superfluous for the reader's understanding by a compositor interested in saving space. E. A. J. Honigmann's examination of Shakespeare's "stability" shows that the compositors took liberties with the stage directions of their manuscripts, both excluding some descriptive directions and expanding indicators of action as they saw fit.[14] However, the directions of The Valiant Scot are sufficiently full to give us some insight into the purposes for which the manuscript must have been used.

We note immediately the richness of the play in off-stage sounds and music, most of the effects being carefully

---

[14]E. A. J. Honigmann, The Stability of Shakespeare's Text (London: Edward Arnold, 1965), pp. 114-115.

preserved in the directions. In the battle scenes, we find the conventional <u>Alarum</u> (II.ii.0.1; IV.iii.17.1); in the ceremonial scenes, we find <u>Trumpet</u> (II.iii.50.1) and <u>Flourish</u> (V.iv.131.1). The armies are led on with <u>Drums</u> <u>and</u> <u>Colours</u> (IV.i.0.1; IV.ii.0.2-3). Absent, however, is any direction for the drum in several instances where the text clearly calls for it:

<u>Wallace</u>. Sound Drums and drown their cries.
(II.iii.12)

<u>Grimsby</u>. Hark! How their friendly drums
Chide them for loytring.
(II.iii.159-160)

<u>Beaumont</u>. What further he intends,
Harke their Drum tels. Here my Commission ends.
<u>Clifford</u>. Lets send him commendations too, beat ours.
(II.iv.250-252)

<u>General</u>. To councell, beat a Drum.
(IV.i.4)

<u>Grimsby</u>. A Drum! Call a Drum.
(V.ii.67)

The sound effects may be so obvious in these cases that the author felt there was no need to indicate them, or else the compositor may have dropped them in the interest of economy. But still we should expect to find each sound effect carefully indicated in a manuscript that was used for prompt copy; the fact that so many drum indications are missing is some evidence that the text was not set from prompt copy.

Off-stage shouts are continually used to expand the action beyond the visible stage. As Wallace and the Scots flee after the duel in which Young Selby is killed, for

18

instance, the cry "Murder! Murder!" is raised off-stage
(I.iii.0.1). Such effects often follow exits or precede
entrances. Before Wallace enters to Sir Jeffrey and Bolt
in the seashore scene, his off-stage calls spark an
exchange:

> Wallace. /from within7 Wa ho ro sol fa, sol fa.
> Bolt. Harke.
> Jeffrey. Peace Bolt.
> Bolt. Nay peace you, good Sir Jeffery, peace, peace.
> Wallace. Sol la, sol la sol la sol la.
> Bolt. Some Faulconer's teaching his Hawke pricksong.
>   Shall I mocke him in's owne key?
> Jeffrey. Do.
> Bolt. Sol fa sol fa, here boy.
>
> (III.i.95-103)

The grimmest use of off-stage effects occurs when Wallace's
foot-boy is murdered before Wallace's own capture. The
off-stage cry, "Helpe, murder!" is the only representation
of that treacherous act (V.iii.11.1).

The properties used in the performance of the play are
as unevenly mentioned as are the sound effects. Most
properties are carefully indicated, but other obviously
necessary ones are omitted. The most visible property used
but not referred to in the stage directions is the table at
which the English governors sit at the opening of the play.
When Wallace enters, he "takes his place" at the "solemne
meeting" and is immediately reproved in terms that seem to
indicate that the players are indeed grouped around a table:

> Selby. Presumptuous Groom, this is a seat for Eagles,
>   And not for Haggards.
>
> (I.1.34-35)

Other examples of properties not mentioned in the directions

19

yet obviously displayed onstage are the "head" of Sebastian
(II.iii.129.2) and the halter which Selby calls a "key" to
end his life (III.1.188). On the other hand, stage directions indicate such properties as Wallace's "stumps"
(II.iv.0.2), Sir Jeffrey's trunk (III.i.0.1), Haslerig's
apples and Wallace's sticks, straw, and flints (III.i.282.2;
III.ii.0.1-2).

Some of the details mentioned in the directions lie
closer to the concerns of the costumer than those of the
property man. The blue caps which designate the soldiers
of the Scottish army are mentioned (IV.i.0.3), as well as
the tattered state of Bolt's squad (II.iv.64.1). Other
similar designations are: "Wallace all bloudy" (II.iii.0.1);
"Selby miserably poore" (III.i.185.1); "Haslerig, poore as
th'other" (III.i.282.1).

The details of stage traffic are sometimes unclear.
The great majority of entrances are indicated by a simple
"Enter . . . ." However, during the great battle scene in
Act IV, where Mentith is brought onstage immediately after
a messenger departs to the English headquarters, the direction is specific: "Enter Mentith at another door." Again,
in scene ii of Act II, where there is a simultaneous
entrance by two groups from different doors, the direction
seems to be cut short:

    Enter Haslerig one way; Selby and
    Sir Jeffrey with Friar, Old Wallace, and
    Peggie /enter another way/.

20

The outstanding case of an entrance not designated in the directions is perhaps the most interesting from the viewpoint of theatrics. During the battle in Act IV Wallace stands disengaged, refusing to fight, on a hill to the rear of the action. Our indication of his presence is given by an exchange between Edward and Bruce during a brief respite in the battle:

> King. Stay, Bruce, what's yonder on the hill?
> Bruce. They are Collors.
> King. Why do they mangle thus their Armies limbes?
>   What's that so farre off?
> Bruce.   Sure 'tis the Reare,
>   Where burns the black brand kindles all this fire,
>   I meane the Traytor Wallace.
>   (IV.ii.59-64)

Wallace, a flag bearer, and an extra or two have climbed to the upper stage or gallery where they view the battle. Wallace's entrance is not designated, but his position is made clear when Mentith enters to beg his aid for the suffering Scottish army:

> Mentith. For honours sake come downe, and save thy
>   Countrey.
>
> Wallace. Why then descend amaine.
>   (IV.iii.24-31)

J. W., here, makes use of the "above" to gain the elevation Wallace would have if he viewed the battle from an actual hill. This shows full use of the facilities of the Elizabethan stage, but the stage directions do not reflect the staging of the scene.

An examination of the handling of names in the stage directions reveal some interesting points. The order of

21

the listing shows typical arrangement by rank, but it also reveals management of the dramatic situation. The designation for I.iv is:

<u>Enter</u> King Edward, Elinor, Percy, Beaumont, Grimsby, Prince, Sebastian, Bruce.

Bruce enters last, as is fitting for a character separated from the others by his disaffection (he is being refused the crown of Scotland by Edward). Throughout the play he will stand apart, torn between his sworn fealty to Edward and his natural loyalty to his homeland. Sebastian, too, enters late, out of the order of rank. He will appear out of rank in Act II, disguised as a common follower in an embassy to Wallace which will lead to tragedy both for himself and, ultimately, for Wallace. The Prince seems to be out of the order of rank, also, but he may be a "ghost" or mute character like Hereford in V.iv.46.3. He does not speak and is not mentioned thereafter in the play. He may represent a role left over from an earlier authorial intention, or he may be a surplus character cut from the acting version of the manuscript. The characters in this stage direction, then, fall into two groups: those who enter according to their place in the English court, and those who enter late, perhaps out of step or lagging behind. The arrangement seems to bear dramatic significance.

There is also a curious indecision about the number of characters on stage in certain stage directions. In one case it may be that we glimpse the author making up his

mind on the number of characters as he writes. In I.i,
Selby enters with "other gallants" to help guard
Peggie. When the Gallants re-enter later in the scene,
they are spoken of as "2 Gallants." In the opening direction of I.iii they are "the two Gallants." The author
seems to be feeling out the number of characters he will
need: having written speaking parts for the first Gallant
and second Gallant, he decides that only two are required.
Somewhat different is the case of the opening direction to
Act II, where Grimsby enters with "two or three followers."
Here the number of characters is left to the discretion of
the theater bookkeeper, who would know how many extras were
available to fill out the scene. As the characters do not
speak, there is no need for the author to specify the
number of Grimsby's followers.

One bit of evidence to indicate that the text has not
been carefully prepared for production is the confusion of
Grimsby and Graham in IV.iii. At this point one section of
the Scottish army including Grimsby is encircled by the
English in a counterattack that ends in the death of all
the trapped Scots. Not only is the death of Grimsby described in action, it is spelled out in the stage directions
(IV.iii.35.3-4). However, Grimsby appears alive again in
V.ii. In both of these two scenes, Grimsby speaks and is
addressed by name, so it is clear that the mistake is not a
passing slip by the compositor. An examination of the

source of the battle scene, Hary's <u>Wallace</u> (XI.392-395), indicates that the actual Scottish friend of Wallace killed at Falkirk was Graham. The importance of this confusion for our purposes is that it indicates an authorial manuscript, for no bookkeeper would allow such a major contradiction to stand in a text intended for use in a production.

The stage directions and speech headings, then, provide some evidence that the manuscript derives from the playwright himself. We have seen that the stage directions include "ghost" characters, that they are silent in some cases where one would expect explicit testimony, and that an important character is resurrected in the act following his death on stage. Though the evidence is not absolutely conclusive, it seems reasonable to infer that the manuscript from which the play was printed was never used in the playhouse. E. K. Chambers supposes that the normal procedure in producing plays was to revise the author's draft for theatrical purposes:

> There is, indeed, little direct evidence, one way or other; but what there is points to the conclusion that the 'original' or standard copy of a play kept in the play-house was the author's autograph manuscript, endorsed with the license of the Master of the Revels for performance, and marked by the bookkeeper or for his use with indications of cuts and the like, and with stage-directions for exits and entrances and the disposition of properties, supplementary to those which the author had furnished.[15]

---

[15]E. K. Chambers, <u>The Elizabethan Stage</u> (1923; Oxford: Clarendon Press, 1951), III, 193.

The manuscript from which The Valiant Scot was set had never passed through this process of revision. If the play was staged before the date of the printing, another copy of the play must have been used by the actors.

The manuscript may have gone through one further process, at least as far as stage directions were concerned. This was the "correction" or simplification of the copy by the compositor as he cut out extraneous matter in order to abbreviate the printing job. The only evidence we have on this matter is the fact that the text of the play seems fairly coherent and unified. It appears that the compositor respected the lines of the play proper and that the substance of the manuscript passed through his hands without drastic changes.

II.   THE PRESENT EDITION

Only once since the original 1637 edition has The
Valiant Scot been edited--in a 1905 dissertation by John
Linton Carver at the University of Pennsylvania. R. L.
Widman of the University of Pennsylvania Department of
English informs me that this edition has disappeared:

> Professor Baugh has suggested that the edition of
> 1905 possibly was in manuscript and hence has not
> survived transference to the library archives
> from the Graduate School or has not been put into
> the library at all. It is highly unlikely that
> the thesis was prepared from any copy-text other
> than the extant copy of 1637 in our Rare Book
> Room.[16]

Such an edition, prepared according to nineteenth-century
notions of copy-text and attempting to reconstruct a single
copy of the work, would be sadly inadequate by modern
standards.

The present edition provides The Valiant Scot with a
complete editorial treatment designed to make the play
accessible to students of Renaissance drama. Following the
models of F. T. Bowers' definitive editions, The Dramatic
Works of Thomas Dekker and The Works of Beaumont and
Fletcher, I have established my critical, old spelling
text, basing it (as outlined above) on a full collation of
twenty copies of the 1637 edition. Generally I follow the

---

[16]Letter dated 2 April 1969.

style of my copy-text, especially in regard to spelling, capitalization, and the use of italics; these may preserve at least some of the orthographical habits of the author. I have silently regularized the division of words, except in those cases in which the sense may be affected by a re-adjustment of the word division. With regard to the punctuation, I have had to make many changes in order to clarify obscurities. I have not attempted to make the punctuation conform to modern practice in all cases, but have felt free to emend the original rhetorical punctuation for the sake of sense and clarity. Thus, many of the commas which make up practically all the marks within speeches have been replaced by semi-colons or full stops. A certain freedom in the treatment of punctuation seems justifiable, for it is this feature of early texts that possesses the least authority, and usually owes more to the compositor or printing house than to the author.[17] However, all changes in punctuation, as well as those in the other accidental features of the text, have been recorded in an appendix entitled Emendations of Accidentals.

Also included in the Emendations of Accidentals is the dash introduced into the text in order to indicate comple-tion of an aside in a continuous speech. The direction /Aside7 is placed at the head of a speech which is not

---

[17]Fredson Bowers, Textual and Literary Criticism Cambridge Univ. Press, 1959), p. 126.

generally addressed to the body of actors on stage. In speeches which shift from _aside_ to regular discourse, the dash indicates the point at which the transition occurs.

The stage directions of my edition follow the conventions of the period, being set in italics except for the proper names. The directions have been silently normalized in spelling and punctuation. Entrances and more elaborate directions are centered throughout, while exits are placed at the right margin. Stage directions have been emended or added as seems necessary to clarify the action; all additions are placed in square brackets. Substantive emendations have been defended in the notes. Those few directions which appear in the margins of the 1637 quarto have been centered in this edition so as to be consistent with the others, but such changes of placement are also listed among the _Emendations of Accidentals_. Q was printed with act, but not scene, divisions. I have supplied scene divisions, following the rule that a new scene begins at the point where the stage is cleared of living characters. At the ends of I.ii, II.ii, and III.i, bodies are left on stage to be discovered in the following scene. In these cases, I have noted the presence of the bodies in the annotations and have indicated a new scene. The act and scene divisions are given in Latin, conforming to the example of Q (e.g., "_Actus_ I").

Speech headings have silently been made consistent

with the most common form of the name appearing in $\underline{Q}$, and spelled out fully. The name of Wallace's wife is spelled Peggie, despite our usual modern spelling of this common name. Within the text, however, the spelling of $\underline{Q}$ is followed in names as well as in other words, without regard for consistency. I have silently modernized archaic letter usages in the text--i for j, u for v and v for u--and replaced ornamental letters with conventional type. The long f is replaced by modern s in all cases. Abbreviations, including the tilde, have been expanded and the spacing of contractions regularized. Running-titles, catchwords, and signatures have been eliminated.

My apparatus, which is designed to clarify the text and present background information useful to a serious student of the play, has been modeled after that in Professor Charles R. Forker's edition of James Shirley's The Cardinal (Bloomington, Ind., 1964) and the "Revels Plays" series published by Methuen under the editorship of Clifford Leech. From these models I have taken a practice for numbering the lines of stage directions that are separate from lines of verse. If the line to be indicated appears in a direction initiating a scene, a zero follows the Roman numeral of the scene, followed in turn by the number of the line within the direction, both set off by periods. For example I.ii.0.3 indicates the third line in the direction beginning Scene ii of Act I. In directions within the body

of the scene, numbering is counted from the preceding
spoken line, the number of which replaces the zero of an
initial direction.

My textual footnotes are placed immediately below the
text, separated from the commentary by a rule. These notes
record all substantive emendations of Q. The form of the
footnote consists of the line number, my reading, a square
bracket, and the rejected Q reading. The following example
demonstrates my practice:

31. Some⟩ Save Q.

This note indicates that the term "Some", which appears in
line 31, was originally "Save" in Q. This emendation is
then defended in the commentary.

My running commentary on the text appears below the
textual footnotes at the foot of the page. These notes are
designed to aid the reader in a variety of ways. Difficult
terms are glossed; obscurities in dictation and style are
clarified. This is especially true of the Scots dialect,
much of which is so unfamiliar that virtual translation is
required. As befits a treatment of this semi-anonymous
play, sources and parallels are pointed out to show the
author's familiarity with the work of his dramatic predeces-
sors or his use of commonplace ideas and rhetoric. From
such evidence we learn more about J. W.'s knowledge of the
drama and about the way he approaches the task of composition. In the commentary footnotes, I quote original texts

verbatim and literatum except for the yogh and the long $\int$, which I have silently modernized.

III. THE QUESTION OF AUTHORSHIP

The major unsolved problem in regard to The Valiant
Scot is the question of authorship. The few critical exam-
inations of the play to date have all dealt first with this
question, but none has reached a satisfactory conclusion.
The main difficulty, of course, is the lack of authoritative
external evidence linking the play with a specific writer.
The initials on the title page are scarcely enough to guide
us, especially since they match the initials of the publisher, John Waterson. It may be a coincidence that
Waterson's initials fit the "J. W., Gent/Ieman/" of the
title page, though it is equally possible that Waterson,
either not knowing the actual author or not caring to
mention an obscure figure, had the play printed with his
own initials. That they happened to match those of John
Webster may have been an additional advantage in promoting
a lucrative sale of the quarto.

The play is dedicated to James, first Duke of Hamilton
and second Earl of Cambridge.[18] Hamilton was perhaps the
natural patron for a play on the theme of the unification
of England and Scotland, for after his return from the
Thirty Years' War in 1634 he was Charles I's principal
advisor on Scottish affairs. He held an hereditary

[18]See the biographical account in DNB, VIII, 1063-1067.

influential position, possessed great estates in both England and Scotland, and led the royalist cause in the Scottish Parliament. As a military leader, his career was disastrous. In 1631 he assembled and led to Germany an ill-fated expedition to aid the Protestant forces, at that time commanded by Gustavus Adolphus, in the Thirty Years' War. It is presumably to this expedition that William Bowyer alludes when he styles himself in the dedication to Hamilton "one amongst your meanest followers in your Lordships practicall life of a Souldier." Very little is known about William Bowyer. Carver points to a "Will: Bowyer, Knight" who was admitted Master of Arts at Oxford in 1605.[19] However, it seems unlikely that this Sir William Bowyer (1588-1641) of Knypersley, Staffordshire, Member of Parliament from 1621-1646, would have occasion to serve under Hamilton.[20] His son, William (1614-1637-41?), may possibly have served briefly in Germany before or after his matriculation at Exeter College, the same Oxford college earlier attended by Hamilton. He had been admitted to Gray's Inn in 1632, but disenchantment with legal study may have sparked a military adventure, for Sir William in his will of 1637 very pointedly bequeathed to William his entire

_____

[19]Carver, p. 92, quoting from Anthony Wood, _Fasti Oxonienses_.

[20]Josiah C. Wedgewood, _Staffordshire Parliamentary History_, in _Collections for a History of Staffordshire_ (London: Harrison and Sons, 1920 and 1922), II, part I, 20-21.

library except for his law books. Yet, as the Staffordshire Bowyers were Puritans, and leaned toward Parliament in their political sympathies, it may be doubted whether William would dedicate "the light dressing of a play" to a royal favorite such as Hamilton. Perhaps a stronger candidate is the William Bowyer of Denham, Buckinghamshire, who was admitted to Jesus College, Cambridge, in 1628.[21] That he was created baronet barely six weeks after the Restoration indicates loyalty to the royalist cause. His son befriended John Dryden and helped the poet with technical matters in his translation of Virgil's Georgics.[22] As the association with Dryden suggests both a literary and a royalist tradition in the family, this Sir William Bowyer is perhaps our strongest candidate for the dedicator of The Valiant Scot. However, there is no real evidence for a connection of either the Staffordshire or the Buckinghamshire Bowyers with the theater. Professor R. G. Howarth suggests still a third family of Bowyers:

> The dedicator may have been a brother or cousin of the actor Michael Bowyer (each of whose short-lived infant sons was in succession christened William) and a member of a family whose most prominent representative was William the Keeper of the Tower Records: he died unmarried in 1622. In 1636 or 1637 Michael left Queen Henrietta's Company, then decimated, for the King's Men and may have been in possession of the script of The

[21]John Venn and J. A. Venn, *Alumni Cantabrigienses* (Cambridge: Cambridge Univ. Press, 1922), I, 194.

[22]Kenneth Young, *John Dryden: A Critical Biography* (1954; New York: Russell & Russell, 1969), p. 190.

> *Valiant Scot* owned by the former, which he en-
> trusted to William as the one likeliest to make a
> successful appeal for patronage to an interested
> notable.[23]

Whoever William Bowyer was, it is doubtful that he had a

hand in writing the play, though Friedrich Huch, in a mono-

graph dated 1901, assumes that "William Bowyer" is a

pseudonym for the author whose initials are "J. W."[24] I

tend to agree with Bentley, who reads the phrase in the

Dedication "what I have I bestow upon you" as suggesting

the possessor of a manuscript, rather than its author.[25]

The most forthright attempt to link *The Valiant Scot*

with an actual J. W. is that of Professor R. G. Howarth,

who attributes the play to John Webster. He sees William

Bowyer as the "editor" of this chronicle play which he

believes Webster wrote late in his career under the influ-

ence of Shakespeare's history plays.[26] Howarth's attribu-

tion of the play to Webster is based on impressionistic

evidence which consists primarily of a tragic flavor he

views as particularly Websterian, and of "characteristic

devices or conventions" such as,

> an illustrative Aesopian apologue, reflections on

---

[23]"The Valiant Scot as a Play by John Webster,"
Bulletin of the English Association: South African Branch,
9 (1965), 5.

[24]Ueber das Drama The Valiant Scot (Hamburg: M.
Lekmann, 1901), pp. 1-2.

[25]Bentley, Jacobean and Caroline Stage, V, 1234.

[26]Howarth, pp. 3-8.

> death and on life in relation to it, a requiem,
> ghosts warning of approaching calamity, irony in
> both speech and situation (especially allied with
> anticipations and repetitions, foreshadowings and
> echoes, often in sombre guise), pairing and
> balancing or opposition of characters, rhymed
> couplet "sentences" and clinching statements or
> conclusions (above all at scene-ends), together
> with reflections of other Elizabethan plays.[27]

This is obviously too general a list of characteristics on
which to base a case for Webster. In his common-sense
review of the problems of studies of attribution, Internal
Evidence and Elizabethan Dramatic Authorship, Samuel
Schoenbaum warns against such "canonical impressionism"--
the inclination "to make oversimplified descriptive pro-
nouncements and pass oversimplified value judgments."[28]
Most of Howarth's support for the attribution of The
Valiant Scot to Webster is totally swept away by Schoenbaum's First Principles (especially number seven) for
avoiding disaster in this kind of study: "Intuitions,
convictions, and subjective judgments generally, carry no
weight as evidence."[29] Even the single piece of specific
evidence (other than the initials) produced to link The
Valiant Scot with Webster's canon--the use of the phrase
"letters of mart" at II.iii.104 which appears also in A
Cure for a Cuckold by Webster and William Rowley--proves
valueless upon examination. Not only does use of this

---

[27]Howarth, p. 7.

[28](Evanston: Northwestern Univ. Press), p. 193.

[29]Schoenbaum, p. 178.

phrase go back to the fifteenth century (see _OED_), but it occurs in _A Cure for a Cuckold_ within a scene attributed wholly to Rowley by H. D. Gray and divided between Rowley and Webster by F. L. Lucas.[30] No linguistic parallel can have authority if the work referred to is itself of doubtful authorship.

Still, the possibility that John Webster might be the J. W. of the title page deserves the fullest consideration. To this end, and also for the sake of exploring the nature of the play as fully as possible, we must consider what Professor Howarth calls "the strongest evidence of Webster's hand . . . characteristic devices or uses of convention."[31] Therefore, we shall examine the devices mentioned by Howarth which appear in both _The Valiant Scot_ and in Webster.

The first device mentioned by Professor Howarth is the illustrative Aesopian apologue which shows up in the first scene of _The Valiant Scot_ (lines 106-116). Here Graham dissuades Old Wallace from appealing for aid to King Edward by means of a fable which tells of sheep eaten after their appeal to King Lion. Graham introduces the fable with the words: "I have heard a story." This opening varies from the formula used by Webster to introduce his fables, all of which open in more direct fashion:

---

[30]_The Complete Works of John Webster_, ed. F. L. Lucas (1927; London: Gordian Press, 1966), III, 15. The scene discussed is Act II, scene iv.

[31]Howarth, p. 7.

```
I'll tell you a tale
                           (The White Devil, II.i.335)

I'll tell you a tale
                           (The White Devil, IV.ii.222)

Dost thou know what reputation is?
I'll tell thee
                  (The Duchess of Malfi, III.ii.119-120)

Sad tales befit my woe:  I'll tell you one
                     (The Duchess of Malfi, III.v.124)
```

The closing, as well as the opening of Graham's tale, varies from the formula used by Webster. Unlike Graham, the speaker in the Webster plays makes specific application of the moral of his fable, either through direct reference, such as "Only I will apply it to your wife" (The White Devil, II.i.354), or through the "so" of the simile formula used in the fables of The Duchess of Malfi. Moreover, Graham's tale is shorter and more closely tailored to the dramatic situation than are Webster's apologues. The Aesopian story of the Lion's administration compares, point by point, to King Edward's rule over Scotland through venal officials. Even the "Lambe" stolen by the fox is a conventional image for a young girl and thus fits exactly the case of the abducted Peggie. On the other hand, Webster's fables relate only obliquely to his plays. Though the application usually fits the dramatic situation thematically, the characters and the plots of the fables do not parallel the action of the play very exactly. Thus, Graham's tale is more organic to the context in which it appears than are Webster's fables, which tend to seem digressive.

The second convention mentioned by Professor Howarth as linking The Valiant Scot to Webster consists of "reflections on death and on life in relation to it." Webster's plays reflect a tone of disillusionment with the world and abound in references to death as a final release from a bitter life. To Webster, courage in facing death is the one vital thing in life.[32] The many references to death are so striking that Lucas, in an attempt to correct those who see Webster as obsessed by the subject, reminds us that quotations about "worms in winding-sheets and yews in graves" were commonplace.[33] Webster is distinguished first by the quality of the horrors. Though these are part of the melodramatic machinery of the typical revenge play, Webster amplifies and repeats them until they tend to overpower the Christian moralizing about heavenly reward--the other side of the conventional view of death. Another distinguishing feature which adds to the peculiarly gloomy tone of Webster's plays is bitter satire. In self-conscious fascination, the characters discuss their own situations and the corrupt society in which they struggle. Brooke sees this penetrating satire in every character and in nearly every speech.[34]

---

[32]Works of Webster, I, 39.

[33]Works of Webster, I, 35.

[34]Rupert Brooke, John Webster and the Elizabethan Drama (London: Sidgwick & Jackson, 1916), p. 121.

Both the charnel-house reflections and the satire are
lacking in The Valiant Scot. Despite the great number of
deaths in the Wallace play, death is viewed either as an
opponent to be honorably confronted, or as the door to a
better world. There is little dwelling on the melancholy
and the morbid. Death comes swiftly, through murder or
battle, without the torment that adds so much of the
macabre to Webster's Italianate plays. The characters die
with a prayer on their lips, commending their spirits to
heaven. The play is especially rich in comments of resignation to fate and of trust in providence. Unlike The
White Devil and The Duchess of Malfi, where opportunistic
characters plot and connive "in a mist" for power, wealth,
and pleasure, The Valiant Scot is closely superintended by
a higher power. There is no sense of a malignant universe,
but rather of one in which even the sacrifices which are
necessary to the tragic plot and which result from human
misjudgment are part of a larger movement which culminates
in the Anglo-Scottish union of the conclusion. Likewise
missing from J. W.'s play is the pervasive satire of
Webster's style. Even in scenes of conflict, the characters
generally accept each other at face value and prefer open
abuse to the hidden stabs and acrid cynicism of Webster's
typical exchanges. The passages where satiric comment does
appear--as in the slurs on Peggie's "honesty" by Mentith
(I.v.16-19)--are so few as to stand out from the general

40

texture of the play.

In his linking of the conventions of Webster's dramas with those of The Valiant Scot Professor Howarth seems to me most persuasive when he speaks of "irony in both speech and situation (especially allied with anticipations and repetitions, foreshadowings and echoes, often in sombre guise)." Dramatic irony, of course, is not the unique property of Webster, and in any case there seem to be differences in degree, especially if we take as normative Webster's two major tragedies where the irony is more emphatic and obvious than in The Valiant Scot. However, Webster and the author of The Valiant Scot do share similar forms of irony. Yet, such parallels could be adduced for hundreds of plays, for they stem from a method fundamental to much Elizabethan drama. This method involves the open presentation of dramatic conflict, as opposed to the hidden or cloaked presentation of, say, the Fletcherian school. By openly presenting to the audience all the stages of conflict, the playwright provides the viewer with an ironic perspective, which permits him to compare the limited view that the characters express of their situations with what the viewer himself knows to be the full or "real" view. This method sacrifices effects of surprise, the sudden discoveries that dazzle audiences in Fletcher's dramas, but it has the advantage of allowing for a deeper pattern of significance as the audience increasingly penetrates into the situations and the relations between characters.

The direct or open irony in The Valiant Scot is conventional, yet it does provide some effective drama. A very human, though morbid, touch, similar to Imogen's confusion over the bodies in Cymbeline (IV.ii), is Peggie's running to kiss the fallen Young Selby when her mind leaps naturally to the conclusion that it is her lover, Wallace (I.iii.2-3). Wallace's disguised visit to the English camp in Act III provides for a whole range of ironic effects from his grim jokes about the maimed Glascot and Mountford to his own involvement in Percy's scheme to entrap him. As distinguished from these incidents where the audience is aware of each trick or maneuver, Edward's sudden crowning of Bruce in Act V seems different in kind. The change of heart is not prepared for and so belongs to another order than the effects we have been observing throughout the play. The sudden resolution leaves us unsatisfied. This is not true of those few scenes in Webster's plays where the audience is as surprised by a sudden revelation as are the characters onstage. Flamineo's arising after being "shot" by Vittoria and Zanche in The White Devil (V.ii) surprises the audience as much as it shocks the two women. However, we accept Flamineo's use of uncharged pistols as consistent with his cynical nature and with the atmosphere of treachery and intrigue that defines the ethos of the tragedy.

Professor Howarth lays stress on the irony which arises from the anticipations and echoes in the play. The most notable example of this in The Valiant Scot is the prophetic warning of Friar Gertrid, which is repeated much later in the play by the ghosts of Act V. Four acts are thus darkened by the fatal prophecy so lightly cast aside by Wallace when it is first delivered. A limited but more precise example of this device is the use of the Judas theme in Act V. Clifford's symbolic gift of silver pieces has the effect of impressing upon Bruce how disloyal his fighting for Edward against Scotland has been.

> Clifford.   Oh bitter scorn, with Judas
> I have betray'd my Master, my dear Country,
> And here's the embleme of my treachery,
> To hasten to some tree, and desperate die:
> Twelve sterling silver pence.
>
> (V.i.28-32)

The following scene finds Coming and Mentith plotting to betray Wallace for ten thousand crowns, the significance of which is later pointed out by Clifford: "Damn'd Judas to thy Country-man and friend" (V.iv.74). Both Mentith and Coming immediately reap the punishment of their treason, as they had themselves predicted (V.ii.15-21). Their betraral of Wallace also recalls the prophecy of the Friar and the speeches of the ghosts.

Apart from this device of ironic foreshadowing and echoing, The Valiant Scot shares with Webster's dramas the balancing or opposition of characters. Again we are dealing with patterns common to drama as the playwright

43

seeks to establish an antithesis of forces in the various conflicts of the play. Thus, if Young Selby is aided by two gallants in his attempt to steal away Peggie, he is opposed by Wallace aided by his own two followers. However, this sort of formal balance is so common in Renaissance drama as to be almost useless as an indicator of personal style.

Another device mentioned by Professor Howarth is the requiem--the set piece of mourning. Probably the most famous Websterian example of this elegiac form is Cornelia's song as she sits "winding Marcello's corse" in The White Devil:

> Call for the robin-red-breast and the wren,
> Since o'er shady groves they hover,
> And with leaves and flow'rs do cover
> The friendless bodies of unburied men.
> Call unto his funeral dole
> The ant, the field-mouse, and the mole
> To rear him hillocks, that shall keep him warm,
> And (when gay tombs are robb'd) sustain no harm,--
> But keep the wolf far thence, that's foe to men,
> For with his nails he'll dig them up agen.
> . . . .
> Let holy church receive him duly
> Since he paid the church tithes truly.
> (V.iv.95-108)

It is true that in the call for the robin-redbreast to cover the bodies of the friendless dead and in the fact that the dirge is in rhymed verse Cornelia's dirge does resemble Wallace's last words to his dead enemies, Selby and Haslerig (III.ii.5-13):

> However both did die
> (In love or hate) both shall together lie:
> The Coffin you must sleep in is this Cave,

Whole heaven your winding sheet, all earth your
grave;
The early Lark shall sadly ring your Knell,
Your Dirge be sung by mournfull <u>Philomell</u>.
Instead of flowres and strewing herbs take these,
And what my charity now fails to do,
Poor Robin-redbrest shall. My last adue.

However, the differences are more significant than the
similarities. Even the verse pattern is different, for
Wallace's speech is written in pentameter couplets, while
Cornelia's song opens with an <u>a</u> <u>b</u> <u>b</u> <u>a</u> quatrain and is made
up of both tetrameter and pentameter lines. The signifi-
cant elements in Wallace's dirge point to a different
source. Let me list them that we may deal with them in an
orderly fashion:

(1)   The robin-redbreast is mentioned as the friend to
      the unburied dead.

(2)   Flowers and herbs are mentioned as the proper
      cerements.

(3)   The speech is addressed to the dead themselves.

(4)   The dead are made fellows in the grave despite
      the fact that they were enemies in life.

(5)   The speech expresses an attitude of charity and
      forgiveness.

All of these elements appear in Shakespeare's <u>Cymbeline</u> in
the scene where "Fidele" and Cloten are buried (IV.ii.218-
229; 283-290). Arviragus mentions the robin ("ruddock") as
the sexton to friendless dead (224-229):

The ruddock would
With charitable bill--O bill, sore shaming
Those rich-left heirs that let their fathers lie
Without a monument!--bring thee all this,
Yea, and furred moss besides when flowers are
none,

45

To winter-ground thy corse.

Rather than the "leaves and flow'rs" of Webster's song,
Wallace speaks of covering the bodies with "flowers and
strewing herbs." Shakespeare's lines mention the same
specific coverings:

> Here's a few flowers, but 'bout midnight more.
> The herbs that have on them cold dew o' the night
> Are strewing fitt'st for graves.
> (IV.ii.283-285)

While Cornelia's song is addressed to the mourners,
Wallace's lines are addressed to the dead themselves.
Similarly, Arviragus's first speech of formal mourning is
addressed to his dead friend. Most significant, however,
are the fellowship of the dead and the tone of forgiveness
of the mourners. Wallace does not know that Selby has just
been killed by Haslerig, but he buries them together,
commenting: "However both did die (In love or hate) both
shall together lie." They were his ancient enemies and
had, indeed, murdered his wife and father; yet, in a spirit
of forgiveness Wallace performs the rough rites available
to him and commends the deceased to heaven. The situation
in Cymbeline is an exact parallel. Belarius and his sons
do not know that Cloten had been an enemy to Imogen, whom
they know as "Fidelio," though they do know that Cloten has
abused and attacked them. Despite this, in a spirit
similar to Wallace's, Belarius buries them together in
charity. From these resemblances in theme and tone, it
seems likely to me that the requiem in The Valiant Scot was

46

suggested by the scene in <u>Cymbeline</u> and thus had no necessary connection with the requiem in Webster's <u>The</u> <u>White</u> <u>Devil</u>.

The presence of ghosts who warn of approaching calamity is another element which Professor Howarth sees as linking Webster with J. W. In this case, we will first examine the handling of the ghosts in <u>The</u> <u>Valiant</u> <u>Scot</u>. There are two scenes in which spirits intrude upon the action of the play. Selby, drowsing by the fire in Act III, suddenly starts up with a cry. He explains to Wallace:

> A slumber took me, and me thought old <u>Wallace</u>
> Clapt me upon the shoulder with one hand
> And with the other pointed to his wounds,
> At which I started, spake, but know not what.
> (III.i.264-267)

Before his own death, in a scene similar to the procession of ghosts in Richard III (V.iii), Wallace is visited by the ghosts of his three murdered loved ones, Friar Gertrid, Old Wallace, and Peggie. Though not visible to Grimsby, they are seen by Wallace and by the audience. Speaking in couplets, the ghost of the Friar warns Wallace of three things: that he will die by the third night; that Bruce will be his "bane;" and that Wallace needs to care for his soul. The ghost of Old Wallace passes wordlessly across the stage as Wallace cries out in horror. Peggie's ghost enters last, mourning for Scotland's loss as implied in Wallace's imminent death. She repeats the Friar's warning against Bruce, yet mysteriously adds: "<u>Bruyce</u> sall not

47

hurt thee" (V.ii.120) Like the ghost of King Hamlet in
Shakespeare's play, she exits with a couplet announcing the
approach of morning when spirits must depart, though she
must return to her rest and not to Hamlet's purgatorial
flames.

The ghosts of The Valiant Scot are radically different
from Webster's spirits in The White Devil which, alone
among Webster's plays, utilizes this form of the supernatural. Stoll describes Webster's ghosts as "spectacles":

> Spectacles I call them, for neither of the ghosts
> speaks; the one is frankly nothing more than the
> mental image of his sister, and the other, with
> his pot of lily-flowers and skull, casting earth
> on Flamineo, is little more than a symbol of
> death, a slightly operatic omen of evil.[35]

These silent manifestations, with the emblematic flowers
and skull, do little more than add to the gloomy atmosphere
and prepare for Flamineo's approaching death. The ghosts
of The Valiant Scot represent a reversion to an earlier
technique in that they foretell doom and affect the action.
Wallace's observation of Selby racked by guilty apparitions
causes a change in his intentions. Instead of avenging
himself upon the defenseless Selby, Wallace resolves to
leave revenge to the heavenly powers which so visibly
disturb the murderer. Thus, in this indirect manner, the
invisible spirit troubling Selby acts like the ghost of
Montferrers in Tourneur's The Atheist's Tragedy (II.vi) who

---

[35]E. E. Stoll, John Webster (Cambridge: Harvard
Cooperative Society, 1905), pp. 117-118.

directs the hero to leave revenge to God. The ghosts which
appear in Act V of J. W.'s play, on the other hand, make
little difference in the plot, for Wallace does not change
his plans in response, nor do they reveal any secrets to
the audience. They function mainly in a thematic way,
enforcing the sense that providence seeks to warn man
against unwise acts despite the tragic hero's stubborn
insistance upon following his own will.

Finally, Professor Howarth points out the use of
"rhymed couplet 'sentences' and clinching statements or
conclusions (above all at scene-ends)." On the face of it,
this is a telling point, for one of the most characteristic
devices of both The Valiant Scot and of several of Webster's
works is this very element. Webster's use of the rhymed
couplet, however, is strikingly uneven from play to play.
His first major work, The White Devil, has almost as many
couplets as The Valiant Scot,[36] while his second major
play, The Duchess of Malfi, has about half that number.
The Devil's Law-Case and A Cure for a Cuckold have very few
couplets, and those mostly at the ends of scenes where such
usage is conventional. Then, perhaps because of the
influence of Webster's possible collaborator Thomas Heywood,
Appius and Virginia has even more couplets than does The

---

[36]Though there is some uncertainty as to the number of
intentionally rhyming lines, I count 86 rhymes in The White
Devil, 40 in The Duchess of Malfi, 100 in Appius and
Virginia, and 98 in The Valiant Scot.

<u>Valiant</u> <u>Scot</u>. Examining the uses to which the couplets are put in Webster's tragedies and in <u>The Valiant Scot</u>, we find some interesting differences. To begin, we might notice that rhyming lines are used in <u>The Valiant Scot</u> for many more purposes than merely "sentences" and conclusions. Boasts, curses, images, laments, pleas, praises, prophecies, and threats are all emphasized by the use of couplets, as are the speeches of characters when they strike down their enemies and of victims when they expire. Any especially forceful or emotional statement may be rhymed. The early Webster plays tend to use couplets gnomically, most often for aphorisms and exit lines. In all the three plays by Webster that make extensive use of couplets, we find the rhyming used in images--especially elaborate similes--much more than is J. W.'s practice. Webster's tendency is to use the couplet for decorative purposes, whereas J. W. tends to use rhymes for dramatic emphasis at powerful moments throughout the play. Not only the use, but the form of the rhymed lines is distinctive in <u>The Valiant Scot</u>. A great number of the rhymed lines in this play contain material extraneous to the thought bound together by the rhymes. Consider the first example in the play:

> Use rein or bitt? By this all doubts are cleer'd;
> 'Tis alwayes better to be lov'd then fear'd.
> (I.1.14-15)

The first two feet of the line belong to a sentence that is syntactically separate from the aphorism pointed up by the rhymes. It is stretching the term somewhat to call this a couplet in Howarth's sense. At any rate, it is quite different from the practice of Webster, the great majority of whose couplets are syntactically independent of what precedes. Also, more of the couplets in The Valiant Scot are split between different speakers than is the case with Webster. In the use of couplets, as in the other conventions and devices pointed out by Professor Howarth, The Valiant Scot seems distinctly different from the major plays of Webster.

The above discussion has been concerned specifically with Professor Howarth's arguments, but there is further evidence that John Webster is not the "J. W., Gent." of the title page. In a series of articles in Studies in Bibliography, Cyrus Hoy examines the Beaumont and Fletcher canon using the linguistic habits of Fletcher and his collaborators in an attempt to identify the various hands involved in the work. Hoy's ambitious attempt to identify the authors of disputed works by an examination of their habitual use of alternative linguistic forms makes use of pronominal forms (ye and y' for you), verbal forms (hath and ha' for have; doth for do), and contractions. He is particularly careful to take account of bibliographical problems such as possible interference with the transmission of specific usages by a compositor. However, he demonstrates that the available evidence can be exceedingly

51

valuable for purposes of attribution. It would, of course, be impossible to establish an absolute case for authorship of The Valiant Scot when so much of the history of the manuscript is conjectural, but the evidence of involuntary linguistic habits can establish a strong degree of probability for or against a particular author's hand in the play.

Hoy examines the linguistic evidence for Webster's work in Part IV of his study, which is concerned with Webster's possible share in The Honest Man's Fortune and The Fair Maid of the Inn. The following table presents the linguistic evidence for Webster's habits, based on Lucas's edition of The White Devil, The Duchess of Malfi, and The Devil's Law-Case:[37]

	ye	y'	hath	doth	'em	them
WD	1		42	17		71
DM	2		55	28	3	80
DLC	2	5	1	2		55

	i'th'	o'th'	a'th'	h'as	's	ha'
WD	32	11	8	2	19	
DM	31	20		1	15	
DLC	46	11	11		20	1

Hoy notes the dramatic "discrepancy between the high rate of occurrence of hath and doth in the two tragedies, and

---

[37]Hoy, 12 (1959), 103.

the negligible use of the forms in the tragicomedy of The Devil's Law-Case." Leaving this inconsistency aside, we observe a fairly consistent pattern throughout the three plays: you is much preferred over its alternatives (ye and y'); them dominates over its substitute ('em); and Webster makes unusually rich use of such contradictions as i'th' (in the), o'th' (of the), a'th' (at the), and 's (his). Hoy adjuges this pattern as "a reasonably distinctive one."[38]

Turning to a slightly expanded table which I have con-structed for the linguistic evidence in The Valiant Scot, we find a quite different pattern:

ye	y'	'ee	hath	doth	'em	'um	them
39	7	1	12	3	17	5	7

i'th'	o'th'	h'as	's	ha'
3	1		8	12

In the case of The Valiant Scot, we find a fairly large number of substitutes for them, and very slight use of i'th' and o'th' contractions. We also see a moderately frequent use of ha' contractions in The Valiant Scot, whereas Webster makes practically no use of this form. It should be pointed out here that a number of the substitutes for you and the ha' contractions appear in passages of Scots dialect where such forms might be regarded as a deliberate imitation of a

---

[38]Hoy, 103.

local pattern of speech.[39]

But, allowing for this possibility, it is obvious that The Valiant Scot reveals a pattern totally distinct from that to be found in Webster's plays. In none of the categories of usage do we find parallel habits. In order to attribute The Valiant Scot plausibly to Webster, we should have to posit an almost complete revision by scribe or compositor down to the smallest linguistic features of the text.

From our examination of the conventions and devices of style together with the linguistic characteristics of The Valiant Scot, we have seen that there is very little likelihood that John Webster is J. W. Who the author may be, we cannot say. The play is quite derivative in theme and language. It would be possible to compile a list of verbal similarities and echoes linking it stylistically to a number of earlier playwrights, especially to Thomas Dekker, Thomas Heywood, Philip Massinger, William Rowley, and Cyril Tourneur, in addition to John Webster. The solution to the problem of authorship may well await the development of more sophisticated tools of analysis along the lines of those developed by Cyrus Hoy.

---

[39]Peter B. Murray calculates that in The White Devil and The Devil's Law-Case Webster averages sixty contractions made with a preposition plus "it" ("with't") and sixteen contractions made with a verb plus "it" ("see't"). See his table in A Study of John Webster (The Hague: Mouton, 1969), pp. 266-267. In contrast, The Valiant Scot has twelve contractions of prepositions with "it" and fifteen contractions of verbs with "it".

IV. THE DATE AND TOPICAL SIGNIFICANCE OF THE PLAY

The quarto of The Valiant Scot provides no evidence
for the date of composition nor does it contain any information about theatrical production of the play. Since the
printed edition and the entry for 26 April 1637 in the
Stationers' Register comprise the only evidence available,
any attempt to date the play must depend upon evidence
within the text itself. One example of such internal
evidence is the allusion to "lachrymae" (I.iv.54), which
refers to John Dowland's 1608 composition, "Lacrimae or
seaven Teares figured in seaven passionate Pavans." This
allusion establishes 1608 as a probable early limit, though,
as Dent notes, the phrase "to sing lacrimae" was not really
common until the 1620's.[40]

The only attempt made to establish a precise date for
The Valiant Scot is that of R. G. Howarth, who places the
play c. 1625 on the basis of two allusions in the text. In
II.iii, Wallace, grieving for the deaths of his wife and
father, demands:

> But bid relentlesse Edward
> Send in the pyrats Haslerigg and Selbye,
> And in their hands letters of Mart subscribed,
> To make me Master of my owne revenge.
> (II.iii.102-105)

---

[40] Robert W. Dent, John Webster's Borrowing (Berkeley:
Univ. of California Press, 1960), p. 313.

Howarth believes that this allusion to letters of Mart
(i.e., letters of Marque, documents which license priva-
teering) is connected with a similar reference in John
Webster and William Rowley's _A Cure for a Cuckold_ which
"serves to date the play in the same year and to link the
two."[41] He thinks that both the J. W. and Webster-Rowley
allusions refer to England's adoption of letters of marque
in February 1625 for use against Spain. A second allusion
seems to point to the same year. Rallying the Scottish
army in IV.i, Wallace says:

> Lets in our rising be, or in our falls,
> Like bels which ring alike at Funerals
> As at Coronations; each man meet his wound
> With self-same joy as Kings go to be crown'd.
>   (IV.i.46-49)

Howarth sees in these lines an allusion to the death of
James I on 25 March 1625, and to the succession of Charles
I. "The play," Howarth points out, "ends with a coronation,
that of Bruce as Robert I of Scotland, and with the conjunction of the two realms under Edward I of England, thus
recelebrating topically the union of 1603, so renewed
through Charles."[42] This is suggestive, but since the
emphasis is placed on the coronation, rather than the
funeral, it would seem logical to posit a slightly later
date. Charles I was crowned on 2 February 1625/26, and it
could well be that the author was remembering rather than

---

[41]Howarth, 6.

[42]Ibid.

anticipating the coronation bells.

Of course, the reference to a coronation, especially
in a history play, might well be innocent of topicality,
but other evidence in the play also points to 1626 as the
probable date of composition. The court scene in Act I
elaborately introduces an element that is dropped after that
scene so that not a single direct mention of it occurs
later in the play. This is Edward's dispute with France,
which appears to be introduced into the play for no reason
other than to explore the theme of Anglo-French relations:[43]

> In expedition of this holy warre
> When France in person was enjoyn'd to march,
> To work his safetie we engag'd our own,
> Casheer'd his fainting souldiers, and on promise
> Of so much gold at our return, suppli'd
> The French designes our selfe; and is our love,
> And losse of bloud, halfe which at least had
> drop'd
> Out of French bosomes, quittant with owe none?
> Pillage and play the free-butter for more.
> (I.iv.58-66)

It is true that in Scene iv we are introduced to such
important characters as King Edward, Bruce, Percy, and
Grimsby. However, Grimsby switches his support to Wallace
as a result of a quarrel with Percy in this scene over
Grimsby's handling of a diplomatic mission to France.
These developments do not require that so much attention be
devoted to France. Not only does this concern with France

---

[43]There is, however, an indirect mention of the enmity
between France and England in II.iv.227-230, when Beaumont
reports Wallace's proposed trip to France to seek aid for
Scotland.

direct our thoughts away from Scotland, the focus of the
play, but it creates loose ends. What is the outcome of
Edward's "French wars"? How does Bruce, supposedly comman-
ding the French expedition, turn up in Scotland? The play
does not settle these questions.

If the Anglo-French difficulties do not justify the
attention given them within the structure of the play,
perhaps an impulse other than the artistic one prompted J.
W. We notice that the japes of Sir Jeffrey and Bolt in Act
III are continued far out of proportion to their importance
in the structure of that act. The playwright obviously expanded these comic roles because he knew the audience would
respond to their humor. It may well be that he included
much of the court scene for a similar reason: he knew that
the audience for whom the play was written would respond
with approval to its political overtones. The popularity
of political satire with London audiences can be estimated
by the overwhelming success of Middleton's anti-Spanish A
Game at Chess (1624), only the most notorious of the numerous plays of the period which cater to political bias.

No source exists for a dispute/of the sort vaguely
outlined in Edward's outburst; moreover, it is unhistorical.
Edward I had many difficulties with Philip the Fair, but
there is no record of a war stemming from unappreciated aid
sent to France. However, Edward's charges roughly describe
English displeasure with France in the 1620's, displeasure

which led to a war between the two countries that lasted from 1626 to 1629.

In 1624, the Duke of Buckingham and Cardinal Richelieu arranged a treaty between England and France according to which the two nations were to form a grand alliance against Spain, England's traditional enemy. Under the terms of this pact, Charles was to receive in marriage a French princess, Henrietta Maria. In return, the English were to raise an army under the adventurer Count Mansfield for use on the Protestant side of the Thirty Years' War. But at least two insoluble difficulties stood in the way of an accommodation between England and France: first, the secret treaty bound Charles to relax the severe laws against English Catholics--a policy which Protestant public opinion would hardly permit; and, second, no less disturbingly, France was in the process of stamping out an armed rebellion by the Huguenots who, as fellow Protestants, enjoyed English popular sympathy. The alliance soon soured, for the English not only demanded that the French cease mistreating the Huguenots but insisted even more ardently that substantial French aid be forthcoming against Spain. Royal instructions to the English ambassador in Paris on 11 February 1626 contain two points brought up by Edward in his speech against France (I.iv.58-66): "his Majesty's great charges both by sea and land" and the fact that "the diversion in Germany concerneth chiefly the security of

France."[44] An English audience of 1626 would easily
identify the "holy warre" of which Edward speaks with the
grand Protestant alliance against the encroachments of
Catholicism, and respond to suggestions that France was not
fulfilling the obligations expected of her. The steps so
heroically proposed by Edward to redress the situation may
well have been intended to reflect the preparations begun
early in 1627 to relieve the Huguenots at Rochelle by an
attack on the Isle of Rhé.

Though the description of the "French designs"
parallels English political moves of 1626-27, there is a
firmer indication of political satire in the characters of
Queen Elinor and of Grimsby. Though trusted enough to be
an ambassador on a delicate diplomatic mission, Grimsby
rebels against his prince out of resentment at Edward's
handling of a quarrel in which he is involved. Grimsby's
revolt is based upon an incident in Hary's Wallace, though
the quarrel with Percy is J. W.'s invention. Grimsby's
pride, as well as his traits of character as described by
Edward and Percy, are elements which the playwright added.
These details strongly suggest Charles I's unpopular
advisor, George Villiers, Duke of Buckingham.

Buckingham was notorious as the architect of the
ruinous foreign policy of James I and Charles I. In 1626

[44]S. R. Gardiner, History of England . . . 1603-1642,
5th ed. (London, New York, and Bombay: Longmans, Green,
and Co., 1886), VI, 55.

his mishandling of affairs was rapidly launching England into a war with France at the same time that she was at war with Spain. Buckingham was identified with the French alliance, unpopular since its very inception, and was thus a suitable object for J. W.'s scorn as embodied in Percy's charges of diplomatic failure. In his attack on Grimsby, Percy mentions points which square with popular feeling against Buckingham in the London of the day:

> Grimsby, thou canst do well in Garison:
> Weare shamoys for a grace, project for bloud,
> Make eight dayes to one week, turn executioner,
> And hangman-like send fifty in one morning,
> To feed the Crows, and live upon dead pay.
>   (I.iv.9-13)

First is the charge that Grimsby is a garrison, as opposed to a field, officer. Though Lord Admiral of the English fleet, Buckingham never saw action until his ill-fated expedition against the Isle of Rhé. His position of command had been purchased by his good looks, his charm, and his courtly presence. Public awareness of Buckingham's unmartial background is seen in a contemporary song:

> Reioyce, brave English gallants,
>   Whose anncestors wonne France;
> Our Duke of Buckingham is gone
>   To fight and not to daunce.[45]

Buckingham's rich wardrobe was so notorious that since his embassy to Paris in 1624 his name had been a symbol to the French of satorial magnificence. Percy alludes to this

---

[45]"Poems and Songs Relating to George Villiers, Duke of Buckingham," ed. F. W. Fairholt in Early English Poetry . . . , Percy Society, 29 (London: Percy Society, 1851), 14.

delight in clothing when he refers to Grimsby's "Weare⟨Ing⟩ shamoys," i.e., expensive and luxurious clothing, "for a grace" (I.iv.10). Gifted with courtly bearing and a rich appearance, Buckingham had risen meteorically in the court of James, who delighted in male splendor. The Stuart monarchs had showered gifts and offices upon him to the extent that either James or Charles could well have reproached him, as Edward does Grimsby, with "The many favours we have grac'd thee with."

The darker attributes of which Percy accuses Grimsby likewise have their place in the popular view of Buckingham. As the expeditions planned by the royal minion failed, a chorus of voices cried out that he was enriching himself at the expense of the poor conscripts marched off to the Netherlands, to Cadiz, and to the Isle of Rhé. In a contemporary satire "Upon the Duke," the ghost of the recently assasinated Buckingham is made to admit:

> The flood of my ambition swell'd soe high
> . . . .
>   it spared not to spill
> The liues and blood of myne owne countrey men,
> And if I loved one, I hated ten.[46]

It is Buckingham's unrelenting hatreds, mentioned in the final line, that Grimsby's unchristian refusal to forgive Percy at the urging of Edward seems to reflect. Though he has some reason to feel aggrieved, Grimsby, by placing personal revenge above his duty to his king, is like the

---

[46]"Poems and Songs Relating to . . . Buckingham," 40.

the evil Cardinal Winchester in Shakespeare's I Henry VI of
whom this passage reminds us:

> King.   Then joyn hands,
>   Our subjects both, the native of two Lands.
> Percy. Friends Grimsby.
> Grimsby. /Aside/ Friends in shew,
>   But in my brest bloudy revenge lies ambush't.
>   (I.iv.47-51)
>
> GLO. See here, my friends and loving countrymen.
>   This token serveth for a flag of truce
>   Betwixt ourselves and all our followers.
>   So help me God, as I dissemble not!
> WIN. /Aside/ So help me God, as I intend it not!
>   (III.i.137-141)

Most Englishmen in 1626 would not have doubted that Buckingham could be guilty of such a treason. The whole
portrait of Grimsby, then, could be a warning to Charles
that Buckingham's full-blown arrogance could easily turn to
ingratitude and betrayal.

  If Percy's comments to Grimsby portray the popular
view of Buckingham, the few lines given to Queen Elinor
reflect one aspect of Charles's dearly bought queen,
Henrietta Maria. As a character in the play, Elinor is one
of the politically unattached figures urging charity and
consideration to both English and Scots. This portrayal
may derive from the sources, for both Hary and Holinshed
treat Queen Elinor well. However, her comment, "Edward
will be more kind to Christians" (I.iv.56), would bring an
instant response from an audience who feared, not without
justification, that Henrietta Maria was using her influence
to win toleration for English Catholics. Her marriage had

63

been designed to symbolize the new French alliance which in
turn was to be based upon the removal of the punitive laws
against the hated papists. Elinor's term, "Christians,"
taken up immediately by Edward, "Let Christians be more
honest then to Edward" (I.iv.57), could be understood as a
clef for "Catholics." In any performance before the outbreak of the Civil War, Edward's firm response would
probably be met by a hail of applause as suggesting the
firmness which the public hoped Charles would exert against
the domestic pressures of French Catholicism.

The style of The Valiant Scot does little to confirm,
or rule out, 1626 as the date of the composition of the
play. As we should perhaps expect of a chronicle play
written in the last days of a declining genre, the style
seems old-fashioned. It retains the exaggerated language
of the dramatists of the 1590's, along with such dated
devices as apostrophes, personifications, and ghosts. The
play contains little sentiment or introspection; even the
internal struggles of Bruce seem rather a matter of rhetorical convention than psychological probing. In short, The
Valiant Scot seems closer to the wrangling factions and
bustling battlefields of Henry VI than to the grandiose
delusions of Perkin Warbeck.

V. SOURCES OF THE PLAY

Fredrich Huch, writing in 1901, was perhaps the first
to point to the Wallace of Blind Hary as the major source
for the historical parts of The Valiant Scot.[47] This
narrative poem in twelve books, written in the years 1476-
78,[48] describes the career of Sir William Wallace as the
hero in the wars for Scottish independence. From a number
of references to the life of Wallace and from the fuller
accounts of Wallace's battles, Hary draws his basic
material, which is then amplified through invented detail
into an extended, fully drawn portrait of a hero who drives
the English from his Scotland three times before his
betrayal and martyrdom. Hary presents a coherent account
of Wallace's struggles which, if somewhat repetitious, is
nevertheless colorful and vivid. As will be seen below,
the structure and characterization of The Valiant Scot owe
much to Hary's Wallace.

Hary's poem was available to J. W. in at least five
Scots editions published between 1509 and 1620. If we may
trust the slim evidence of a single work, the 1570 edition
of the Wallace, published by Robert Lekpreuik in Edinburgh,

---

[47]Huch, p. 12.

[48]Hary's Wallace, ed. Matthew P. McDiarmid (Edinburgh
and London: William Blackwood and Sons, 1968), I, xvi.

was the specific source used by J. W. For the Lekpreuik
edition alone substitutes "refrene" for the authoritative
"restreyn" (Wallace, XII.1110) in the line from which
"Alace, fra mourning wha sall thee refayne?" (V.ii.117) is
borrowed.

John Linton Carver, in the only study to explore the
connection between the Wallace and The Valiant Scot, points
out the above echo, though he fails to distinguish between
the editions of the Wallace. His explanation for the sub-
stituted term is that the playwright unconsciously echoed
another line in the previous book: "Was na man thar fra
wepyng mycht hym rafreyn" (XI.583).[49] This echo is one of
the three examples of parallel phrasing noted by Carver.
There are, in addition, three other parallel passages that
deserve notice. The first passage is more an echo of theme
and image than of language:

        So bett I am with strakis sad and sar.
        The cheyle wattir vrned me mekill mar.
                                (Wallace, V.383-384)

        I'me with his /Neptune's7 beating bruis'd, weary
              cold, weak,
        Liquor'd soundly.

                                (III.i.119-120)

The other two echoes appear in the ghostly laments of Act V.
The first of these is the use of an image, "for him dy'd on
tree" (V.ii.119), that appears several times in Hary's
Wallace: I.236; V.1029; VI.845; VIII.1287. The second

---

[49]Carver, p. 84.

echo is the use of two lines of the narrator's comment on Wallace's spiritual state at the time of his capture:

> For as off wer he was in sumpart yrk,
> He purpost than to serue god and the kyrk.
> (Wallace, XII.961-962)

In the play, this comment becomes a warning to Wallace by the ghost of the Friar that Wallace needs spiritual regeneration:

> Wallace beweere, me thinks it thee should irke,
> Mare need hast thou to serve God in the Kirke.
> (V.ii.101-102)

Despite the small number of echoes from Hary's Wallace, the language of The Valiant Scot is not especially distinctive. Although the playwright does not rely extensively upon verbal effects of the fifteenth-century poem, his idioms and phrasings, the particular turns of speech, are similar to those in other playwrights of the early seventeenth century. The jests of Bolt and the boasts of Wallace are drawn largely from a linguistic reservoir available to anyone widely steeped in the drama of the period. Many parallels can be found between the language of The Valiant Scot and such playwrights as Dekker, Massinger, Middleton, Rowley, and Webster, though the borrowing is more often one of idea or image than the actual transcription of words. The playwright's borrowing habits can be seen most clearly perhaps in his use of Shakespeare's early history plays, which are rich in effects of dramatic presentation that show up again and again in The Valiant Scot. From such

67

plays as the three parts of <u>Henry VI</u>, <u>Richard III</u>, and
<u>Richard II</u>, J. W. draws incidents, as well as images, to
link together or to add dramatic interest to the material
drawn from Hary's <u>Wallace</u>. J. W. does not unblushingly
copy whole speeches word for word from Shakespeare; he
takes the rhetorical occasion and the ideas, but rewrites
the speeches for his own purposes. The borrowing may be
slight, involving but a phrase or two. Clifford's protest
at the treachery of Percy:

> Intrap a fo? Sure 'tis no <u>English</u> word,
> <u>Clifford</u> at least was ne're acquainted with't.
>
> (II.iv.168-169)

seems to owe its origin to Shakespeare's:

> Submission, Dauphin! 'Tis a mere French word.
> We English warriors wot not what it means.
>
> (<u>I Henry VI</u>, IV.vii.54-55)

A whole speech may be drawn from a Shakespearean model, as
is the speech of Wallace at the opening of Act II in which
he attempts to draw the loyalty of his fellow Scot, Grimsby,
from the English (II.i.5-15). It is modeled on Joan La
Pucelle's speech in <u>I Henry VI</u> wherein the maid of Orleans
persuades Burgundy to switch his loyalty back to the French
(III.iii.44-51). Each passage opens with a line or two of
complaint to the listener, then pleads with him to "look
on" the sufferings of his country. Each dwells on the
misery within the humble family and uses the image of the
wounded breast of his country:

> Behold the wounds, the most unnatural wounds,

Which thou thyself hast given her woeful breast.
                    (I Henry VI, III.iii.50-51)

        Look upon the wounds
And mortall stabs of that distressed breast
That gave thee suck.
                                        (II.i.8-10)

Ideas from different plays may be combined in a single
passage of The Valiant Scot. In I.i, Old Wallace relinquishes his staff of office to the English commissioners:

    Old Wallace. To what my King commands
            I humbly bend, resigning on my knee
            Both Staffe and Office.
    Selby.   Which thus Selby breaks
            Over thy head.
                                        (I.i.47-50)

This incident is drawn from the similar action of Gloucester
in 2 Henry VI, II.iii.32-34, while Selby's breaking the
staff is taken from the report of the same incident in
Richard II (II.ii.59 and II.iii.27).

    Whole scenes in The Valiant Scot are modeled on Shake-
spearean sources. The court scene (I.iii) in which Percy
and Grimsby contend before King Edward, who attempts to
make peace, is influenced by similar scenes in Shakespeare,
notably I Henry VI, III, i. The execution scene in which
Peggie, Old Wallace, and Friar Gertrid are slaughtered
draws its stylized form from similar scenes in 3 Henry VI
(I.iii; I.iv; V.v). Devices borrowed in this scene are the
use of multiple executioners, parallel speeches among the
victims who beg for mercy and among the executioners who
refuse the pleas, and the justifying of the killings as
revenge for earlier killings. In his study of The Valiant

<u>Scot</u>, Huch notes the resemblance of the seashore scene of
Act III to Shakespeare's <u>Pericles</u>, II.i.[50] He calls
attention to the similarity in words, situation, and tone.

At least one important element in the structure of the
play is drawn from Shakespeare's <u>I Henry VI</u>. The last
scene of Act I and the opening scenes of Act II are modeled
upon the corresponding scenes in the Shakespeare play. The
first acts of both plays end on a note of celebration by
the opposing party, which has won important victories over
the forces represented by the hero. Both the French of <u>I
Henry VI</u> and the English of <u>The Valiant Scot</u> give a banquet
that ends disastrously, for in each case their enemies
counterattack while the banqueters are still befuddled by
festival cheer. The similarity of the passages in which
the counterattack is urged makes it probable that genuine
Shakespearean influence was involved:

> This happy night the Frenchmen are secure,
> Having all day caroused and banqueted.
> Embrace we then this opportunity
> As fitting best to quittance their deceit
> Contrived by art and baleful sorcery.
> (<u>I Henry VI</u>, II.i.11-15)

> The town of Lavercke, peopled
> Only with <u>English</u> pride and overjoyed
> With thy surpriz, all are made drunk with mirth,
> Bonefires, bels, banquets, and the devill and all
> Invite our swords to their sad funerall.
> (II.i.56-60)

Wallace's sudden reversal of fortune, from condemned
prisoner to leader of the victorious Scots army, is thus

---

[50]Huch, p. 7.

patterned upon the account of the English army in Shakespeare's play.

While most of the plot was taken from Hary's Wallace
touched up by incidents from Shakespeare, a few important
details derive from Holinshed's Chronicles. In the case of
Old Wallace's defiance of the English commissioners who
demand he produce documents attesting to his ownership of
his lands, J. W. used Holinshed's account of the Earl of
Surrey's resistance to the same illegal demands of Edward
I.[51] Holinshed reports that it was the English lord who
drew out his sword as sufficient evidence of his possession
of his land; in The Valiant Scot Old Wallace declares that
his son Wallace will "shew evidence sufficient--Mine, my
deere Fathers, and my Grandsires sword" (I.i.72-73). The
stirring incident adds color and interest to the Scots'
resistance of the English tyranny.

The history of Scotland in Holinshed's compilation was
translated from Hector Boece's Scotorum historiae (c. 1527).
The dramatist took several incidents from this section of
the Chronicles to round out the fifth act of The Valiant
Scot. The first scene of this act finds Clifford sending
to Bruce a pair of spurs and twelve silver pence as a
symbol of his Judas-like betrayal of Scotland. Hary does
not mention this action in his Wallace,but the biography of

---

[51] Raphael Holinshed, The Chronicles of England, Scotlande, and Irelande (London: George Bishop, 1577), II, 798.

71

Bruce in the Chronicles refers to the incident though with
a different sender:

> The Erle of Glocester immediately after that
> Robert Bruce was departed from the kings presence,
> sent to him .xii. sterling pennies, wyth two
> sharpe spurres, whereby he coniectured his meaning
> to be, that the best shift for him was to auoyde
> out of the ways in moste speedy wyse.[52]

In the drama this action helps to motivate Bruce's decision
to turn against the English, a matter swiftly decided in
the Wallace, but agonized over in the play.

In Scene ii of this act, Wallace replies to Edward's
last demand that he surrender with a threat of his own to
invade England:

> For my appearance tell him this, I'le dyne
> On Christmas day next in his English Court,
> And in his great Hall at Westminster, at's owne boord,
> Wee'le drink Scotch healths in his standing cups of
> gold.
> (V.ii.50-53)

The source of this speech is probably a passage in Holinshed
where Wallace threatens to spend Easter in England:

> he willed the Englishe ambassadors to declare
> from hym unto king Edward, that he purposed to
> hold his Easter in Englande (if God fortuned him
> lyfe) and that in despite of king Edward and al
> such as would beare armour against him.[53]

The change in the holiday may be due to the elaboration of
the threat, Christmas ordinarily being a more festive
social occasion than Easter. Wallace's speech stresses the
revelry of the victorious Scots who will celebrate at

---

[52]Holinshed, I, 310.

[53]Ibid., I, 304.

Edward's own holiday board.

While Hary refuses to dwell on the manner of Wallace's death, Holinshed describes the gruesome execution. Wallace was quartered after his hanging as an "ensaumple to other." Holinshed's phrase was possibly the source of Mentith's statement that Wallace was taken alive "to th'end the world May see the publique shame of an Archtraytor" (V.iv.68-69). Again, Hary does not mention the death of Coming, while Holinshed describes Bruce stabbing "the foresayde Comyn a sore blowe in the belly."[54] In both these cases, Holinshed's account provided information needed by the playwright to conclude his play satisfactorily. One slight bit of verbal evidence that it was Holinshed's account, rather than an earlier translation of Boece by John Bellenden that J. W. consulted, is Holinshed's use of the phrase "the yoke of bondage,"[55] which appears in The Valiant Scot at I.iv.93. Though not an exotic image, the phrase does not appear in Shakespeare, nor in the OED; it may well be drawn from the few pages of Holinshed that deal with Wallace's career.

This weaving together of details and incidents drawn as needed to fill out the outline of the play is a characteristic of J.W. In his use of the Wallace, he ranges freely through the poem, selecting details that fit his dramatic conception which he then rearranges together with

[54]Holinshed, I, 310.
[55]Ibid., I, 307.

bits from other sources and with original material to
create the finished drama. To aid the reader in locating
these scattered passages, Carver listed twenty-five
parallels between the _Wallace_ and _The Valiant Scot_.[56]
Carver's references were to an edition of the _Wallace_ which
since been superseded and, of course, to his own (now
missing) edition of _The Valiant Scot_. Below are listed the
same references according to the present edition and to
McDiarmid's edition of Hary's _Wallace_. Four parallels not
noted by Carver are also included.

Incident	VS	Wallace
Tyranny of Haslerig and Thorne	I.i.1	VI.107
Wallace's wife desired by		
Englishman	I.i.82	V.665
Death of Young Selby	I.ii.41	I.203
Haslerig in England	I.iv.68	VI.280
Queen intercedes with Edward	I.iv.80	VI.289
Grimsby turns to Wallace	II.i.1	VI.297
Friendship of Graham and Wallace	II.i.24	V.437
		VI.119
Massacre of Laverck	II.i.56	
	II.ii.14	VI.230
Wallace meets uncle and parson	II.i.25	V.351
Wallace's marriage	II.i.62	VI.48
Friar's speech	II.i.66	II.346
Death of Wallace's wife	II.iii.1	VI.191
Wallace and the English heralds	II.iii.51	VI.349
Disguised Wallace to English camp	II.iii.146	VI.434
Douglas, Macbeth, and Wintersdale	II.iii.160	VI.771
Wallace's swim	III.i.110	V.380
Wallace's hunger	III.i.114	XII.554
Death of Selby and Haslerigh	III.i.186	VI.235
Battle of Falkirk, Wallace to		
the rear	IV.i.1	XI.60
Bruce in the English army	IV.ii.59	XI.203
Defeat of the Scots	IV.iii.1	XI.245
Death of Graham	IV.iii.34	XI.377
Interview of Bruce and Wallace	IV.iii.38	XI.442
		XI.527

[56]Carver, p. 79.

Incident	VS	Wallace
The "blood-drinking" taunt	IV.iv.69	XI.527
Bruce refuses to fight against the Scots	V.i.19 V.iv.23	XI.720
Wallace's defiance of Edward	V.ii.48	VIII.1086
Ghosts and visions appear to Wallace	V.ii.93	XII.360
Betrayal of Wallace	V.iii.1	XII.979 XII.995
Wallace slays Mentith	V.iv.90	XII.149

From this list it can be seen that most of the material in
the play was at least suggested by Hary's Wallace. Carver
explains that some of the incidents are but slightly mentioned in the poem while others follow closely the lines of
the original narrative. Book VI of the Wallace provides
much of the material for the first two acts of the play,
while Book XI, which deals with the battle of Falkirk,
provides the material for Act IV. The last act of the play
derives many of its details from Book XII, which deals with
the betrayal and death of Wallace.

More interesting than the account of the details
actually woven into the play are differences of emphasis
given by the playwright to materials which he chose to
utilize. The attitudes and values of the play often contrast significantly with those of the Scottish bard. The
poet and the playwright, for example, stress different
values in their respective treatments of the battle between
Wallace and Young Selby. Hary emphasizes Wallace's refusal
to bear abuse and his courage in the face of numbers, but

75

the incident is little more than a common street brawl. In
contrast, J. W. emphasizes the seventeenth-century code of
honor as the two combatants withdraw from their followers
and punctiliously observe all the niceties of the _duello._
Young Selby's refusal to take advantage of Wallace's lost
sword demonstrates a chivalric magnanimity that would have
disturbed the earlier poet, who believed the object of
fighting to be the killing of one's enemies. J. W. is as
much concerned with how one acts as with the mere success
of his action. This same distinction in ethical sophisti-
cation can be seen also in the journey of the disguised
Wallace to the English camp. Hary's Wallace undertakes a
purely functional mission, spying out the establishments of
the enemy in preparation for the Battle of Biggar. The
valiant Scot, however, has no motive other than to demon-
strate his courage in what his followers liken to an epic
deed: "So _Hercules_ sought honour out in Hell" (II.iii.169).
The courage and the imagination shown in the action become
their own justification.

We notice in addition that to a great degree language
now replaces action in the portraiture of Wallace. The
Wallace of Hary's poem is a busy man, winning dozens of
battles, small and large, in Scotland and in France, and
rescuing his country from the English no fewer than three
times. In the play, however, we _see_ only minor heroics.
Wallace never defeats the English; indeed, he stands aloof

from the only major battle that is staged. But he
repeatedly defies King Edward in the most heroic terms, and
is spoken of by the other characters as Scotland's savior.
The audience accepts this rhetorical "Wallace" as a representation of the historical warrior, who was still mentioned in popular ballads. Though it is probable that
additional heroic actions involving Wallace were worked
into the staging, the only Englishman the printed text
requires him to kill is Young Selby, and then, of course,
in fair fight. Wallace even refrains from avenging himself
personally on Selby and Haslerig. By evading the dramati-
zation of bloodshed on the part of the Scots, the poet
avoids alienating his audience from the hero of the play, a
hero who is implicitly anti-English.

Another alteration designed to make the play acceptable
to an English audience is the creation of the "neutral"
character who supports justice and honor whether it appears
on the English or on the Scottish side. Such figures as
Thorne, Clifford, the Queen, and the Friar evidence a dis-
placement of patriotism (so strong in Hary's poem) by honor
as the supreme standard of the play. A character carries
negative charge in the ethical pattern of the play not
because he represents a particular nationality, but because
he falls short of the code he is expected to maintain.
Thus we have both Scottish and English villains. And
Clifford, loving virtue even in an enemy (as Prince Hal

admires Hotspur in Shakespeare's I Henry IV), can expose
Bruce's false position in the English camp to him, even
though the act seems to fly in the face of English policy.
Hary's Wallace expresses a much more single-minded patriotism. His view of the English is blunt: "Our ald Ennemys
cummyn of Saxonys blud, That neuyr yeit to Scotland wald do
gud" (I.7-8). According to the values expressed throughout
the work, the hero of Hary's poem is justified in confessing
before his death that he slew "nocht halff enew" Englishmen
(XII.1386), for his simple duty lay in killing any English
male found alive above the Tyne.

Rather than killings on the part of the title character,
the dramatist stresses Wallace's acts of redemption. Act
III explores the possibility of a new Wallace, almost as
though he might become one of the "neutral" characters mentioned above. When he has the murderers of his wife and
father at his mercy, this "new" Wallace refuses revenge,
preferring to leave Selby and Haslerig to God's judgment.
It is clear from the haste with which this judgment is
fulfilled that this development in Wallace's character is
meant to be approved by the audience. However, the character lapses again into the conventionally heroic mode upon
his return to the political arena. The warning of the
Friar's ghost in Act V indicates that Wallace has neglected
personal growth for the sake of political success: "Mare
need hast thou to serve God in the Kirke" (V.ii.102).

Still it is the political Wallace who becomes the agent of Bruce's redemption by winning the latter's loyalty back to Scotland, as he had earlier won Grimsby's. The Bruce of Hary's _Wallace_ is ambitious in a way that the author of _The Valiant Scot_ suggests by showing him importuning King Edward in the first act. In the poem it is Bruce who seeks parley with Wallace (XI.442-449), and it is Bruce, again, who arranges the rendezvous at which Wallace is captured. J. W., at this point, fuses two separate meetings between Bruce and Wallace in order to compress the time between the Battle of Falkirk and the capture of the hero. In the poem, the fatal meeting is arranged after the meeting agreed upon during the battle. J. W. conflates the two episodes deliberately in order to gain dramatic economy. Both parleys were arranged by Bruce in order to assure himself Scots support for his claim to the throne. By having Wallace initiate the discussion, J. W. emphasizes the role of his hero as an active seeker of legitimate order in Scotland. This impression is strengthened by his explanation to Mentith and Coming of his intentions:

Wallace. Oh Sir John Mentith I have crackt the Ice
    To a designe, which if it will succeed,
    England no more shall strike, nor Scotland bleed.
Coming.
Mentith. } Lets be partakers, deare sir.
Wallace. What will you say, if I winne Bruce from the
    English?
Mentith. The happiest day that ever shone on Scotland.
Coming. And crowne him King?
Wallace. That's the up-shot must crowne all.
                               (V.ii.68-75)

This view of Wallace as the political savior of Scotland
through the conversion of a defector is completed when, on
being dragged off to execution, he instructs Bruce:

> Only it grieves me that I have not freed
> Scotland my native soile from tyranny.
> Bruce, thou hast a Kingdome, lose it not.
> (V.iv.107-109)

We may note here that Wallace's execution is carefully
prepared for in the play. After the deaths of his loved
ones in Act II, he is an isolated figure who performs his
actions alone. Alone, he visits the English camp in Act II,
submits to God's judgment in Act III, withdraws his troops
from the Scottish army in Act IV, and is captured in Act V.
Even his closest Scottish friends betray him. Moreover,
his language bespeaks a self-destructive tragic hero half-
consciously pursuing his own death. In such lines as, "I
will on Were certain death against my bosome bent" (II.iii.
151-152), he seems recklessly to throw himself into danger's
path as seeking release from his loneliness and suffering.
That a tragic end is to be his fate appears most clearly in
his identification of himself with Death: "Death of my
selfe is part; I'le never flie my self" (IV.i.44-45). The
nature of the death that does close his career as, betrayed
by friends, he is hanged on a "tre" and takes upon himself
the guilt of a rebellious Scotland in order to free his
people, suggests more than a casual analogy to Christ.
Merged with, but ultimately rising above, the warrior-
chieftain of the Wallace and the ballads, is the self-

sacrificing redeemer of an entire nation.

As mentioned above, the dramatist softens Bruce's ambition. J. W. makes a significant change in order to depict Bruce as a suitable Scots hero to the more refined culture of the seventeenth century. In his parley with Bruce on the battlefield at Falkirk (IV.iii.55-59), Wallace instructs Bruce to dip his hands into Scottish blood to test the English response to his heroics. Such an action is unnecessary in the poem since Bruce has already been drenched in the blood of the Scots whom he cut down in battle. The change allows Bruce to appear before the audience as untainted by the blood of his own, though Clifford has already reported his deeds against the Scots (IV.iv.68-70). It also imparts to Wallace yet greater credit for the eventual conversion of Bruce, for the test demonstrates to his disloyal compatriot the scorn with which the English regard his equivocal position.

Bruce's final decision to ally himself with his countrymen is dramatized in his refusal to fight against the Scots. Whereas in the Wallace Bruce tells King Edward that he will no longer fight his fellow Scots, the playwright has him express his refusal to Clifford at a time when, ironically, the capture of Wallace has rendered more fighting against the Scots unnecessary. This change makes it possible for Bruce to dedicate complete loyalty to Scotland without breaking openly with Edward. Thus, Bruce can give

81

to Scotland the loyalty which befits a Scots patriot and monarch. At the same time, when Edward voluntarily crowns him King of Scotland in the same scene, Bruce can swear a vague fealty to a generous Edward. Wallace's sacrifice has cleared the Scots of the guilt of rebellion, while Bruce's execution of Coming, the person responsible for the betrayal of Wallace, is made to settle all accounts in a morally forced distribution of rewards and punishments. Carver comments on the unsatisfactory nature of the ending but concludes that it is "perhaps the happiest possible one in the days when the Stuarts were on the English throne."[57] It does enable the playwright to create an unhistorical settlement that gives their due to both the Scots and the English in a feudal prototype of the conjunction of both kingdoms under the Stuart dynasty.

[57]Carver, p. 82.

VI. STAGE HISTORY

The sole account of a production of The Valiant Scot
is in an anonymous Puritan pamphlet of 1641, Vox Borealis:
or, The Northern Discoverie. The work is in the form of a
dialogue between two Scots, one living in London and the
other with the Scots army threatening the north of England;
their exchange of "news" contains a humorous attack on the
policies of the royalist party. As one of his playful
references to song and drama, the London-based Jamie relates
that the "poore players of the Fortune play-house" staged a
play called The Cardinal's Conspiracy, in which they filled
the stage with ecclesiastical trappings:

> But wofull was the sight to see how in the middest
> of all their mirth, the Pursevants came and seazed
> upon the poore Cardinall, and all his Consorts,
> and carryed them away. And when they were ques-
> tioned for it, in the High Comission Court, they
> pleaded Ignorance, and told the Archbishop, that
> they tooke those examples of their Altars, Images,
> and the like from Heathen Authors. This did some-
> what asswage his anger, that they did not bring
> him on the Stage: But yet they were fined for
> it, and after a little Imprisonment gat their
> liberty. And having nothing left them but a few
> old Swords and Bucklers, they fell to Act the
> Valiant Scot, which they Played five days with
> great applause, which vext the Bishops worse then
> the other, insomuch, as they were forbidden Play-
> ing it any more: and some of them prohibited ever
> Playing againe.[58]

---

[58] Vox Borealis (London: "Margery Mar-Prelat," 1641),
unpaged. The account is repeated in A Second Discoverie of
the Northern Scout (London: B. W., 1642). Portions of the
account are reprinted in Gerald Bentley, The Jacobean and

In his discussion of The Valiant Scot, Gerald Bentley discounts the importance of this reference. Since the suppression of The Cardinal's Conspiracy was mentioned in a letter dated 8 May 1639, the warming over of this incident two years later for propaganda purposes seems too pat and casts some doubt on the credibility of the other half of the story:

> If he /the author of Vox Borealis/ were so slippery about his dates, can he be relied upon in his statement about The Valiant Scot, especially when the title (taken as referring to the noble Scottish Presbyterians and the salutary drubbing they gave the enforcers of episcopal tyranny in the Bishops' Wars) is such a magnificent and unindictable jeer at the bishops?[59]

It is impossible to prove or disprove absolutely the assertions of the "Northern Scout's" pamphlet, but I believe the writer deserves more credit than Bentley grants him. The slipperiness about dates is an aspect of the form of the pamphlet. The two Scots are depicted as meeting together after long absence, whereupon they bring each other up to date on the incidents of the past several months in London and in Scotland. The author of the "Epistle" admits the fragmentary nature of the "news." Thus we receive a desultory, but presumably reliable, account of events, both political and artistic, that relate

---

Caroline Stage, I, 277-278, while the entire Vox Borealis is rather inaccurately reprinted in The Harleian Miscellany (London: Robert Dutton, 1809), IV, 422-441.

[59]Bentley, The Jacobean and Caroline Stage, V, 1235.

to Scottish-English relations.

Moreover, it seems clear that the body of the pamphlet
was written several months before the date of publication.
It is not the author who claims that the news is fresh
early in 1641, but the pseudonymous printer, "Margery Mar-
Prelat." The approximate date of composition can be established by noting Jamie's reference to the "new invented
oathes" with which Scots would be forced from their own
point of view to swear against God, conscience, and country
--an allusion to the open-ended "Etcetera Oath" announced
by the Episcopal Convention in May of 1640. Jamie's threat
to drive "that false papisticall traitor Rothwen, and all
of his knaveries, out of the Castle" indicates that the
writing was done before the surrender of Edinburgh Castle
by Patrick Ruthven in September of that year. It is, therefore, from the perspective of the summer of 1640, rather
than from the spring of 1641, that the "Scout" is reviewing
the news. Since this shortens the period between the
supposed presentation of the play at the Fortune and the
composition of Vox Borealis, the information may be somewhat more reliable than Bentley allows.

But of greater significance in weighing the truth of
the anecdote is the use to which it is put. Jamie is
relating the abuses of the bishops against "poets and
players" to show that even the merry fellows are abused.
The difficulties of the Fortune players are recounted after

Jamie's discussion of the punishment of two balladeers, one of them a royalist. The whole section is a digression to lighten the political satire. A play of words on the name of the drama provides a clever transition back to the more serious political discussion when Willie says, "Let the Bishops be as angry as they will, we have acted the _Valiant Scot_ bravely at _Berwicke_." This quibble on the title of the play is in the spirit of much of the pamphlet which mocks Laud and the other ecclesiastical authorities through puns and jests drawn from plays, songs, and games. However, it is unlike the mere playing with names in such allusions as the one that changes Heywood's _The Royal King and the Loyal Subject_ to _The Loss of a Loyal Subject_. The account of the performance is narrated in some detail with specific reference to the props and the length of the run, and it is tied in with the closing of _The Cardinal's Conspiracy_, for which we have corroborative evidence. Like the _Conspiracy_, which was apparently staged in an effort to criticize the high church prelates,[60] _The Valiant Scot_ contains elements certain to offend the royalist party in 1640--a Catholic friar, tyrannous English officials, and the glamorous Scottish rebels. Archbishop Laud and his staff were not necessarily tolerant of the drama merely because of their

---

[60]Bentley, _The Jacobean and Caroline Stage_, I, 277, quotes Edmund Rossingham as writing: "Although they allege it was an old play revived,...yet it was apparent that the play was revived on purpose in contempt of the ceremonies of the Church."

royalist politics,[61] nor would they be slow to shut down
such a deliberately irreverent performance by a suspect
company at that sensitive time.

It is true that the incident described in the pamphlet
is effectively suited to the political purposes for which
it was supposedly used, but rather than assume that it was
created for this effect, it seems reasonable to suspect
that it had a basis in fact. The memory of such an incident
would almost certainly be relished as an anecdote with its
strongly partisan flavor and its sharp-edged irony.

We possess no record of a performance of The Valiant
Scot earlier than the 1639 Fortune production. The company
occupying the Fortune Theater at that time was the Red Bull
Company, which Bentley believes was created about 1626 by a
combination of the remnants of Prince Charles's Men and a
provincial troup formerly sponsored by King James.[62]
Professor Howarth believes it "unthinkable that The Valiant
Scot should not have been produced on composition,"[63] but
whether the newly formed Red Bull Company first staged the
play or whether another company owned it we do not know.
The Red Bull Company took exclusive acting rights lightly,
for they twice had to be restrained from acting plays that

---

[61]Lawrence A. Sasek, The Literary Temper of the English
Puritans, Louisiana State Univ. Studies, No. 9 (Baton Rouge:
Louisiana State Press, 1961), pp. 92-93.

[62]Bentley, The Jacobean and Caroline Stage, I, 270-272.

[63]Howarth, p. 5.

87

belonged to the King's Men.[64] Since the one production of which we have any record took place after publication of the quarto, the actors may have simply "borrowed" the play without regard for original rights in the play.

There is no record of a revival of The Valiant Scot at the Restoration or at any time during the eighteenth and nineteenth centuries. On 10 June 1964, Professor Howarth staged a reading of scenes from The Valiant Scot before the South African Branch of the English Association at Capetown. Senior English students, trained by Mrs. S. Osborn, gave a "spirited" reading in conjunction with Professor Howarth's lecture on The Valiant Scot published in the Bulletin of the English Association: South African Branch. This appears to be as close to a modern production of the play as anyone has yet come.

[64]Bentley, The Jacobean and Caroline Stage, I, 270, 279.

88

VII. THE PLAY

The Valiant Scot is perhaps of most interest to the
historian of English drama as the last of the history plays
to be published before the closing of the theaters. Though
I have dated The Valiant Scot before the publication of
Davenport's King John and Matilda (1631) and Ford's Perkin
Warbeck (1633), it was nevertheless composed during the
decline of the genre. For a number of reasons,[65] the urge
to capture in drama the spirit of the past was weakening so
much that the late emergence of Ford's masterpiece forces
us to return to the last decade of the sixteenth century
for worthy comparisons.

The exact position of The Valiant Scot in the tradition
of the history play needs exploration. Ribner characterizes
it as "somewhat in the manner of the episodic history play
play."[66] Howarth is scarcely less vague when he refers to
"the true technique of the chronicle play on English history."[67] Schelling's comment that the play is "a far from
ineffective chronicle in the old manner"[68] perhaps sets the

---

[65]Irving Ribner, The English History Play in the Age
of Shakespeare (1957; London: Methuen, 1965), pp. 266-267.

[66]Ribner, p. 298.

[67]Howarth, p. 7.

[68]Felix E. Schelling, Elizabethan Drama 1558-1642
(1908; New York: Russell & Russell, 1959), I, 306.

tone for later commentators. These opinions probably owe
more to the outward trappings of the play, the battles and
pageantry which do seem to glance backward, than to the
political philosophy which the play evinces.

We have seen that the source for The Valiant Scot is
largely to be found in Hary's Wallace, a book that, like
another of the sources, Holinshed's Chronicles, would have
been regarded as historically authoritative by a seventeenth
century playwright. The derivation of the material from a
historical source is important in establishing the genre of
the play, but, just as important and even more interesting,
are the historical purposes which the play serves. For it
is true that historical matter may be used in dramas that
are devoted to essentially non-historical purposes, such as
the private struggles of the human soul in tragedy (e.g.,
Macbeth or The Duchess of Malfi). However, one of the distinguishing characteristics of the history play as a
separate dramatic genre is the use of historical sources
for serious didactic purposes.[69]

In his study of The English History Play, Irving
Ribner abstracts a number of historical purposes which the
English history play as a type derived from two general
traditions--the classical-humanist and the medieval-
Christian:

[69]Lily B. Campbell, Shakespeare's Histories: Mirrors
of Elizabethan Policy (1947; San Marino, Calif.: The
Huntington Library, 1958), pp. 16-17.

90

Those /historical purposes/ stemming from classical and humanist philosophies of history include
(1) a nationalistic glorification of England; (2)
an analysis of contemporary affairs, both national
and foreign so as to make clear the virtues and
the failings of contemporary statesmen; (3) a use
of past events as a guide to political behaviour
in the present; (4) a use of history as documen-
tation for political theory; and (5) a study of
past political disaster as an aid to Stoical
fortitude in the present. Those stemming from
medieval Christian philosophy of history include:
(6) illustration of the providence of God as the
ruling force in human--and primarily political--
affairs, and (7) exposition of a rational plan in
human events which must affirm the wisdom and
justice of God.[70]

An application of Ribner's criteria to J. W.'s play is

revealing. The Valiant Scot, for example, contains no

nationalistic glorification of England. Since most of the

story is unfolded from the point of view of the Scottish

rebels, it is Scotland that is extolled as the beloved

mother country. England itself is not attacked, though a

number of scornful comments criticize English military

habits (e.g., I.ii.86-92; V.ii.8-13). However, since the

one consistently honorable character is the Englishman

Clifford, these comments are obviously not intended to

blacken English character, but to highlight distinctions

between English and Scottish customs of battle. Also many

personal insults refer to national differences in the give-

and-take of verbal conflict, though these are due to the

particular dramatic situation rather than to a desire to

censure either people in blanket fashion.

-----

[70]Ribner, p. 24.

Those historical functions which are expressed in the play are, primarily, the use of the past as a guide to the present and the use of history to document political theory. Also important are the analysis of contemporary statesmen and the illustration of God's providence in human, especially political, affairs.

The providential theme is stressed at only one point in the play, the deaths of Selby and Haslerig in Act III. However, it is clear that the notion of God's Will being worked out in history pervades the play as a whole. We find passing mention of the providential idea in scattered comments throughout. In a passage where Haslerig urged the English to action, the reference to providence is a mere verbal convention, a commonplace of usage; this much appears from the emphasis of the speech which is on human, rather than divine, agency: "'Tis time for providence to stirre....We must prevent it" (I.vi.4-10). A later passage in which Mentith describes the capture of Wallace conceives of the hand of heaven as intervening in human affairs despite the opinions of men:

          We struck
     The Stagge to the ground, and thought him dead,
     But heaven put backe the blow of purpose.
                                        (V.iv.64-66)

In the third act, J. W. brings out the workings of providence both in speech and in action. Here Wallace has within his grasp the revenge which he swore against Selby, who had murdered his father. Selby is ill and weak; Wallace

92

has but to lift his hand to take his revenge. Yet he

willingly relinquishes to heaven his duty of vengeance:

> Unlesse I be a devill (tho I have cause
> To kill thee) yet my quicke hand shall eschew it;
> Thy carelesse confidence does bind me to it.
> This mercy which I show now is for Gods sake,
> In part of payment of his showne to me.
> If I should kill thee now, thou owest me nothing;
> Live, and be still my debtor; I shall do thee
> More harme to give thee life, then take it from thee.
> Heaven in my fathers bloud who is chiefe sharer,
> Shall strike for me a revenge more just and fairer.
>   (III.i.273-282)

Wallace's refusal to yield to the impulse for private

revenge is in line with orthodox thought: "Elizabethan

moralists condemned revenge as illegal, blasphemous, im-

moral, irrational, unnatural, and unhealthy--not to mention

unsafe."[71] The orthodox position was that the evil-doer

must be left to the hands of God. By refusing revenge,

Wallace joins with the heroes of A Woman Killed with Kind-

ness, The Malcontent, and The Atheist's Revenge, plays in

which the hero "suffers base injury but whose major virtue

is his explicit refusal to take revenge."[72] And the ortho-

dox position is quickly vindicated in the immediate and

ironic murder of Selby by Haslerig, his partner in tyranny,

in a futile struggle over the food left by Wallace. Upon

the heels of Selby's murder follows the death of Haslerig,

who is mistaken for Wallace by Sir Jeffrey and his followers.

---

[71]Eleanor Prosser, Hamlet and Revenge (Stanford: Stanford Univ. Press, 1967), p. 10. See also Fredson Bowers, Elizabethan Revenge Tragedy, 1587-1642 (1940; Princeton: Princeton Univ. Press, 1956), pp. 8-14.

[72]Prosser, p. 66.

Sir Jeffrey, who had been the third killer of Wallace's
loved ones, makes manifest the pattern of providence working
through men--the principle of the guilty punishing one
another. The blood guilt remains on the stained hands, and
Wallace, the injured party, stays untainted:

> Just heavens ye have bestow'd my office
> Upon some other; I thank ye that my bloud
> Stains not my hand.

(III.ii.3-5)

But the providential scheme may be seen to operate
throughout the play in a larger sense. The overall action
represents the slow, painful process of reestablishing
legitimate and traditional relations between Scotland and
England. This process will be examined in detail hereafter,
but we might note at this point the structural balance of
positive and negative ethical forces, typical of the tradition of the morality play. In the first scene, we are
presented with a distinction between the English who seek
to tyrannize over Scotland and the sympathetic but feeble
Thorne who seeks rather to rule. King Edward, like Gorboduc
torn between the counsel of his flatterers and that of
Eubulus, must choose between the viewpoints of Percy, the
"politician," and Clifford, the man of honor. Even Wallace
has the equivalent of a good angel to advise him against
the self-destructive course he follows. When he ignores
Friar Gertrid's advice, the cleric's prophecies one by one
come true until Wallace himself falls, betrayed by his own
kind.

Another consideration which informs The Valiant Scot
is that of the mirror of contemporary statesmanship.
Certain characters and incidents seem to comment directly
upon the affairs of the writer's own time. The most prominent example is the court scene (I.iv) where, as we have
seen, Grimsby's unsuccessful mission to France suggests the
Duke of Buckingham's clumsy negotiations with France in
1625-26. Queen Elinor's position as peacemaker with the
"Christians" of France may reflect Queen Henrietta Maria's
interest in her native France. King Edward, of course,
corresponds to King Charles.

Still more important to The Valiant Scot are the more
far-reaching political motives of the play. The use of
history to present policy and to document political theory
can be seen both in the relations between England and Scotland and in the important characters of the play. The
dominant political theory examined is that vital matter
explored in so many Elizabethan plays--the relationship
between sovereign and subject. This relationship is explored from both directions: we are invited to regard the
government of King Edward as an exercise in arbitrary
authority, at the same time judging the career of Wallace
as an example of understandable, if unjustifiable, rebellion.

The fact that Wallace is both the titular hero of The
Valiant Scot and the historical hero of Scottish indepen-

dence must not bind us to the fact that he is presented as
a misguided and shortsighted rebel against legitimate order.
For the play substantiates Edward's claim to ultimate
authority over Scotland as well as England. Grimsby admits
that Edward won the crown of Scotland by conquest, a per-
missible means of gaining rule provided one opposes a
legitimate enemy (II.i.4).[73] According to orthodox political thought of the day, however, one's own sovereign could
not be a legitimate enemy.[74] The universe tended to be
viewed as a fixed order bound together by interconnections,
so that a rebel rose up not only against his prince, but
against "his country, his countrymen, his parents, his
children, his kinfolks, against God and all men heaped
together."[75] Shakespeare dramatizes this distinction
between legitimate conquest and illegitimate rebellion when
he makes the weak Henry VI admit that the Lancastrian claim
to the throne is based on rebellion:

> My title's good, and better far than his.
> WAR. Prove it, Henry, and thou shalt be King.
> K. HEN. Henry the Fourth by conquest got the
> crown.
> YORK. 'Twas by rebellion against his King.
> K. HEN. /Aside/ I know not what to say. My
> title's weak.--
>
> (3 Henry VI, I.ii.130-134)

---

[73]Hugo Grotius, De Jure Belli et Pacis, ed. William
Whewell (Cambridge, 1853), III, chapters vi and vii.

[74]Ribner, Appendix A, pp. 305-312.

[75]Homily Against Disobedience and Wilful Rebellion
(1571), quoted in Ribner, p. 309.

Since Wallace and the Scots accept Edward's rule at the beginning of the play, they cannot logically throw it off later.

It is clear that the Scots accept Edward as a legitimate ruler. Old Wallace specifically admits this when he returns the staff of office to Edward's representative:

> To what my King commands
> I humbly bend, resigning on my knee
> Both Staffe and Office.
>
> (I.i.47-49)

It is to the English officials that the Scots appeal for succor as to the rightful magistrates of their land. Bruce acknowledges Edward's rights over Scotland when he begs the crown from his hands, acknowledging a form of imperial suzerainty. Thus, the Scots themselves admit that Edward has gained a clear and legitimate authority over Scotland.

Yet the play also depicts a disturbing breakdown in the political order that makes rebellion understandable. The opening scene demonstrates the corruption of English rule in Scotland, corruption that overthrows property rights in the case of Old Wallace and that splits families in the case of Graham. From this corruption stems the private warfare of Wallace and Young Selby, as well as the civil war which pits Scotland against England.

It is these actual grievances of the Scots that ultimately lead to Wallace's defiance of King Edward as an illegal ruler or tyrant. For there was a view which opposed the "Tudor doctrine of obedience." A number of

97

Renaissance writers followed Medieval thinkers like John of
Salisbury and Marsiglio of Padua in justifying tyrannicide.[76]
An unworthy ruler could be deposed and executed if his
regime was so oppressive as to force the people to rise up
against him. As in Shakespeare's Richard III, a subject
people might throw off the bonds of fealty sworn to a conqueror if he treated them as slaves rather than as newly
acquired free subjects. On this basis Wallace justifies
his rebellion to Grimsby:

        Look upon the wounds
    And mortall stabs of that distressed breast
    That gave thee suck; see thy poore brethren slaves,
    Thy sisters ravisht, and all out-rages
    That bloudy Conquest can give lycense to;
    See this, and then aske Conscience if the man
    That with his bloud seeks generall reformation
    Deserves the name of Traitour.
                                    (II.i.8-15)

A closer view, however, indicates that Wallace is mistaken
in his assessment of English intentions. From Edward's
instructions to the leaders of the army sent into Scotland,
we learn that the oppressive actions were initiated by
Selby and Haslerig for their own profit. Edward gives
orders that the rights of the Scots citizens are to be
maintained, while tyrannous officials are to be punished:

    If any officer of ours transgresse
    Our will, or go beyond his bounds prefix'd
    Wee'l have his head; he our high worth depraves,
    That our free subjects seek to make his slaves.
                                    (I.iv.83-86)

In fact, Selby and Haslerig are relieved of their positions

---

[76]Ribner, p. 311.

and sent penniless into banishment as a punishment for the very crimes that inspire Wallace to revolt. Had Old Wallace actually petitioned the King, as he suggests doing at I.i. 105, the whole chain of events might have been cut off at the beginning.

Even after rebellion has broken out, Edward attempts to heal the breach without bloodshed. At least three times the King sends to Wallace demanding his submission and offering redress of wrongs. Wallace, however, refuses to credit Edward's good faith, which is perhaps not surprising after he has witnessed Percy's plot to trap him (II.iv.167-201). But the embassy of Glascot and Mountford appears to have been a genuine effort on the part of Edward to reclaim the Scots peaceably to their duties as subjects. The exchange highlights both Edward's generosity and Wallace's false grounds for rebellion:

> if your Countreys wrongs
> Grow from abuse in Edwards substitutes,
> You shall have equall hearing, and the wrongs
> Punish't in the deservers.
> Wallace.   This should not be English,
>   Or if it be King Edward is no tyrant.
>   (II.iii.82-86)

At this point, where a just settlement seems possible, Wallace avoids accepting Edward's justice; instead he switches the discussion to his desire for personal revenge for the death of his wife, father, and chaplain. The revenge which he takes upon the ambassadors on the basis of a legal technicality effectively excludes him from

Edward's pardon at the end of the play.[77] Though he does not lose the sympathy of the audience, he becomes the symbol of rebellion to both Scots and English alike. It is Wallace who lacks generosity at the critical moment; he must, therefore, be sacrificed to clear the path for the final reconciliation.

More interesting than the career of Wallace--insofar as the political thought of the play is concerned--is the view of King Edward's rule which the dramatist presents. The attitude to monarchy embodied in the play modifies to some extent the orthodox doctrine of obedience. Edward is depicted as wavering between two concepts of authority: that based on force and that based on honor. The distinction appears in the first scene where Selby and Haslerig debate with Thorne. Throughout the rest of the play, the two views are represented by Percy and by Clifford.

Percy is closest to Edward in the court scene, for indeed the King styles him his "honor'd second in all inward combats" (I.iv.22). Percy seeks his goals through cunning rather than through honorable directness. He sets the snare for Wallace and approves of Edward's scheme to procure Wallace's death through bribery. Arrogant to inferiors, he causes Bruce's disaffection by his cruel jest against the Scot. He ungenerously refuses to see Bruce in action at Falkirk. When he spies Bruce "muffled" he sneaks

---

[77]See the commentary on II.iii.123-126.

off to report his discovery to the King rather than face
Bruce openly. His criticism of Grimsby, whose later
actions belie every statement made about him by Percy, may
well reflect self-doubt.

That element of King Edward's character which is
extended in the character of Percy is apparent in the monarch's attempt to rule Scotland through English deputies
rather than restore the legitimate Bruce to the throne. As
Wallace points out (II.iii.98-99), Edward is responsible
for the acts of his subordinates; thus, his selection of
Selby and Haslerig as administrators corresponds to his
choice of Percy as advisor. The same impulsive selfishness
that makes him delay in granting Bruce his inheritance
splits up his court when he reproves Grimsby for defending
his honor against Percy, and causes him to send away Bolt
when the soldier offers his coat as a royal seat. In each
case, second thoughts result in an attempt to repair the
damage, but the realm suffers from Edward's short-sighted
initial response.

Clifford represents the man of honor, the proper
counselor for a king. He is courageous in battle and in
counsel; he counters even Edward when the King sponsors
unworthy policy (IV.iv.56). He is generous and gives full
credit to Wallace and the Scots for their virtue. He hates
the small-mindedness of Percy's jests against Bruce and
suggests to Bruce the ambiguity of his position in the

English court. Both Wallace and Bruce attest to Clifford's nobility, his concern with ideals rather than with narrow expediency. For the sake of virtue, Clifford will turn against his own nation if Englishmen force him toward a dishonorable position. He therefore sets a moral standard for the entire action. His refusal to countenance Percy's plot against Wallace symbolizes the supreme rule of honor, which even Edward must obey to hold the hearts of virtuous subjects. The play assumes mutual obligations between lord and subject; the King must obey law lest his follower be released from his duty. When Clifford, like Bruce, turns against Edward's rule, we see honor as a higher principle than patriotism or fidelity to the prince. J. W. here shows a modification of orthodox political doctrine. In 1626, the subject might question his duty of obedience in a way that would have been dangerous thirty years earlier. Despite the reiterated claims to divine right, Charles I was under the constant necessity of justifying his position by both pragmatic success and by principle.

Just as the character of Percy reflects some traits of Edward, so Clifford also reflects some characteristics of the King. In the court scene we see Edward maintaining his honor against France with a scrupulousness of which Clifford could only approve. As noted above, he reconsiders hasty actions that might be unworthy of him. Though in the heat of battle he refuses mercy to the surrounded Scots (IV.iii.

33-34), he ultimately joins England and Scotland in the traditional, legitimate union toward which the play has been moving. His assurance to Bruce that he "value/s7 honour above conquest" (V.iv.134) indicates that either the disadvantage of force or the example of Clifford has won him over to rule by honor. Yet it is significant that the final speech, conventionally given to the leading character who remains alive, is assigned to Clifford. Clifford maintains his choric function to the end.

The uncertainty as to Edward's motivation for returning the crown of Scotland to the legitimate prince seems to be a weakness in the play, for there is no preparation for this decision other than the presence of Bruce throughout the play. Edward instructs his followers to observe Bruce (I.iv.107), and he inquires about the Scotsman's conduct at Falkirk, but we have the impression that Edward distrusts Bruce rather than that he is testing his loyalty. The abruptness of the shift in attitude toward Bruce contributes to the effect of a patched-up ending, although the conclusion culminates important themes that the dramatist has been developing throughout the play.

There are other examples of unsatisfactorily motivated conduct in the play. The sudden decision to betray Wallace on the part of his life-long companions, Coming and Mentith, is disturbing. Only in one aside when Mentith jests at Peggie's morals (I.v.16-19) do we feel anything but complete

identification with Wallace's cause. If The Valiant Scot
were a Fletcherian play, with sudden shifts in intention
for the sake of theatrical surprise, such switches might be
expected. However, J. W.'s usual practice--as, for instance, with Grimsby's change of loyalty--is carefully to
prepare for such alternations; therefore, such sudden
inconsistencies disturb out expectations.

Act III provides a number of such problems. To begin,
Wallace's shipwreck is not explicitly connected with his
trip to France. Carver, on the basis of Selby's and Haslerig's changes in fortune, speculates that an interval of
several months has lapsed between acts.[78] Such an obvious
point could easily be clarified by a simply statement by
Wallace or by Ruge-crosse, the Scottish herald who announces
Wallace's return from his reported shipwreck. Also, there
seems to be no reason why Selby should not make a more
satisfactory explanation of his banishment and inform us
about Edward's proceedings in Scotland. Completely un-
explained is the presence of Bolt and Sir Jeffrey Wisacres
in a civilian capacity. It may be that in the clean-up of
the Scottish administration Sir Jeffrey was put out to
pasture as Justice of the Peace in a poor district of Scotland, but the text is silent on the matter. Also, Sir
Jeffrey's character seems to undergo a change. In Act I he
is a tool of the English commissioners. In practically

---

[78]Carver, p. 103.

every speech, he voices his faith in "policie," though he refuses to commit himself when asked for advice. It is he who performs the routine of the Commission, manhandling prisoners, publishing proclamations, and arranging banquets. In Act II, he slays the Friar, shouting, "Thus religion dies" (II.ii.23). When Sir Jeffrey reappears in Act III, he is a comic, wisecracking butt for Bolt's jests. He never once mentions "policie," his perpetual refrain in the first act. Though it is not very significant in light of Wallace's bedraggled condition, Sir Jeffrey fails to recognize in Wallace the person at whose hearing in I.vi he had been present. Taking all the evidence together, the name seems to be the only link between the character of the first acts and that of Act III. It is possible that at some point in the writing process two characters were collapsed into Sir Jeffrey, a convenient form of "doubling" for the actor.

On the other hand, Bolt is the same irrepressible joker wherever he appears. Though his place changes from that of corporal to clerk, and his puns accordingly from military to legal vocabulary, he remains lively, witty, and capable. Overbearing to his own inferiors, he is unabashed before his betters. Nevertheless, a more meticulous dramatist would have accounted for the shift in positions.

The length of the comic scenes of Act III provides evidence of the difficulty which J. W. had in plotting the

105

play. He skillfully handles the opening scenes as the
tyranny of Selby and Haslerig expands to engulf all the
characters in the play. Except for the digression concern-
ing Edward's "French affairs," the plot progresses
efficiently and economically. It moves through a series of
reversals of ever-deepening seriousness as the Scots and
English commissioners struggle to avenge each preceding
atrocity and contend for control of Scotland under the
approaching threat of royal intervention to both sides.
With the visit of the English ambassadors after the murder
of Wallace's family this development ceases. Wallace's
visit in disguise to the English camp and the seashore
scene of Act III are essentially digressions. Even the
deaths of Selby and Haslerig, though thematically valuable,
are nevertheless improvised and unsatisfactory. For the
restraint shown by Wallace in this act seems inconsistent
with his character elsewhere; we seem to see J. W. pulling
the strings, and so falsifying his own creation. When
there is no longer need for revenge, Wallace ceases to act
except for making contact with Bruce, the action which con-
stitutes his enduring success. During the final two acts,
interest is focused on Bruce. The playwright's handling of
Bruce's growing disaffection with the English is excellent,
as the character reacts to all the major characters before
determining to devote himself to Scotland--at a time when
the capture of Wallace makes a break with Edward unneces-

sary. If the play wanders during the middle scenes, it opens strongly and closes effectively.

In his extended comparison of the kingdom of the sea to that on land (III.i), Bolt describes the fishy domain as a highly structured community in which the different types of fish have functions according to their natures. Like the world in which the characters of the play struggle, the kingdom of the sea has a real possibility for order, yet "as great men here eate up the little men, so Whales feed upon the lesser fishes" (III.i.59-60). This is the central problem of the play. Both the rulers and the ruled abuse their positions in a general decay of degree and duty. The kingdom degenerates through several degrees of instability until civil war results. The image patterns of the play reflect this degeneration. Music, generally seen in the Renaissance as reflecting order and harmony, here threatens through allusions to the dirge-like Lacrimae (I.iv.54) or to execution music to make Death smile (II.ii.6-7). The important group of animal images that runs throughout the play expresses the dehumanizing effect of the civil disturbances. Both sides see their opponents as domestic animals to be butchered or as prey to be hunted. Wallace, for example, is ultimately struck to the ground like a "Stagge" (V.iv.65). A second major group of images, the storm images, express either the struggles or the emotions of the combatants. The third important group, the references to the heavens and to the stars, reflects two aspects of man's attempt to adjust to an unstable universe. The large number of references to fate and to the stars as controlling human destiny demonstrates the feeling of human weakness, of being swept blindly along by events. Countering this are the references to providence and to ultimate hope in heavenly bliss, which depict the pious trust that the sufferings of this life may be redeemed in another. These image patterns are not at all original with J. W., yet they are tightly unified with the themes of degeneration and decay in the kingdom on land.

Though the language of The Valiant Scot is not its high point, it is certainly worth careful consideration. There seem to be two general aspects of the style of The Valiant Scot: an energetic, quick, serviceable manner, used basically for exposition and action, and a slower, more deliberate and formal modification of this style for scenes of rhetorical occasion.

Most of the dialogue of Act I, in which characters are introduced and the plot machinery set going, reflects the first style. The speeches tend to be short; the majority of words tend to be monosyllabic. A large number of run-on lines contributes to the effect of energy, as do also the lines split between different speakers. Not a few of the lines are metrically uneven, many of them squeezing in eleven, twelve, or even thirteen syllables. As befits such

a medium for unselfconscious action, images are short,
designed for emphasis rather than for pictorial effect.   J.
W. draws heavily on aphorisms to give authority to the
statements of his speakers, rather than to create more
wordy argument in verse as Massinger might do.   An example
of this efficient style is Edward's speech in I.iv.   This
speech of thirteen lines is much longer than the norm for
this act, but it is packed with matter as King Edward gives
a number of orders and comments on his policy:

> Let messengers be sent
> To question the proud Rebell, and if Grimsby
> Faile in his plot, Northumberland and Clifford
> Shall second him in armes; so slight a fo
> Must not detain us from our French designes.
> Our Queen has all our brest, and tho we might
> Justly perhaps confine your liberty,
> Bruce, we inlarge it, giving you command
> in our French wars. /Aside/ Observe him neerly Lords;
> I have read this maxime in state policie:
> Be sure to weare thy danger in thy eye;--
> France lights a Comet, Scotland a blazing Star;
> Both seeke for bloud, wee'le quench 'um both with war!
>   (I.iv.99-111)

Many of the speeches of Act II run as long as the
above example.   Much of the interest in this act is devoted
to psychological or ceremonial matters; hence, J. W. modu-
lates to his more rhetorical style.   Wallace's apostrophe
to his dead friends is a good example:

> First pray pardon me,
> If like the working of a troubled sea
> My bosome rose in billows, for though the windes
> That rais'd the storme be downe, yet the deare ruines
> Lye still in view, a father and a wife.
> Age, beauty, and religion, for thee
> Thousands shall weep, as many wives
> Shed purple teares for thee, as many Church-men
> Offer their reeking soules in sacrifice;

109

Court, City, Church, the Chamber of your King,
The Chaire of State shall be no priviledge.

(II.iii.87-97)

Since Wallace is here displaying his emotions, the rhetorical pitch of the speech is higher than that of King
Edward's speech quoted above. Wallace's speech is carefully
built around a number of rhetorical figures from the
opening apology for his emotion (<u>anangeon</u>) to the allitera-
tive series of nouns in the subject of the last clause
(<u>hypozeugma</u>). We note the elaborate image of the sea-storm
with which Wallace describes his weeping and the "ruines"
of the storm, the corpses before him; the address to "age,
beauty, and religion" which represent his three dead friends
(<u>antonomasia</u>); and the promise of revenge which, by the
shift in address from his dead friends to the English ambassadors, becomes a threat of revenge (<u>cataplexis</u>). This
highly wrought style seems doubly mannered by contrast with
the terse language of the basic style of the play. In this
passage, the emotional occasion justifies the strained
expression, but there are a number of passages in which the
language is inflated to the point of extravagance. The joy
of the rescued Wallace at the opening of Act II passes the
bounds of logic and taste:

> In heaven or in a slumber, who resolves me?
> Speake: am I dead, or living? or asleep?
> Or all, or both, or neither? Tell me fate.
> Me thinks I see my Father, warlike <u>Graham</u>,
> The Fryer--What <u>Peggie</u> too? I prethee joye
> Do not ore-flow my sences. Deerest friends,
> <u>Pegg</u>, <u>Father</u>, <u>Coming</u>, <u>Mentith</u>, <u>Graham</u>, see
> I am new moulded, and here stands the creature

> That by a warrant granted from the Queene
> Form'd me from out a second Chaos, breath'd
> New life, new motions, new dimensions.
> To tell the story were to shame the world,
> And make all mankinde blush.
>
> (II.i.21-33)

It may be that we are meant to suppose this speech the language of hysterical relief as is suggested by "I prethee joye Do not ore-flow my sences," but such emotional instability is hardly the overall impression we get of Wallace's character. At another point the effect of the language is almost one of parody:

> How shall we save her? Singly as I am
> I will oppose me 'gainst the town of Lavercke,
> Swim the vast moat, and with my trustie sword
> Hew down the Castle gates, dishinge the doores,
> File off her irons, and through a wall of steele
> Attempt her rescue.
>
> (I.v.34-39)

Wallace's hyperbolic reaction to his father's news about the capture of Peggie is so overwritten that it seems an ironic imitation of such popular romances as Sir Bevis of Southampton.

Despite occasional lapses in taste, however, the verse of The Valiant Scot is generally well suited to its dramatic purpose. Even those passages that present syntactical problems would probably be understood by an audience in the context of dramatic exchange.

Prose makes up a sizable proportion of the language in the play. The passages in Scots dialect are vigorous and racy, though Carver feels that the dialect itself is a poor

111

imitation of actual Scots speech.[79] The forceful spirit of
the language perhaps accounts for the over-robust character
of Peggie, whose vituperative speech oversteps the bounds
of decorum. The English prose exchanges of Bolt and Sir
Jeffrey are short, swift, and idiomatic. Under the strain
of never-ending wordplay, the jests sometimes fall flat and
the prose becomes tedious, but Bolt's exuberance is often
fresh and delightful. Like the verse, the prose is uneven
and inconsistent, but it often surprises by its excellence.

As we have seen, The Valiant Scot provides a fresh
view of the career of Wallace in that his revolt is por-
trayed as a symptom of the disorder resulting from Edward's
attempt to rule Scotland without the legitimate king. Yet
Wallace is a symptom that must be removed for the restoration of health to Scotland. His tragedy lies in the fact
that he responds to actual grievances, yet blindly follows
out his course even after Edward has removed the grievances.
His achievement is that he restores Bruce's sympathies to
the Scottish people over whom he is to rule. Through the
sacrifice of Wallace, J. W. establishes a delicate balance
between English and Scottish claims in which an ideal
(though somewhat unconvincing) order is restored to both
kingdoms.

The Valiant Scot is perhaps typical of many of the

---

[79]Carver, pp. 98-101.

hundreds of English Renaissance plays that have received little critical attention in that it is neither an excellent nor a bad play. At points the structure seems to falter: the characters of Wallace and Edward at times lack clear motivation; the language occasionally rises above or sinks below the proper tone for the occasion. Yet in such scenes as the court scene (I.iv) and the battlefield scenes of Act IV, J. W. handles a many-stranded action smoothly and interestingly. The Valiant Scot is a serious, though spotty, effort to revive a moribund dramatic form.

THE VALIANT SCOT

BY

J. W. GENT.

1637

PERSONS

Edward I, King of England

Beaumont ⎤
Clifford ⎬ English lords
Percy[1] ⎦

Glascot ⎤
⎬ English ambassadors to the Scots
Mountford ⎦

Sebastian, Nephew of Queen Elinor

Haslerig ⎤
Selby ⎬ English commissioners ruling over Scotland
Thorne ⎦

Young Selby, Son to Selby

Sir Jeffrey Wisacres, a comic Justice of the Peace

Bolt, Sir Jeffrey's clerk

Robert Bruce (Earl of Carrick[2]), Heir to the Throne of
                                                Scotland

Old Wallace

Wallace, Son to Old Wallace

Friar Gertrid

---

[1]Percy is several times styled by the title, "Earl of
Northumberland"; however, the title was not created for the
Percy family until 1377 (DNB, XV, 839).

[2]Bruce is several times styled by the title, "Earl of
Huntington"; however, the title (properly, "Earl of Huntingdon") was vacant between 1237-1337 (The Complete Peerage,
ed. H. A. Doubleday, Duncan Warran and Lord Howard de
Walden, VI /London, 1926/, pp. 647-648.

Graham, friend to Wallace and father of Peggie

Coming ⎫

Mentith ⎬ Supporters of Wallace

Grimsby ⎭

Douglas ⎫

Mackbeth ⎬ Scots Lords

Wintersdale ⎭

Scottish General

Ruge-crosse, a Scottish Herald

Elinor, Queen of England, wife to King Edward

Peggie, Graham's daughter and Wallace's wife

Gallants, Messingers, Heralds, English Soldiers, and
Scottish Soldiers[3]

---

[3]Mentioned in the stage directions but not given
speaking parts are Prince /Edward7 and Herefor/d7 (see
Introduction, p. 22).

To the right Honorable <u>James</u>, Marquesse <u>Hamilton</u>,
Earle of <u>Cambridge</u> and <u>Arran</u>, Lord of <u>Even</u>,
<u>Ennerdale</u> and <u>Arbroth</u>, Master of the Horse
his Majesty, Steward of the Honour of <u>Hampton</u> Court,
Gentleman of the Kings Bed-chamber, and Knight of   5
the most noble Order of the Garter, <u>and</u> <u>one</u> <u>of</u> <u>his</u>
<u>Majesties</u> <u>Privie</u> Councell in both Kingdomes.

Right Honorable,

<u>Mens</u> <u>actions</u> <u>have</u> <u>not</u> <u>their</u> <u>difference</u> <u>alwayes</u> <u>from</u> <u>the</u>
<u>relation</u> <u>of</u> <u>their</u> <u>persons</u>, <u>for</u> <u>hee</u> <u>that</u> <u>presented</u> <u>his</u>   10
<u>King</u> <u>with</u> <u>a</u> <u>dish</u> <u>of</u> <u>water</u>, <u>having</u> <u>nothing</u> <u>else</u>, <u>made</u>
<u>the</u> <u>gift</u> <u>acceptable</u>. <u>I</u> <u>would</u> <u>use</u> <u>the</u> <u>application</u> <u>to</u> <u>my</u>
<u>selfe</u>, <u>having</u> <u>been</u> <u>one</u> <u>amongst</u> <u>your</u> <u>meanest</u> <u>followers</u>
<u>in</u> <u>your</u> <u>Lordships</u> <u>practicall</u> <u>life</u> <u>of</u> <u>a</u> <u>Souldier</u>: <u>what</u>
<u>I</u> <u>have</u> <u>I</u> <u>bestow</u> <u>upon</u> <u>you</u>, <u>and</u> <u>doe</u> <u>hope</u> <u>though</u> <u>it</u> <u>be</u>   15
<u>clothed</u> <u>in</u> <u>the</u> <u>light</u> <u>dressing</u> <u>of</u> <u>a</u> <u>Play</u>, <u>it</u> <u>will</u> <u>not</u>
<u>be</u> <u>denied</u> <u>your</u> <u>Lordships</u> <u>acceptance</u>, <u>since</u> <u>it</u> <u>contains</u>
<u>the</u> <u>Character</u> <u>which</u> <u>History</u> <u>hath</u> <u>left</u> <u>to</u> <u>Posterity</u> <u>of</u>
<u>your</u> <u>own</u> <u>truly</u> <u>valiant</u> <u>Countriman</u>: <u>I</u> <u>most</u> <u>humbly</u> <u>beg</u>
<u>pardon</u> <u>for</u> <u>my</u> <u>boldnesse</u>, <u>and</u> <u>that</u> <u>I</u> <u>may</u> <u>continue</u> <u>knowne</u> 20
<u>to</u> <u>your</u> <u>Lordship</u>, <u>at</u> <u>the</u> <u>becomming</u> <u>distance</u> <u>of</u> <u>your</u>
<u>Honours</u> <u>truly</u> <u>honourer</u>, <u>and</u> <u>humblest</u> <u>servant</u>.

10-12. <u>for</u> . . . <u>acceptable</u>⌉ This allusion appears to
refer to a story similar to that of the widow's mites
(<u>Mark</u>, XII, 42).

11. <u>dish</u>⌉ i.e., dishful, cupful.

17. <u>Character</u>⌉ formal delineation of qualities.

117

Your Lordships most humble

servant and Souldier,

William Bowyer.

THE VALIANT SCOT

Actus I. /Scena 1/

Enter Haslerig, Thorne, Selby, and Sir Jeffrey
Wiseacres. /Haslerig, Thorne, and Selby take
their places at the table./

I.i. The place of the scene is a council chamber in
the Castle of Laverk (Lanark). The properties required for
this scene, a table and four chairs, have presumably been
carried on stage in full sight of the audience and will be
removed in the same way at the end of the scene. Richard
Hosley's examination of staging at the Globe Theater ("The
Discovery-Space in Shakespeare's Globe," Shakespeare Survey,
12 (1959), rpt. in The Seventeenth-Century Stage, ed. Gerald
E. Bentley /Chicago and London: Univ. of Chicago Press,
1968/) indicates that furniture is "discovered" only in
scenes that are "essentially 'shows,' or disclosures, of a
player or object invested with some special interest or
significance" (pp. 211-212). Otherwise, stage-keepers
physically transport the properties in plain sight of the
audience to create the "setting" for normal action. George
F. Reynolds asserts that the table of the council scene,
like the bar of the trial scene can also be assumed as
being present without explanation (The Staging of Elizabethan Plays at the Red Bull Theater 1605-1627 /1940; rpt.
New York: Kraus Reprint Co., 1966/, p. 82). If we take as
literally true the 1641 account of a production at the Red
Bull in which the only properties were "a few ragged foils"
(cf. Introduction, pp. 83-88), that production at least had
the furniture fancied as being present. However, as the
"place" of Old Wallace is significant in the action of the
scene, we may assume that the dramatist expected furniture
to be physically present.

Thorne. Fellow colleagues, since it hath pleas'd our King,

    Renowned Edward, of his speciall favour

    To spheare us in this height of eminence,

    And make us rulers over Scotland,

    Lets shew our selves worthy the dignities   5

    Conferred upon us.

Selby.   That's not by lenity,

    For howsoere the armed hand of war

    Has made them ours, they are a Nation

4. make⌐ maks Q.

---

    3. spheare⌐ set aloft, place above the common reach
(as a planet is placed among the heavenly spheres, OED, 3b).
    4. make⌐ The Q reading ("maks") may represent a con-
traction of "make us" without the standard apostrophe, as
in the parallel case of "toth' the" in I.ii.35. In each
case, the contraction is unnecessary as it is followed by
the contracted term. On the other hand, as the term is
generally spelled "make" throughout the text, the Q form
may simply be a compositorial error.
    6. That's⌐ The pronoun refers to the act of showing
themselves worthy of their dignified place, i.e., We don't
show ourselves worthy of our place by lenity.
    7. howsoere⌐ i.e., notwithstanding that.
    armed hand of war⌐ Cf. William Rowley, A Shoemaker
a Gentleman: "wee are youths whom the rough hand of Warre
hath ruin'd" (I.ii ⌐sig. C⌐). Cf. also Richard II: "and
the hand of war" (II.i.44⌐).
    8. Has⌐ The Q reading "Ha's) represents a peculiar
spelling pattern in this play. The regularity with which
this spelling appears indicates that it is used deliberately, and is not a compositor's slip. The only other examples
of this spelling which this editor has seen are in John
Fletcher ⌐?⌐, The Bloody Brother (London: T. Allott, 1639),
sigs. Iiv, I2, I2v, and in John Tatham, The Francies Theater
(London: R. Best, 1640), sigs. A4v and B3v.
    they⌐ i.e., the Scots.

Haughty and full of spleen, and must be manag'd

With straighter reins and rougher bitts.

<u>Thorne.</u>   Ahlas,   10

I finde them easie, tractable and mild.

Autority may with a slender twine

Hold in the strongest head; then what needs tyranny

Use rein or bitt? By this all doubts are cleer'd;

'Tis alwayes better to be lov'd then fear'd,   15

---

9. spleen7 hot or proud temper.
    manag'd7 This technical term for directing or con-
trolling a horse introduces the image, developed in the
next six lines, of Scotland as an unruly horse to be
mastered.
    10. straighter7 tighter, firmer. This image refers to
the taut line of the reins on a horse under firm control,
as opposed to the loose arc of the reins when a horse is
"given his head."
    12. Autority7 Authority. <u>OED</u> preserves several seven-
teenth-century cases in which the early spelling "aut--" or
"auct--" is preserved.
    13-14. what . . . bitt7 Though no longer employed in
modern English, the impersonal verb "needs" is common in
Elizabethan usage. As in this sentence, it often follows
"what" and elides parts of the following subordinate clause.
This question might be paraphrased: "What need is there
that tyranny should use rein or bit?" (Cf. Abbott, 297 and
<u>OED</u>, 12b).
    14. clear'd7 cleared away.
    15. 'Tis . . . fear'd7 Thorne is here opposing well-
known Machiavellian principles which govern the policy of
the other three. Cf. <u>Machiavelli's</u> The <u>Prince</u>: <u>An Eliza-</u>
<u>bethan Translation</u>, ed. Hardin Craig (Chapel Hill: Univ. of
North Carolina Press, 1944), p. 72: "from hence risethe a
question whether it be better for a prince to be beloved or
feared, feared or loved, both dowbtlesse are necessarie,
but seinge it is harde to make them drawe both in one yoake,
I thincke it more safetie . . . to be feared then loved."
Thorne's attitude is typical of the moderate nature of the
man which is distinctly J.W.'s conception: Hary characterizes him as "a felloune sutell knycht" (VI, 113) and an
enemy to Scotland.

And by your leave, Sir <u>Thomas</u>,

We have good reason to defend our own.

<u>Selby</u>. You are as cleer of danger, and as free from foes--

<u>Haslerig</u>. As he that holds a hungry wolfe by th'eares.

The principles are true: trust not thy wife   20

With secrets, nor thy vassall with thy life;

Sound example proves it.

<u>Jeffrey</u>. And private policy confirms it. I could urge

reason why, shew cause wherefore, and speake to purpose

whereby, but my betters are in place, I know them to   25

---

17. defend our own7 i.e., defend those entrusted to us
(cf. line 8).

18. foes7 It is quite possible that this Q reading
should be emended to "fears" in order to complete the couplet after the standard form of the proverb (Tilley W603).
Identical rhymes are found in Tilley's quotation from
<u>Tottel's</u> <u>Miscellany</u>: "Who . . . Shalbe as free from cares
and feares, As he that holds a wolfe by the eares" (I, 148,
line 24). Cf. also <u>The</u> <u>White</u> <u>Devil</u>: "I do love her, just
as a man holds a wolf by the ears" (V.1.154-155).

20-21. trust . . . life7 No source for the form of
this proverb has been found. The basic ideas are commonplace, however; cr. Tilley, "Do not tell your wife all you
know" (W347a); "A woman conceals what she knows not" (W649);
and "So many servants so many enemies" (S242). This idea
is embodied in Hotspur's refusal to answer Kate's questions
in <u>1</u> <u>Henry</u> <u>IV</u>: "Constant you are, but yet a woman. And
for secrecy, No lady closer, for I well believe Thou wilt
not utter what thou dost not know, And so far will I trust
thee, gentle Kate" (II.iii.111-115).

23. policy7 political craftiness, associated with
Machiavelli. Sir Jeffrey's use of this term acts throughout
this act as a comic refrain to the serious plotting of his
superiors. Without ideas himself, Sir Jeffrey places his
faith in his favorite political term, almost as Richard II
does in the term "king" (<u>Richard</u> <u>II</u>, III.ii.85). Cf. I.i.
101-102, I.vi.11, and I.vi.110.

be pregnant, and a ready wit's worth all.

Selby. For our owne safeties then, and Englands honour,

Let not us lose what our King hardly wonne.

Haslerig. To that effect called we this solemne meeting

To which we have summon'd divers: chiefly Wallace,   30

Late Sheriffe of Ayre, which office tho the King

Conferred on me, the haughty Scot thinks much

To tender up; observe his insolence.

Enter /Old/ Wallace, and takes his place

/in the remaining chair/.

Selby. Presumptuous Groom, this is a seat for Eagles,

And not for Haggards.

Old Wallace.   Selbie 'tis a seat,   35

I, and my Grandsires Grandsire have enjoyed

And held with worship, and till Edwards hand

Remove me from't, Wallace will still posses't.

---

26. pregnant/ imaginative, resourceful, wise.
    wit's/ intelligence is, cleverness is.
27. For... safeties/ i.e., For the safety of ourselves.
28. hardly/ with difficulty.
30-31. Wallace . . . Ayre/ In Hary's Wallace it is
Wallace's uncle that "schirreff was of Ayr" (I.316-317).
Wallace's father was dead before the events of the poem
took place (III.111).
33. tender/ surrender, resign.
34. Groom/ tender of horses, hence inferior person.
35. Haggards/ hawks caught when adult, hence wild and
untamed.
37. worship/ distinction, honor.
38. still/ always, continuous.

<u>Selby</u>. Proud Wallace dares not.

<u>Old</u> <u>Wallace</u>. <u>Selbie</u>, both dares and doe, and must, and will!

Tho subject unto <u>Edward</u>.   41

I'me <u>Selbies</u> equall both in birth and place;

Tho in mine Office, <u>Edward</u> joyn'd you with me,

He never made you ruler over me.

<u>Haslerig</u>. You'le finde he did. Reade that Commission, 45

And tell me then, if <u>Selby</u> or your self

Be Sheriffe of Ayre.

<u>Old</u> <u>Wallace</u>.   To what my King commands

I humbly bend, resigning on my knee

Both Staffe and Office.

<u>Selby</u>.   Which thus <u>Selby</u> breaks

---

40. dares and doe7 This case may represent a compound verb divided into two separate verbs as the <u>hendiadys</u> represents a divided noun phrase. The compound verb would be "/Wallace7 dares do," meaning that he dares act despite any opposition. Upon the division of the verb, the "doe" was not changed to be parallel in form with "dares." Perhaps because of the unexpected tense, the present "doe" seems more emphatic than would the grammatical "does."

42. place7 rank and position.

47-49. To . . . Office7 This scene perhaps echoes Gloucester's resignation of staff and office in 2 <u>Henry</u> <u>VI</u>: "Here, noble Henry, is my staff. As willingly do I the same resign As e'er thy father Henry made it mine" (II.iii.32-34). In both cases a faithful servant willingly gives up his position under pressure from scornful and irresponsible political opponents.

49-50. Which . . . head7 In <u>Richard</u> <u>II</u> (II.ii.58-59) Worcester breaks his staff upon resigning Richard's stewardship to flee to Bolingbroke. Selby here shows contempt for Old Wallace by snapping the sheriff's wand above the head of the kneeling Scot. He also indirectly shows contempt for King Edward through this abuse of the symbol of royal office.

Over thy head, and now proud Sir acknowledge   50

<u>Selby</u> your Ruler, and with your place resigne

Your Castle and your Lands.

<u>Old</u> <u>Wallace</u>.   That's not inserted

In your Commission. What the King

Has given I surrender. For my Lands

They're still mine own, were purchas'd with the sweat 55

Of my deer Ancestors! and ere I lose

A pole, a foot, I or the smallest turfe

A silly Larke may build on, I'le lose life.

<u>Selby</u>. At your own choice, either your lands or life,

Of both.

<u>Old</u> <u>Wallace</u>. Of neither! Royall <u>Edwards</u> mercy   60

Sits above Selbies malice.

<u>Selby</u>.   Surly Groom,

51-76. resigne . . . lawfull⌐7 This passage derives
from Holinshed's account of the Earl of Surrey's reply to
Edward I's demand that all landholders exhibit their "evi-
dences, as theyr charters, deedes, copies, & other writings"
by which they held their lands (<u>Chronicles</u>, II, 789).
Surrey drew forth a rusty sword, crying, "By this instrument
. . . doe I holde my landes, and by the same I entende to
defende me from all those that shall be aboute to take them
from me" (II, 790). See Introduction, pp. 71-73, for a
discussion of J. W.'s use of Holinshed as a source.
    57. pole⌐7 rod, lineal unit of measure equal to 16.5
feet.
        I⌐7 Aye.
57-58. smallest . . . on⌐7 Cf. <u>The</u> <u>White</u> <u>Devil</u>: "you
would dig turves out of my grave to feed your larks" (IV.ii.
65-66). Cf. also <u>The</u> <u>Duchess</u> <u>of</u> <u>Malfi</u> (IV.ii.128-130).
    58. silly⌐7 innocent.

Mercie's for subjects; by what Evidence,

Charter or Service, do you hold your Land?

Old Wallace. Selby by none! That title which I had

    I have given my sonne, a boy of that proud temper,   65

    As should he heare thy insolent demand,

    Would pluck thee from thy seat, and lay thy head

    A satisfaction at his fathers feet.

    But heavens forbid it; Selby thus it stands,

    Thou hast my Office, and my sonne my Lands.   70

Selby. He must shew how he holds 'em.

Old Wallace.   So he can,

    And Selby will shew evidence sufficient--

    Mine, my deere Fathers, and my Grandsires sword.

    He weares good evidence about him, Selby.

    And will upon the least occasion   75

    Both shew and prove it lawfull.

Haslerig.   If the sword

    Be your best plea, y'ave but a naked title,

    And by our autority we here command

---

    62. Evidence7 title-deeds; cf. The Devil's Law-Case:
"I sent you the Evidence of the peece of land I motioned to
you for the Sale" (I.1.57-58).
    63. Charter7 deeds of conveyence of property (OED, 2b).
    Service7 To "hold in service" means to hold in the
capacity of a tenant. Selby here questions the terms by
which Old Wallace holds his land as a tenant.
    68. satisfaction7 tribute, especially that exacted in
a duel.
    77. naked7 empty, legally of no force (with a quibble
on the meaning of "unsheathed").

You and your sonne at our next generall meeting,

To bring in your Surrender, or undergo   80

The penalty of traytors.

Enter Sir John Graham.

Graham. Oh you the patrons of poore injur'd subjects,

Do Graham justice. Selbies riotous sonne

Assisted by a crew of dissolutes

Has stole my onely daughter, and intends   85

A violent Rape, or which more cuts my soule

A forced marriage.

Selby.   Inconsiderate foole,

The boy affects her, and with my consent

Intends a lawfull marriage; 'tis a favour

Her betters sue for.

Graham.   Oh let 'um hate; my bloud   90

Shall never enter league nor hold alliance

With him that hates my Country.

82-87. Oh you . . . marriage⌐ Hary reports that it was
not Selby but Haslerig whose son sought Wallace's wife:
"For Hesilryg had a mater new begone And hyr desirde in
mariage till his sone" (V.665-666). Graham's role as
Peggie's father is completely J.W.'s invention. "Ane agyt
knycht" (V.438), Graham is one of Wallace's most trusted
followers in the poem, and is killed at the Battle of Falkirk (cf. IV.iii.35).
  87. Inconsiderate⌐ thoughtless.
  88. affects⌐ fancies, loves.
  90. bloud⌐ i.e., "flesh and blood," daughter
  91. enter league⌐ make a covenant or alliance.

Selby.   Rest your thoughts.

He has her; if he likes her he shall wed her,

And Graham as a dowry shall enjoy

Thy present state, revenues, goods and Lands.   95

Fret out thy soule, he shall.

Graham.   Shall?

Selby.   I Sir, shall.

It's the highest favour conquest can afford,

For a slave to joyn alliance with his Lord,

And Wallace see present surrender made

Or look for storms.   100

Jeffrey. So say I too, and 'tis not the least part of

policy, neither.

        Exeunt ⌊Selby, Thorne, Haslerig, and Jeffrey⌋.

Old Wallace. Will have my Lands!

Graham.   Inforce me give a dower!

Misery decre'd above comparison.

Old Wallace. Complain unto the King.

Graham.   The King alas.   105

I have heard a story how the subtle Fox

---

95. state⌋ estate; property, possessions (cf. OED, 36).
96. I⌋ Aye.
106-116. I have . . . death⌋ The precise source for
this version of the fable is not known. Philip Harry, in
"A Comparative Study of the Aesopic Fable in Nicole Bozon,"
University Studies of the University of Cincinnati, 2nd
ser., 1, No. 2 (1905), pp. 34-38, traces the development of

Having stole a Lambe, the family of sheep

Drew a petition, and with full consent

Prefer'd it to the Lion. He imploy'd

'Bout earnest and more serious businesse,   110

Appoints the Beare Commissioner, to take up

This bloudy difference. The Beare impannels

A partiall jury all of Wolves, they choose

The Fox their Fore-man, they consult and finde

The sheepish Nation guilty, and with generall breath, 115

Cast, judge, condemnd, and sentenc'd all to death.

<u>Old</u> <u>Wallace</u>. Men should have souls.

<u>Graham</u>.   But tyrants being no men,

Have consequently none. Complaints in slaves

Are like to prayers made over dead mens graves,

---

the fable from "<u>Ovis Canis et Lupis</u>" of Phaedrus (Book I,
Fable 17) to <u>Bozon</u> (Fable 55, c. 1320). Bozon's version is
quite similar to that in <u>The Valiant Scot</u>: the Sheep is
condemned after complaining to the Lion against the Wolf
who has stolen her lamb. A contemporary Aesopian apologue
with points of resemblance is found in <u>The Telltale</u> (V /p.
113/). In this fable the lion temporarily entrusts his
reign to the ass, who disguises himself in a lion's skin to
terrorize the forest subjects. The lines describing the
lion's absence are similar in theme and language to lines
109-111: "this lion king of the forest being vpon some
weighty Cause to trauaile did for the time of his absence,
Confer the Charge of his scepter . . . to the asse." As
very little work has been done on <u>The Telltale</u>, the significance of this resemblance is not certain. For a comparison with the Aesopian fables of Webster, see Introduction,
pp. 37-38.
    112. bloudy/ involving bloodshed.
    116. Cast/ convicted; cf. Massinger, <u>The Emperor of</u>
<u>the East</u>: "I am cast: A jury of my patronesses cannot quit
me" (I.i. /Works, p. 244/).

Nor heard, nor pitied. Heaven has impos'd a curse,   120

Which suffrance in time may cure, complaints make worse.

Old Wallace.   Then as it is lets bear't, win heaven to

                friend;

He that begins knows when and how to end.

                                 Exeunt.

121. suffranc_e7 sufferance; patient endurance, long-
suffering.
123. He that begins7 "He" probably refers to God
through whose will things are begun, Himself having no
beginning. Tilley (B257) cites Fergusson: "Everything has
a beginning (God excepted)." The actual quotation is:
"All things hath a beginning (God excepted)" (Fergusson's
Scottish Proverbs, p. 4).

/Actus I, Scena 11/

Enter Young Selby, and /two/ other

gallants guarding Peggie.

Young Selby. Maske her! Come Peg hide your Scottish face.

Peggie. Why shild I hayd my Scottis face? My Scottis face

　　is as gude as yare English feace; 'tis a true Scotties

　　feace.

Young Selby. I know 'tis sweet, Peggy, and because   5

　　'tis not a picture for every Painter to draw forth,

　　let this curtaine be pind before it.

　　I.11. The place of this scene is a street in Lanark.
Selby and the Gallants enter with drawn weapons (cf. 11.
11-12).
　　1. Maske her/ The custom of masking brides is referred
to in Dekker's The Shoemaker's Holiday (V.11.98-113).
　　2-3. Why . . . feace/ "Why should I hide my Scottish
face? My Scottish face is as good as your English face;
'tis a true Scottish face." Note the irregularity of the
dialect spelling as an extra "e" is added to "Scotties" and
to "feace" in line 3.
　　5-7. because . . . it/ W. J. Lawrence, Pre-Restoration
Stage Studies (1927; New York: Benjamin Blom, 1967), pp.
111-116, discusses the Elizabethan practice of covering
valuable pictures with curtains and the application of this
practice to drama, particularly to the closet scene in
Hamlet (III.iv). He cites Twelfth Night: "we will draw
the curtain and show you the picture" (I.v.251-252).

/He attempts to veil Peggie who

pushes aside the veil.7

Peggie. Hange yare flee-flaps! Na Scottis woeman is

asheamed a that luke, that the master painter abuife

guifes her; whare mun I gangand now? Fay, fay, fay,   10

what lossell am I that am hurrand thus till and fra

with sweards and wapins? Whay mun backerd men gang

fencing and florishing about me? Am I yare may-game?

Young Selby. No Peggy, th'art my prisoner, but here's

thy jaile.   15

/He attempts to embrace her; she steps away.7

8-13. Hange . . . may-game7 "Hang your fly-flops /fly
swatters7! No Scottish woman is ashamed of that look that
the master painter above /I.e., God7 gives her; where must
I go now? Fie, fie, fie, what losel /worthless person7 am
I that /I7am hurried thus to and fro with swords and weapons? Why must backward /perverse7 men go fencing and
florishing about me? Am I your may-game?"
    8. Hange . . . !7 "Hang" is here used as an impreca-
tion, a strong expression of anger.
    13. fencing and florishing7 figurative for the brandi-
shing of swords by the English gallants hustling Peggie off
to a forced marriage.
         may-game7 object of sport, especially a sport such
as one of the Robin Hood games associated with May Day. Cf.
The Devil's Law-Case: "he seemes a Gyant in a May-game"
(IV.ii.145-146).
    14-15. th'art . . . jaile7 Cf. A Cure for a Cuckold:
"An . . . my Neck and Arms Are still your Prisoners. Bon.
But you shall finde They have a gentle Jaylor" (I.ii.211-
214).

Peggie. Are yee my jalor? What kin bin you to the

hangman? Senu you? Whare's hee? Wha is that

foule loone amang you, that mun be my hangman?

Young Selby. Here's no man here your hangman, or

your jailor. 20

Peggie. Wha then be you?

Young Selby. Your friends that hold you only in

bonds of love.

Peggie. I reckand mickle your luife! Fay upon sike

16-18. Are yee . . . hangman⁊ "Are you my jailor?
What kin be you to the hangman? Say you? Where's he? Who
is that foul rogue ⁊loon⁊ among you, that must be my hangman?" Not knowing why she is being kidnapped, Peggie's
distraught mind moves from the mention of "jail" to the
idea of "hangman."

16. bin⁊ be. This subjunctive form was used in questions, especially those implying doubt or appeal. Abbott
(299) cites Othello: "Where be these bloody thieves?" (V.
i.64). Note line 18, where dialect spelling "bin" is
replaced by standard "be."

17. Senu⁊ Say; see Carver, p. 100. He speculates
that "Senu" may be a misprint, though it appears twice in
the text.

Wha⁊ Who.

18. loone⁊ lout, dolt. Cf. Macbeth: "thou cream-
faced loon!" (V.iii.11).

24-28. I reckand . . . helters⁊ This is a confusing
passage. The first sentence may be taken as bitter irony:
"I reckon ⁊value⁊ much your love!" The next sentence makes
sense only if "the" is read as "thee"; however, this
spelling appears nowhere else in Peggie's speech. If we
adopt this reading, the rest of the passage may be modernized thus: "Fie upon such love, you old felon thief,
loving my father's silver as you love me. I'd rather be a
Scotchman's whore than an Englishman's wife to be driven to
the Church with halters." There remain rough places.
Though the gerund clause "luifand the trueman's . . . me"
is connected by the address to "you", it hangs loosely to
the rest of the sentence. The two "luifand's" are ambiguous,
as the first is clearly a gerund, while the second is a verb.

luife, the awd fellon theef, luifand the truemans   25

siller as you luifand me. I'de rather be a Scutch-

mans whore, then an Englishmans waife, and be

dreave toth' Kirke with helters.

Young Selby. Tell mee what proud Scot loves thee,

what Scot dare touch thee now th'art Selbies?   30

Peggie. Hang thee, hang thee foule meazel'd lowne!

Carver points to the second as evidence of J.W.'s careless-
ness in the use of dialect (p. 100). The participle
"dreave" is another example of an awkward attempt at Scots
dialect. Joseph Wright, The English Dialect Grammar (1905;
Oxford: Clarendon Press, 1968), p. 291, lists a number of
dialect participle forms of "drive" which lack the ending
"en". None of these is Scots; but this form may have
reflected a Scots flavor to J.W.
    25. truemans/ her father's. This word contrasts
Graham's honesty to the mercenary nature of the English.
    28. dreave . . . helters/ Refers to the English custom
of having bridegroom's men lead a bride to the church by
her arms as if by force. Cf. Beaumont and Fletcher, The
Scornful Lady, "Were these two armes incompast with the
hands of Bachelers, to leade me to the Church" (I.i.148-149).
This custom is discussed in John Brand, Observations on
Popular Antiquities (London: Chatto & Windus, 1913), pp.
363-364.
    31-35. Hang . . . bange/ This is a confusing passage.
The first sentence is clear, but "What Scuttishman . . .
case" makes no sense in the light of contemporary grammar.
It would require at least two emendations to clarify the
sentence as it now stands. Without evidence for these
changes beyond the evident confusion of the line, we may
only speculate that "What" may have been originally something like "If that" and "his" should be "my". Assuming
that these changes were justified, the passage could be
modernized: "Hang you, hang you, foul measled /infected
with measles, filthy/ loon! If that Scotsman /who/ dares
give his love /to me/ understood my case, you should go no
further on God's dear earth; my lover should strike you
down as butchers do cattle."

What Scuttishman darres guiff my luif understood

my case.

On Gads deare earth yow sud no farder gange;

As butchers kie toth' grund he sud yow bange.   35

2 Gallant. All mildnesse is in vain, take some rough

course.

Young Selby. Toth' Church, away! I'le marry her there

by force.

1 Gallant. Away with her.   40

            Enter Wallace, Coming, and Mentith;

                 Peggy runs to Wallace.

2 Gallant. Younder's Wallace and's crue.

35. toth'⦎ toth the Q.
41. crue⦎ true Q.

---

    35. kie⦎ kine, cattle.
         butchers . . . grund⦎ This is the first use of
"butcher" in the play to suggest a brutal, wholesale killer.
Cf. II.i.17, IV.1.71 and V.iv.30.
         toth'⦎ The Q reading ("toth the") provides a con-
traction that is unnecessarily followed by the contracted
term; cf. I.i.4. This type of mistake is usually caused by
a momentary lapse of memory on the part of the compositor.
    41. crue⦎ The Q reading "true" is not reasonable in
the light of the insults of the following exchange. The
complimentary evaluation "true" would fit poorly with the
general attitude of the English toward the Scots. Moreover,
"The Devill and's dambe" of the following line clearly
refers to a plural object; otherwise this standard expression would be worded "the devil or his dam" (cf. 1 Henry VI,
I.v.5). The mistake could be one of memory failure in the
substitution of one similar word for another on the part of
a swiftly-moving compositor, or more probably a mistake in
the misreading of similar letters. McKerrow describes the
Elizabethan lower case "c" as "Not unlike the lower part of
an upright t" (p. 346).

Young Selby. The Devill and's dambe bee't, budge not.

Peggie. O my luife, these Sotherne Carles mickle wrang

    'gainst mee warcke, and now wad force mee gang

    untill the Kirke, and marry Selby. Wallace my Jo,   45

    not I!

Young Selby. Unhand that beauteous prize, proud

    slave, 'tis mine.

Wallace. Slave! Th'art a villain Selby.

Young Selby. Are ye so brave?   50

Wallace. Look to my wench.

Coming.
Mentith. } Kill 'em.

---

42. Devill . . . dambe/ devil and his dam. This is a common expression; cf. Tilley (D225).

43-46. O my luife . . . not I/ "Oh my love, these Southern /English/ churles work much wrong against me, and now /they/ would force me to go to the Church, and marry Selby. Wallace my Jo, I will not!" (cf. OED, 6d).

43-44. Carles . . . warcke/ The reversed word order of this clause is an example of anastrophe, possibly designed to elevate Peggie's language at this emotional moment.

44. force mee gang/ i.e., force me to go. The omitted "to" of the infinitive following such a verb as "force" was common in Elizabethan English. Abbott (349) points out that such verbs, when they acted as auxilliaries, retained this license. Cf. The Two Gentlemen of Verona: "I'll force thee /to/ yield to my desire" (V.iv.59).

45. Jo/ sweetheart (Scottish term of endearment); cf. II.iv.194, though "Joe" is there used jocularly from male to male. The English Dialect Dictionary cites The Poems of Alexander Montgomerie, ed James Cranstoun, Scottish Text Society, 9-11 (Edinburgh and London: William Blackwood and Sons, 1887), p. 187 as the earliest example (c. 1600) of the use of the term for "sweetheart."

52. Coming. Mentith./ There is a strong probability that this speech should be given to one or both of the Gallants. If spoken by Wallace's followers as designated

136

<u>Wallace</u>. We are no Stares to die by dozens.

<u>Young Selby</u>.   Back,

    The quarrel's mine; and if one single Scot

    Proud'st of your swarme dares answer me, step forth. 55

<u>Wallace</u>. Your first man I Sir.

<u>Young Selby</u>. Harke Gentlemen, let not so sleight a

           showre,

    Which yet lies hid and wrapt in one poore cloud,

    Be by rough winds (raiz'd up by you) dispers'd

---

in Q, the give-and-take of the exchange is disturbed.
Throughout the exchange, it is the English who do all the
threatening, as the Scots are interested in defending
Peggie, whom they now hold. Wallace's retort, "We are no
stares to die by dozens" is obviously in answer to a threat
from the English side. Moreover, Young Selby's opening of
his speech in line 53-54 with "Back," indicates a reproof
to his impetuous followers. The nature of this misattribu-
tion cannot be explained by a simple misreading as can other
mistakes in this scene. Would a compositor give this short
exclamation to both Coming and Mentith? Choric responses
are a feature of this play (cf. line 56), but it seems im-
probable that a compositor would create one, even to
replace a soiled or blotted word in the manuscript. Therefore, if this speech designation is incorrect, it must be a
lapse on the part of the playwright.

    53. no Stares . . . dozens/ This unusual image appar-
ently refers to such meteoric showers as the spectacular
display of 28 October 1602.

    53-55. Back . . . swarme/ Note the shift in address
from the Gallants, who are restrained by "Back," to
Wallace's "swarme."

    57-60. let not . . . storme/ This elaborate image
figures the mortal enmity between Young Selby and Wallace
as a shower. Contained at present in the tacit understanding between Wallace and himself ("one poor cloud"), Young
Selby fears that their followers' threats and insults
("rough winds") will spread the antagonism until all are
involved. Needless to say, the meaning is not precisely
worked out in the image, though the intent is clear.

Into a generall storme; too many eyes   60

Of <u>Scots</u> and <u>English</u> shoots quick lightning forth

Already, but your absence will allay

Those fires which else must kindle. Get them away,

Take shelter in yon taverne.

<u>Omnes</u>.   Agreed.

        Exeunt /Peggie, Coming, Mentith, <u>and</u> Gallants.7

<u>Wallace</u>. Look to my <u>Peggie</u>.   65

<u>Young Selby</u>. Guard my love,

    Hee and I will onely exchange cold words.

<u>Wallace</u>. Now Sir, your cold words.

<u>Young Selby</u>. This Scotch Lasse I love.

<u>Wallace</u>. Is that all?

<u>Young Selby</u>.   Yes.

<u>Wallace</u>.   I love her too,   70

60-61. eyes . . . shoots7 Abbott (333) remarks on the common use of singular inflections with plural subjects in Elizabethan English. He explains that often "the subject-noun may be considered as singular in <u>thought</u>, e.g., 'manners'." This is apparently the case with "eyes," which may be thought of as a single unit; cf. Beaumont and Fletcher, <u>Wit at Several Weapons</u>: "now his eyes shoots this way" (II, i /Works, IX, 87).

61. quick lightning7 Associated with the storm image of lines 53-56, "quick lightning" figures the angry looks that precede the "storm" (e.g., hostility). Like lightning, these scowls may kindle fires, unless allayed (tempered, abated) by absence. "Fires," as in IV.11.63, are the actual hostilities to which such storms may lead.

67. cold words7 The phrase "cold words" often precedes a challenge (Tilley W774). Cf. <u>A Cure for a Cuckold</u>: "I know what belongs to a Calm and a Storm too. A cold word with you" (III.ii.40-41).

Can any words more cold strike to your heart?

Young Selby. Is she your wife?

Wallace.   No.

Young Selby.   She's your whore.

Wallace. Umh, neither.

Young Selby. She gangs with me then.

Wallace. But the dewle kens not whither;   75

If you can win her, weare her; she's wholly mine.

Young Selby. She is?

Wallace. She is; our Lasse are not English common,

I'me right Scotch bred, til death stick to a woman.

Young Selby. And to the death thou shalt; no more

                    but this,   80

Thou shalt heare from me Scot.

---

73. Umh⌐ A negative expostulation, often spelled "Umph."
74. gangs⌐ Young Selby is here using Scots idiom.
This may be intentional imitation of the Northern speech to
mock Wallace, who then replies in the same vein. Such
intentional use of a Scots term is found in Percy's threat
of death to the "bawling barnes" (II.iv.138).
75. dewle⌐ devil. See Hary's Wallace (I.432) for
spelling "dewyll."
76. If you . . . mine⌐ Tilley gives two expressions
close to this version: "Win it and wear it" (W408), and
"Woo, wed, and bed (wear) her" (W731). Cf. Jonson, The
Alchemist: "winne her, And weare her, out for me" (IV.iii.
74-75).
78. Lasse are⌐ At this emotional moment, the playwright
may be using a form of the rhetorical figure enallage, a
singular subject with a plural verb. Abbott (471) points
out that the additional syllable is often dropped in plural
cases of names in which the singular ends in "se". See I.
vi.55: "Art thou their Aspies" for an example in which the
number of a noun used as object is changed for rhetorical
effect.

<u>Wallace</u>.   When?

<u>Young Selby</u>.   Instantly.

Make time Sir, of your weapon, time, and place.

<u>Wallace</u>. This Whinyard.

<u>Young Selby</u>.   This.

<u>Wallace</u>.   Our swords do now agree,

And of one length and scantling. Why should not we,

If we must Surgeons have to morrow, or anon   85

If not as good now? 'Tis the English fashion

To swagger it out, and then drink and then fight

And kill in cold bloud having slept sound all night,

---

82. Make time/ The exact meaning intended by the playwright is unknown as "time" appears to be a compositorial
error of anticipation for the same word which appears later
in the line. From the context, the term replaced must have
been something akin to "choice." The challenged party had
the privilege of selecting the place, time, and arms for
the duel.
83. Whinyard/ short-sword.
84. scantling/ measurement.
84-86. Why should . . . now/ I.e., If we must have
Surgeons occasionally, why should we not have them now as
well? The most confusing element in this sentence is the
repetition of the conjunction "if" which merely makes the
question more emphatic. The other two irregularities in
this sentence are common Elizabethan usages: that which
appears as a double negative "not . . . not," is actually a
repetition of the negative for emphasis (Abbott 406); while
the substitution of the adjective "good" for the adverb
"well" is similarly common (Abbott 1).
86-90. 'Tis . . . principall/ For a similarly scornful
description of English arms, cf. V.ii.8-12. A similar
passage in <u>A Cure for a Cuckold</u> characterizes a nation's
habits on the field of honor: "Carry it like a French
quarrel, privately whisper, Appoint to meet, and cut each
others throats With Cringes and Embraces" (V.i.328-330).

And oftentimes all gash'd the seconds fall,

When home in whole skins come the principall.   90

So about words, the Lawyer wrangling stands,

And loses in mean time his clients lands.

Young Selby. Do'st teach me fencing too in thy own

          school?

I'le beat thee or be beaten; one draws short breath.

Wallace. I feele no sicknesse.

Young Selby.   Yet th'art neere thy death.   95

                /They/ fight.

       Enter 2 Gallants, Coming, Mentith.

         Wallace loses his weapon.

1 Gallant. At it so hotly?

2 Gallant. Kill him, 'tis faire.

---

   90. principall/ principal combatants. The singular
form is used to preserve the rhyme with "fall."
   94. one/ i.e., one of us.
   97-101. Kill . . . infamy/ Without stage directions to
indicate the exact course of the action, we must base our
interpretation on the dialogue. The language indicates that
the situation is an exact parallel to that described in
Massinger's The Parliament of Love: "yor foe beinge at yor
mercy it hath been a Custome in you wch I dare not praise
havinge disarmd your enimy of his sword to tempt yor fate
by yeildinge it againe then runne a second hazzard" (IV.ii.
1429-1433 /ed. Kathleen Marguerite Lea (Oxford: The Malone
Society Reprints, 1929)/). It might be noted that Young
Selby has shown heroic magnanimity twice in this scene;
first by removing the followers from the threatening situation, and now by allowing his opponent to regain his weapon.
For a case in which a combatant does attempt to kill a dis-
armed opponent, see Thomas Heywood and William Rowley,
Fortune by Land and Sea (II.i. /Heywood, Works, VI.386/).

<u>Young Selby</u>. Inglorious conquest; for King Edwards crown,

    I'de trample on no enemy were hee down.

    There--if th'art well, part.

           /Young Selby <u>returns</u> Wallace's <u>sword</u>.7

<u>Wallace</u>.   I'le die,   100

    Or in thy heart-bloud wash this infamy.

<u>Young Selby</u>. Mercy on my soule.

                           <u>Dies</u>.

<u>Coming</u>.   He's slain.

<u>Mentith</u>.   Away!

<u>Wallace</u>. Shift for your selves; 'twill prove a stormy day.

                       <u>Exeunt</u>.

99. well7 i.e., unwounded.
103.1. <u>Exeunt</u>7 Note that the body of Young Selby
remains in place as the stage is cleared of "living"
characters between Scenes ii and iii.

A cry within, "Murder, murder!"

Enter Old Selby, Thorne, Haslerig, Peggie,

and the two Gallants.

Omnes. Search! Call for Surgeons! Follow the murderer.

Peggie. Wa is me! Ligs my luife on the cawd ground?

Let me come kisse his frosty mouth.

Old Selby. What Scot is't?

Omnes. Oh, 'tis yong Selby!   5

Old Selby. Ha! My sonne, who slue him?

1 Gallant. That fatall hand of Wallace.

Old Selby. Follow the villain.

Peggie. I'ze jocund and weel now.

I.iii. The place of this scene is the same as that of
Scene ii, Young Selby's body remaining in position.
2-3. Ligs . . . mouth7 These lines are drawn, consi-
derably changed, from Hary's Wallace (VII, 278-279):
"Nakit, laid law on cald erd me beforn. His frosty mouth I
kissit in that sted." These lines are the report of "a
trew woman" to Wallace that his uncle has been killed by
the English in the atrocity known as the "Barns of Ayr."
5. Omnes7 probably refers here to the Gallants.
"Omnes" is used elsewhere to refer to any collective utterance even when only a portion of those on stage speak; cf.
II.iii.126.
9. I'ze7 Use of "is" with the first person pronoun, as
in this dialectical spelling of the contraction "I is," was
a feature of the northern dialect (OED). In the dialect
passages of The Valiant Scot, "I'ze" means not only "I am,"

Haslerig. Lay upon her fast hold.   10

Peggie. Hang me, I reck not.

Thorne. Away with her to prison.

                                        Exeunt.

as in line 9, but also "I will (II.i.71) and "I would" (II.
iv.29). Moreover, use of "is" in dialect passages is not
limited to the first person singular pronoun. "J.W."
employs such uncommon usages as "thou'se" (thou is = thou
wilt ⟨II.i.69⟩ and "wee's" (we is = we will ⟨I.vi.70⟩).
        I'ze . . . now⟩ i.e., I'm jocund and well now
⟨that I realize Wallace is safe⟩.
    11. reck⟩ care.
    12.1. Exeunt⟩ As the stage is cleared, the body of
Young Selby is carried off by Old Selby and the Gallants.

/Actus I, Scena iv/

Enter King Edward, Elinor, Percy, Beaumont,
Grimsby, Prince /Edward/, Sebastian, Bruce.

King. Not all the bloud and treasure we have spent

Like zealous prodigals in Palestine,

Goes half so neer our heart, as that proud France,

Knowing our merit should bar us of our due.

Percy. France dares not.

King.   Yet he does.

Percy.   'Twas not demanded.   5

Grimsby. How, not demanded? Thinks the bold Lord Percy,

That Grimsby dares not (lawfully employ'd) demand.

Percy. But not command.

I.iv. The place of this scene is the English Court.
Thrones are carried onstage in which King Edward and Queen
Elinor take their places.
    2. prodigals in Palestine/ refers to the Biblical story
of the prodigal son in Luke XV, 11-32.
    3. France/ i.e., the King of France.
    6. Grimsby/ Grimsby is drawn from the Scottish herald
in Hary's Wallace who fled from Edward to follow Wallace's
fortunes: "A Scottis man, that duellyt with Eduuard, Quhen
he hard tell that Wallace tuk sic part He staw fra thaim
als preuale as he may. Sekand Wallace he maid him reddy
boune. This Scot was born at Kyle in Rycardtoune" (VI.297-
302). Hary further explains that Grimsby was a pursuivant
in Edward's service, that he was "Off gret statur and sumpart gray" (VI.311), and that Wallace entrusted him with
the Arms of Scotland.

145

Grimsby.   Yes command, Percy.

Percy. Grimsby, thou canst do well in Garison:

Weare shamoys for a grace, project for bloud,   10

Make eight days to one week, turn executioner,

And hangman-like send fifty in one morning,

To feed the Crows, and live upon dead pay.

Grimsby. He's a man worse then dead that--

Percy. Stop thy throat or--   15

Grimsby. What?

Percy.   I'le cut it.

9-13. thou . . . pay⌐ Percy draws a character of
Grimsby as an unscrupulous behind-the-lines officer. He
succeeds in garrison--thus non-combatant--duty, where expensive clothing stands for more than actual merit. He is
also charged with withholding pay from his soldiers and
with sending his men into danger so he can collect their
pay after their deaths.
     10. shamoys⌐ chamois, from which expensive and luxu-
rious clothes were made. Cf. Beaumont and Fletcher, The
Scornful Lady: "let thy bounty Clap him in Shamois" (II.
ii.9-10). Cf. also The White Devil: "Thou hast scarce
maintenance To keep thee in fresh chamois" (III.i.45-46).
          project for bloud⌐ devise bloody schemes.
     11. Make . . . week⌐ Lucas's note to Webster's The
Fair Maid of the Inn (IV.ii.107) explains this allusion:
"an old joke on the unpunctuality of soldier's pay. Cf.
Witch of Edmonton, III.i: "Ask any soldier that ever
received his pay but in the Low Countries, and he'll tell
thee that there are eight days in the week there hard by.'
The captain would thus be able to keep back more of his
men's pay."
     13. feed the Crows⌐ be turned to carrion, i.e., die.
Cf. I.vi.58-59 and V.iv.155 for other forms of this expression. The same idea may be found in the common expression,
"to yield the crow a pudding" (Tilly, C860).
          dead pay⌐ pay received by an officer in the name
of deceased troups; cf. Webster, "Character of A vaine-
glorious Coward in Command" (Lucas, IV, 26).

Grimsby.   Cut throat.

Percy.   'Tis a trade,

   By which few prosper, and yet thou art made.

Grimsby. A man as good as--

Percy.   A hangman.

Grimsby.   A foule blot

   Lies in your throat.

Percy.   Thy foul-mouth, wash it Scot.

Grimsby. In Percies bloud I'le wash't.

King.   Grimsby you leane   20

   Too hard upon our sufferance, and noble Percy,

   Our honor'd second in all inward combats,

   Thou hast too many worthy parts of man,

   To throw thy self on this unequall hazzard;

   Grimsby thou standst so much degreed below him,   25

   Both in descent and eminent qualitie;

   The many favours we have grac'd thee with,

   Blush to have been conferr'd upon a man

   No better temper'd.

_____

   18-19. A foule . . . throat7 This is a mortal insult
that would ordinarily have to be satisfied by duel. The
ordinary form of the insult is "a lie in the throat." In
this case, the "blot" intensifies the insult, perhaps with
the idea that only from some enduring moral stain ("foul
blot") could such an egregious falsehood have come.
   22. second . . . combats7 i.e., primary advisor.
   24. unequall7 The chance of loss is greater for Percy
since his rank is higher than Grimsby's.
   26. eminent qualitie7 exalted rank.

Bruce.   May it please my Soveraigne

   Confirme his grant touching--

King.   The Crown of Scotland;   30

   Some other time. Grimsby th'ast raised

   A storm which showers of bloud can hardly lay.

Grimsby. Dread Liege,

   If all the youthfull bloud that I have spent,

   And wealthy honors that my sword hath wonne   35

   Waving the Christian Standard in the face

   Of the proud Pagan, in the holy Land,

   Merit the name of hangman, Grimsby casts

31. Some⌐ Save Q.

   29-30. May . . . touching⌐ Hary mentions Edward's
broken promise to deliver the crown of Scotland over to
Bruce (XI.1131-1138). However, Bruce's interjection of his
pleas for his kingdom into Edward's peace-making between
Grimsby and Percy is patterned after the "clock passage" in
Richard III (IV.ii.86-119). Though Bruce interrupts only
twice; Edward's "thou keep'st false time" (line 53) indicates numerous interruptions, several of them perhaps
gestures. Like Buckingham's, Bruce's importunity is eventually cut short by devastating irony.
   31. Some . . . time⌐ The OED records no significance
for the original expression "Save other time" before 1806,
and even then the sense would not fit the context. "Save"
must be a compositorial misreading for "Some," which makes
perfectly good sense, and which is sufficiently near in a
handwritten form that the mistake is probable.
   32. storm . . . lay⌐ Cf. Richard II: "And lay the
summer's dust with showers of blood" (III.iii.43).
   35-37. wealthy . . . Land⌐ This passage echoes Richard
II: "Many a time hath banished Norfolk fought For Jesu
Christ in glorious Christian field, Streaming the ensign of
the Christian cross Against black pagans, Turks, and
saracens" (IV.i.92-95).

148

Them and himselfe at royall Edwards feet,

And like an out worn souldier, humbly begs   40

No pension--/aside/ but look Percy--nor yet office

But leave to leave the Court, and rich in stars

To lose more bloud, or win more worth in wars.

King. We will not lose thee Grimsby; valiant Percy,

If love in us, or loyaltie in you,   45

Have any power--

Percy.   My Soveraignes pleasure sits

Above my private passions.

King.   Then joyn hands,

Our subjects both, the native of two Lands.

              /Percy and Grimsby shake hands./

Percy. Friends Grimsby.

Grimsby. /Aside/ Friends in shew,   50

But in my brest bloudy revenge lies ambush't.

---

40. like . . . souldier/ "Decayed" soldiers were given
permission to beg in order to support themselves after
leaving the service.
42. stars/ destiny, viewed as determined by the stars.
48. Our subjects both/ In this vocative expression,
the indefinite pronoun "both" is used appositively, with
the meaning: "Our subjects both of you." For a similar
expression, see 1 Henry VI: "Good Cousins both" (IV.1.114).
        native/ natives, countrymen. The singular form
used in place of the proper plural may be an example of enallage, perhaps to avoid a third word ending in "s" (cf.
line 86).
50-51. Friends . . . ambush't/ This passage echoes a
similar scene in 1 Henry VI, in which the peace-making
efforts of King Henry are undercut by Winchester's aside:
"So help me God, as I intend it not!" (III.1.141).
51. ambush't/ i.e., waiting in ambush.

Bruce. Gracious Liege.

King. Th'art no Musician, Bruce, thou keep'st false time;
We strike a bloudy lachrymae to France,
And thou keep'st time to a Scotch Jigge to armes.

Elinor. Edward will be more kind to Christians.

King. Let Christians be more honest then to Edward!
In expedition of this holy warre

---

53. Th'art . . . time] This line possibly echoes Richard II's soliloquy on the analogy between proportion in human life and musical rhythm (Richard II, V.v.42-48).

54. lachrymae] a sombre tune. The name comes from the first word of John Dowland's popular "Lachrimae, or seven teares figured in seven passionate Pavans . . .", Grove's Dictionary of Music and Musicians, ed. E. Blom, 5th ed. (London: Macmillan, 1954), II, 755. Cf. The Devil's Law-case: "You'l be made daunce lachrimae" (IV.ii.537).

55. Scotch Jigge] the tune to a lively dance, incongruously played as a martial measure.

56. Edward . . . Christians] Hary does not mention the Queen's pleading that consideration be shown the French. She does protest that the Scots are Christians and should be treated as such (see footnote below to lines 80-82). The present mention of the French as Christians, which is repeated in Edward's next words, probably contains a reference to Anglo-French political and religious difficulties in 1626. Charles I's queen, Henrietta Marie, was notorious for her support of Catholics, both French and English. See Introduction, pp. 63-64, for speculation that this repeated term "Christians" from the lips of the French-born queen would be taken to mean "Catholics" by a politically-conscious audience.

57-66. Let . . . more] This passage refers to the English grievances with Catholic France, whose performance in the great alliance against Spain organized by England and the Netherlands ("holy war") was not up to English expectations. England had sent an army under Count Mansfield to fight on the Continent, in what a royal letter of 11 February 1626 called a diversion which "concerneth chiefly the security of France" (Gardiner, VI, 55). The specific complaint that Edward is making is that the French are refusing to acknowledge indebtedness to the English for military aid.

When France in person was enjoyn'd to march,

To work his safetie we engag'd our own,   60

Casheer'd his fainting souldiers, and on promise

Of so much gold at our return, suppli'd

The French designes our selfe; and is our love,

And losse of bloud, halfe which at least has drop'd

Out of French bosomes, quittant with owe none?   65

Pillage and play the free-butter for more.

Enter Haslerig.

The news?

Haslerig.   Dread Soveraigne, Scotland is infected

With a most dangerous surfet; it breaks out

In strong rebellion.

This is your Kingdome Bruce.

---

61. Casheer'd/ paid off (after being replaced by
English troops).
61-63. on . . . selfe/ i.e., In exchange for a French
promise to repay our expenses, we provided the necessary
troops to fulfill French political intentions.
63-65. is . . . none/ i.e., Do the French seek to
ignore their indebtedness to us for our moral support and
our casualties, half of which at least they would have lost
themselves?
65. quittant . . . none/ a debt cancelled without payment.
66. free-butter/ free-booter. This term refers to a
war of reprisal in which a country seeks retribution for
losses by use of such agents as privateers.
66.1 Haslerig/ After Haslerig's arrival, the remainder
of Scene iv derives from Hary's account of the debate in
the English court over the steps to be used against the
Scots (VI.280-316).
68. surfet/ surfeit, sickness arising from excess.

Bruce. I have no hand in't tho.   70

King. Shouldst have no head, did we but think it; whose

    The Chief?

Haslerig.   One Wallace, a fellow meanly bred,

    But spirited above beleefe.

King. Some needy borderer.

    How is our bosome parted, is their power   75

    Of any strength? Bruce, leavy powers for France;

    /Aside7 If we but thought thee touch'd in't--

         Warlike Percy,

    Beaumont and Sebastian fetch him in

    Or with a second and more fatall conquest

    Ruine that stubbonre Nation.

Elinor.   Gracious Edward,   80

    Tho war has made them subjects, heaven defend

    Subjects should make 'em vassals.

---

71. Whose7 i.e., Who is?
75. our bosome7 Edward, speaking as royal personification of the commonwealth, characterizes the falling away
from loyalty by any subject as a division of his own inner
being (cf. OED, 5).
77. touch'd in't7 implicated in it.
79. Ruine7 bring down into great and irretrievable
disaster.
81-82. Tho . . . vassals7 Hary reports that Queen
Elinor pleaded that the Scots be left in peace: "Till him
/Edward7 scho went, on kneis syne can him as He wald resist
and nocht in Scotland gang; He suld haiff dreid to wyrk so
felloune wrang: 'Crystyne thai ar, yone is thar heretage.
To reyff that croune, that is a gret owtrage.' For hyr
consaill at hayme he wald nocht byde" (VI.290-295).

King.   We conceit you;

   If any officer of ours transgresse

   Our will, or go beyond his bounds prefix't

   Wee'l have his head; he our high worth depraves,   85

   That our free subjects seek to make his slaves.

Haslerig. We do not.

King.   See we finde it not.

Elinor.   Let Ellianor

   Win so much favour as to march along;

   The conquer'd 'las, we are neighbours of one clime,

   And live like them subject to change and time.   90

Grimsby. Royall Edward,

   Though Wallace and some spleenfull dissolutes

   Wrong'd with the yoke of bondage cast it off

---

82. conceit7 understand.
84. prefix't7 limited by prescription.
85. depraves7 depreciates, impairs.
86. That . . . slaves7 Cf. The Telltale: "though
subjects, scorne to bee oprest like slaues" (IV /p. 857).
     seek7 This plural verb used with a singular subject
may be an instance of enallage, perhaps to avoid a fourth
word ending in "s" (cf. line 48). However, immediately
following "subjects," "seek" may be a mistaken plural by
attraction.
87. We do not7 i.e., We do not /exceed Edward's will7.
89-90. Tho . . . time7 Queen Elinor is warning against
the arrogance of the conqueror that might forget that both
nations are alike bound by natural moral laws; i.e., Though
our neighbor Scots are unfortunately conquered, it behoves
us to remember that we are also bound to forces beyond our
control and should thus beware of acting arbitrarily.
93. yoke of bondage7 This phrase is not found in
Shakespeare. It may have its source in Holinshed; cf.
Introduction, p. 73.

Let not the whole Land suffer.

King. Nor do we wish it Grimsby. Should the fates   95

But turn the wheele we might with them change states,

Be Scotlands subjects. Let but Rebellion kneele,

Wee'l weare soft mercy, and cast off rough steele.

Grimsby. I'le undertake it.

King.   Let messengers be sent

To question the proud Rebell, and if Grimsby   100

Faile in his plot, Northumberland and Clifford

Shall second him in armes; so slight a fo

Must not detain us from our French designes.

Our Queen has all our brest, and tho we might

Justly perhaps confine your liberty,   105

Bruce, we inlarge it, giving you command

In our French wars. /Aside/ Observe him neerly Lords;

I have read this maxime in state policie:

---

96.   wheele/   of Fortune.
      states/   conditions.
97.   Be . . . subjects/ /We might/ be. The "we" is, of
course, the royal plural and therefore controls the plural
object "subjects."
98.   soft mercy/ cf. Henry V: "We yield our town and
lives to thy soft mercy" (III.iii.48).
99.   it/ It is not clear what Grimsby is proposing to
undertake. Could lines 99-100 be confused, so that Grimsby's
"plot"is to act as messenger to Wallace? His opportune
arrival in Scene vi seems to precede any other messenger
from the royal forces.
104.   brest/ private thoughts and feelings.

Be sure to weare thy danger in thy eye;--

France lights a Comet, Scotland a blazing Star;   110

Both seeke for bloud, wee'le quench 'um both with war.

Exeunt.

109. Be . . . eye/ Tilly lists a number of proverbs
that are roughly similar in meaning: "Nothing secure unless
suspected" (N314); "Suspicion is a virtue where a man holds
his enemy in his bosom" (S1018).
110. Scotland . . . Star/ This phrase refers to the
belief that such astral phenomena are signs of extraordinary
occurrences, such as wars. Cf. Thomas Dekker, The Noble
Spanish Soldier: "But that I must be held Spaines blazing
Starre, Be it an ominous charme to call up warre" (III.i.
83-84).

Enter Wallace, Coming, Mentith.

Coming. Prethee good Wallace.

Wallace.   Ill betides his soule,

   That speaks of goodnesse, thinks or meditates

   Of any goodnesse more then how to free

   Imprison'd Peg.

Mentith.   But heare me.

Wallace.   Laverck Castle

   Weares but a slender bolt of brick.

Coming.   Turn'd mad!   5

Wallace. And say the moat be fifty fathomes deep,

   Fiftie times fiftie, say it reach through to hell,

0.1. Wallace/ yong Wallace Q.

   I.v. The place of this scene is the Scottish camp.
   0.1. Wallace/ Q's "yong Wallace" has been changed in
order to conform to the standard form of this name appearing in the text.
   1. Ill betides/ a subjunctive form, i.e., May ill
betide. Cf. Abbott (364).
   Prethee/ Prithee (colloquial for "I pray thee").
Coming addresses Wallace, who pays no attention because he
is wrapped in his own thoughts.
   5. bolt/ A figurative expression for the wall that
protects the castle, drawn either from "bolt" as part of a
locking system, or from that quality of brick (a "bolt"--as
of cloth) worn by Laverck Castle.

<u>Wallace</u> will swim't.

<u>Coming</u>. Swim't,

   Yes so wilt thrust an oxe into an Eg-shell,   10

   And rost it by Moon-shine, but why should <u>Wallace</u>?

<u>Wallace</u>. Why should proud <u>Selby</u>, though his forward son

   Were justly slain, imprison <u>Peg</u>? Poor Lambe

   She is no murtherer.

                 In my conscience she

   Ne're drew weapon in anger in her life.   15

<u>Mentith</u>. /Aside/ Not at sharp I think, but by your

      leave 'tis thought,

   She has practis'd in private, put <u>Wallace</u>

   To foil, and made him lie at his hanging ward

   10-11. So . . . Moon-shine/ Coming's exaggerated comparison points out the madness in Wallace's boast. Elizabethan drama is filled with allusions to the supposed connection between moonshine and madness. Cf. Dekker's <u>The Witch
of Edmonton</u>: "When the moon's in the full, then's wit in
the wane" (II.i.55-56). Closer to Coming's extravagant
simile is Lambert Simnel's confession in Ford's <u>Perkin</u>
Warbeck: "I would be Earl of Warwick, toil'd and ruffled
Against my master, leap'd to catch the moon" (V.iii.35-36).
   11. why . . . <u>Wallace</u>/ i.e., Why should Wallace (act
as madly as a moon-struck ox)?
   12. forward/ presumptuous, over-bold.
   16. at sharp/ Fighting "at sharp" means serious fencing
with unbated weapons, in contradistinction to fighting "at
foil." The distinction is used figuratively for the purpose
of sexual innuendo (cf. Massinger, <u>The City-Madam</u>: "lying
at your close ward, You have foil'd their betters" (III.i.
38-39).
   17. practis'd/ A pun may be intended between "prac-
tised" in the sense of having exercised with weapons and in
the archaic sense of having intrigued (with Wallace in a
liason).
   18. hanging ward/ a defensive movement (in fencing).

Many a time and oft.

Enter Old Wallace, and Graham.

Old Wallace.   Wher's my sonne?

Wallace. With Peggie, father, manacles of griefe   20

    Hang heavy on my sences.

Old Wallace.   Shake 'em off.

    Shew thy self worthy him that thou call'st father.

    Or Peggie dies.

Wallace.   What thunderclap was that

    Able to waken death or shake the shroud

    From off a dead mans shoulders? Peggie dies?   25

    Should thunder speak it, Wallace would sweare it lies;

    Who spake that, fatall Nuntio?

Old Wallace.   His breath,

    That gave thee being. Haslerig's return'd.

Wallace. Whence, from the Devill?

Old Wallace. From England, and this instant, but thou   30

---

20. manacles of griefe⌐ This phrase may be echoed in
Richard Lovelace's "The Vintage to the Dungeon" (Poems, ed.
C. H. Wilkinson ⌐1930; Oxford: Clarendon Press, 1953⌐, p.
46): "Griefe too can manakell the minde."
   27. Nuntio⌐ nuncio, messenger.
   30-31. but . . . aire⌐ The English threat to kill
their innocent hostage unless Wallace gives himself up
resembles two incidents in Hary's Wallace. In III.273-277,
the English force Wallace to make peace through a threat to
seize his uncle's land if he continues hostilities. In IV.
718-722, Wallace's mistress is threatened with death unless
she betrays her lover.
   30. but⌐ unless (cf. Abbott ⌐120⌐).

· com'st in

And yeeld thy self, her life dissolves to aire.

Wallace. The charitable Angels waft her to heaven.

Graham. Resolve you then to lose her?

Wallace. How shall we save her? Singly as I am

    I will oppose me 'gainst the town of Lavercke.   35

    Swim the vast moat, and with my trustie sword

    Hew down the Castle-gates, dishinge the doores,

    File off her irons, and through a wall of steele

    Attempt her rescue.

Old Wallace.   'Tis impossible.

Wallace. Impossible! What's the news from England?   40

Old Wallace. Grimsby the fire-brand of his Country

    Comes to insnare you; on the heele of him

    Treads a huge army led on by the Queen,

    Percy and Clifford.

Omnes. Torture and death it self cannot divide us.   45

Wallace. Sir John Graham, you shall be the engine

    Our policie must work with; streight give out

    That hearing of the English expedition,

    Our faction is dissolv'd.

---

32. The . . . heaven/ Cf. Hamlet: "And flights of angels sing thee to thy rest!" (V.ii.371).
34. Singly/ Abbott (420) points out that such adverbs of limitation are often transposed; cf. Thomas Heywood, The English Traveller: "singlie of my selfe I will oppose all danger" (IV/Works, IV.737).
47. streight/ immediately.

Graham. What's this to Peggies rescue?

Wallace.   Much, this rumour   50

    Blown through the Land will stay the English forces,

    And give us time and means to strengthen ours;

    That once in act, repair to Haslerig,

    Selby and Thorn, urge Peggies innocence,

    And for her freedom and your own make faith,   55

    To yeeld me prisoner; 'twill be no doubt excepted,

    Your self once pardon'd, and your daughter free.

Graham. What rests for Wallace?

Wallace.   Prosper'd destinie.

    If the great cause we undertake be good,

    'Twill thrive; if not, be't washt in Wallace bloud.   60

                                 Exeunt.

---

55. make faith/ promise.
56. excepted/ accepted.
57. once/ at once.
60. Wallace bloud/ Wallace's blood. Abbott (471)
explains that the possessive cases of nouns that end in
"ce" are frequently written without the additional syllable.

/Actus I, Scena vi7

Enter Haslerig, Thorne, Selby, Sir Jeffrey.

Haslerig. Is it by generall Proclamation voic'd

    That but proud Wallace yeild, Peg Graham dies?

Sir Jeffrey. The Cryers are all hoarse with balling of it.

Haslerig. 'Tis time for providence to stirre; the King

    (I know not upon what complaints) pretends   5

    This rank Rebellion rather took his root

    From wrongs in us, then treacheries in Wallace,

    And sends his forces rather to examine

    And question our demeanours, then their treasons.

    We must prevent it, how think you, Sir Jeffrey?   10

Sir Jeffrey. Troth even as you think, policie must

                prevent it.

            Enter Messenger.

Messenger. Sir John Graham craves conference with

          the Commissioners.

    I.vi. The place for this scene is the council chamber
in the Castle of Lanark.
    3. balling7 bawling.
    5. pretends7 professes, claims.
    6. rank7 flourishing.
    10. prevent7 act before, anticipate.

<u>Haslerig</u>. Admit him.

<u>Enter</u> Sir John Graham.

A man, me thinks, of your experience,

Respect and education should not linke   15

Your self in such a chain of counterfeits.

<u>Graham</u>. Nor have I Lords, but for your best advantage,

And <u>Englands</u> good; traitors and dottrels

Are sold for all alike. He that will take them

Must seem to do as they do, imitate   20

Their vicious actions, strive to take upon him

Their idle follies, joyn companies, and drive

Them into a net suspectlesse.

<u>Haslerig</u>.   So did not <u>Graham</u>.

<u>Graham</u>. Speak not before your knowledge. You detain

My onely daughter prisoner; will <u>Selby</u>   25

And his colleagues free her and pardon me,

If I dissolve the brood of traitors and give up

<u>Wallace</u> in bands?

---

18. dottrels⌉ dupes
19. sold . . . alike⌉ i.e., betrayed for the general
good.
        take⌉ capture.
22. join companies⌉ i.e., join their company.
22-23. drive . . . suspectlesse⌉ i.e., drive them,
unsuspecting, into a net.
24. before your knowledge⌉ i.e., before you have
correct knowledge.
28. bands⌉ bonds.

Selby.   Let's daughter be produc'd.

                         Enter Peggie.

And th'execution for awhile deferr'd,

Though in her cause Selby has lost a sonne   30

And with him all content. So deer I tender

The peace of Scotland and my Soveraignes good,

As give the traitour to the hand of Law

And with her life take thine.

Sir Jeffrey.   Good policie.

Peggie. Aye trowe ye mean not Wallas. His devoire,   35

    And dowty valour merits mare repute

    Nor sike fawe language.

Graham.   A fowle traitour!

---

28. Let's⏉ Let his.
33-34. As . . . thine⏉ Line 34 contains a shift from
the indicative to the imperative mood after "As". The meaning of the sentence up to the change is: "So dearly do I
cherish the peace of Scotland and the good of my sovereign
that..." At this point, Selby changes from a statement
about his own intentions to a command to Graham. Note the
use of the adjective "dear" in place of the adverb "dearly,"
a common Elizabethan usage (cf. Abbott /17). Also, in line
33, "As" has the meaning of "That" when it follows "So" (cf.
Abbott /109).
35-37. Aye . . . language⏉ "Aye, truly you mean not
Wallace. His faith And doughty valour merit more repute
Than such foul language." The lack of agreement between
the singular verb and the two singular nouns as plural subject is not uncommon (cf. Abbott /336).
35. devoire⏉ French for "duty," here meaning "faith,
loyalty." This term is also used in Hary's Wallace (X.36).
36. dowty⏉ doughty; strong, valiant.
37. Nor⏉ Than (cf. English Dialect Dictionary 1).

163

I have converst with Wallace, thrown my selfe

Into his bosome, mingled thoughts with him,

And find him neither worthy of thy love,   40

Nor my alliance.

Peggie. Fay, sa not sea, my bunny Wallace luifes me.

Graham. Yes as a Politician does a knave

For his own ends. Hearing thy death proclaim'd

But he come in, I told him on't; he smiled.   45

I urg'd thy love and constancy; still he smil'd,

And to confirm't he basely has cut off

All his associates, and given up himselfe

Wholly to me.

Peggie.   Hawd there for cherritie,

And wad yee give him to his faes, that gave   50

38-51. I have . . . protect⟋ This exchange resembles
Languebeau Snuffe's urging to Castabella that she forsake
Charlemont in Tourneur, The Atheist's Tragedy (I.iv.37-64).
Compare with lines 38-41, Snuffe's: "Since Charlemont's
absence I have weighed his love with the spirit of consideration, and in sincerity I find it to be frivolous and
vain. Withdraw your respect; his affection deserveth it
not" (37-40).
    42. Fay . . . me⟋ "Fie, say not so, my bonny Wallace
loves me."
    45. But . . . in⟋ i.e., Unless he submit himself to
the English authorities. Cf. OED, 59.F. for this special
meaning of "come in."
    49. Hawd there⟋ "Hold there." i.e., stop, forbear.
    50-51. And wad . . . protect⟋ "And would you give to
his foes him that gave His blood to your protection." The
verb form "protect" is here used as a noun, an instance of
antimeria, the substitution of one part of speech for another. Note that the historical Wallace here impinges on
the dramatic character, for the character in the play has
lost no blood at this point.

His blood to your protect?

Enter Wallace, with a guard, bound.

Graham.   I will and have;

For thine enlargement and my own I have.

No more, here comes the Rebell.

Wallace.   Traiterous man,

Is this thy love? These thy deep promises?

Art thou their Aspies? See Selby here's the hand   55

Cleft thy sonnes heart.

Selby. For which base villain I'le see thee hang'd.

Wallace. Thou knowest not. Thy own eyes may feed

The Crows as soon as mine; Toads and Snakes

May dig their lodgings in thy brest,   60

And Devils make faggots of thy bones first.

But my sentence?

Selby. Here, Graham, for thy service we enlarge

Thy beauteous daughter.

Wallace. A milde exchange; Angels approve it.

Haslerig.   Next,   65

Thee to thy Lands and Offices we restore.

---

52. enlargement/ release from confinement. Cf. use of
the verb in line 63.

55. Aspies/ spies. The archaic plural used at this
dramatic moment in place of the proper singular object is
an example of enallage, a conscious substitution of one
inflection for another to elevate the language.

58-59. feed . . . Crows/ Cf. I.iv.13.

Peggie.   And what for <u>Wallace</u>?

Selby.   Race him from your thoughts.

Peggie.   Rac'd byn his name furth the whayte buke of life

That speaks it.

/Peggie <u>runs</u> <u>toward</u> Wallace; Sir Jeffrey

<u>steps</u> <u>between</u> <u>them</u>./

Sir Jeffrey.   Hence.

Peggie.   Dear <u>Wallace</u>, thoe ane shrude

Hawd not our bands, wee's meet in yander cloud,   70

Whare na fell Southern nowther can extrude,

Nor bar us fra celestiall pulchritude.

Aid gange thy gate till heaven, and as we flay,

Like turtle Dowes wee'se bill and find gude play.

                                   <u>Exit</u> Peggie.

---

67. Race/ Raze, i.e., erase by scraping. Cf. Massinger, <u>The Bashful Lover</u>: "I deserv'd To have my name with
infamy razed from The catalogue of good princes" (I.ii.
/<u>Works</u>, p. 395/).
68. buke . . . life/ in Biblical language, the record
of those who shall inherit eternal life. The <u>OED</u> cites
<u>Philippians</u> IV.3 and <u>Revelations</u> XX.12.
69-74. Dear . . . play/ "Dear Wallace, though one
shroud Hold not the two of us, so bonded together by marriage, we'll meet in yonder cloud Where no cruel Englishman
can either expell us Or bar us from celestial beauty. I'd
match your pace to heaven, and as we fly, Like turtle doves
we'll bill and find good play."
71. fell/ cruel, deadly.
     Southern/ Southerner; an Englishman, as seen from
the perspective of Scotland.
73. Aid/ I'd; a contraction of "I would."
     gang thy gate/ go at your gait, thus "match your
pace."

166

Wallace. Rare resolution; what weak heart would faint,   75

    Having so constant a companion?

    Selby my soul's bound on a glorious voyage,

    And would be free'd out of this jayle of flesh;

    Then hinder not my voyage.

Sir Jeffrey.   'Tis not policie,

    Wee'l rather set it forwards.

Haslerig.   Raise a Gallowes   80

    Fifty foot high. Ye shall not go by water;

    Wee'l send you up a neerer way.

Wallace.   All's one:

    Axe, halter, famine, martyrdome, or fire;

    All are but severall passages to heaven.

    Let my soule go the furthest way about,   85

    Come tir'd with tortures, shooting out my heart.

---

    79. jayle of flesh7 This image of the body as a jail
or prison for the soul is an ancient one. Donne's use of
this image is discussed in Milton A. Rugoff, Donne's Imagery
(1939; New York: Russell & Russell, 1962), p. 79. Cf.
also Shakespeare, 3 Henry VI: "Now my soul's palace is
become a prison. Ah, would she break from hence, that this
my body Might in the ground be closed up in rest!" (II.i.
74-76) and King John (III.iv.17-19). For a contemporary
parallel, cf. Massinger, The Roman Actor: "His soul is
freed From the prison of his flesh; let it mount upward!"
(IV.ii /Works, p. 1617).
    82. All's one7 i.e., It makes no difference.
    86. tir'd7 a falconry term for meat ripped by the beak
of a hawk.
        shooting . . . heart7 This unusual image apparently
means "giving up my life." In the only example I can find,
the poisoned Count in The Telltale says: "yes to shun further scandall I haue shott my hart as boyes kill Crowes at
kandall" (V /p. 1037).

The deepest wounds, like strong Certificates

Find kindest welcome.

Enter Grimsby.

Grimsby.   Stay th'execution,

And having read this Warrant know

'Tis the Queens pleasure, you send in this traitour   90

Under my conduct to the English Campe:

Rebellion of this nature must be search'd,

With sharper torture.

Wallace.   I outdare the worst!

He is no man that is afraid of death,

And Wallace his resolve shall out-live breath.   95

Grimsby. 'Tis but short-liv'd else. First see him bound

And hud-winckt, then leave him to my care.

Selby. Bear with this Rebell, my love.

Haslerig.   My service.

---

87. like . . . Certificates7 This image refers to the
documents formally certifying facts which, if properly
attested, had the whole authority of the law behind them.
Though I have been able to discover no similar expression,
a parallel may be found in Fletcher, The Noble Gentleman:
"mighty Statutes, able by their strength, To tye up Sampson"
(I.i. /Works, VIII, 176/).
   92. search'd7 explored, or probed (as a wound).
   95. Wallace his resolve7 J.W. avoids the standard possessive forms after names ending in "s" or "ce." In this
case he uses the archaic "his," probably to elevate this
heroic line (cf. "By Mars his helm" /II.iv.228/).
   97. hud-winckt7 hood-winked, blindfolded. This expression from falconry refers to the hooding of the hawk to
keep her quiet and passive.

Sir Jeffrey. And my policie to the good Queen and Ladies.

Grimsby. Come Wallace, now your pride draws neer the

        fall.   100

Wallace. Why Grimsby, if I fall,

   'Tis but to gather stronger force to rise;

   For as a ball's thrown down to raise it higher,

   So death's rebound shall make my soule aspire

   The glorious clouds. So long I die secure,   105

   Death cannot threat more then I dare endure.

Grimsby. No not a man more then my private followers;

   The Queen enjoynes it.

                        Exeunt Wallace and Grimsby.

Haslerig. Farwell, valiant Grimsby, and farwell danger.

Sir Jeffrey. Policie and all.   110

101-102. if . . . rise/ Expressions of this Christian
paradox are common. Cf. Richard II: "Mount, mount, my
soul! Thy seat is up on high, Whilst my gross flesh sinks
downward, here to die" (V.v.112-113). Cf. William Rowley,
All's Lost by Lust: "Let my soule rise, altho my body fall"
(V.v.79) and The Duchess of Malfi: "O Penitence, let me
truly taste thy cup, That throws men down, only to raise
them up" (V.ii.348-349).
    103. as . . . higher/ This image refers to the volleys
in tennis in which the speeding ball rebounds high into the
air to deceive the defender.
    104. death's rebound/ Death is here figured as the
court or field from which the ball rebounds.
    aspire/ aspire to. Abbott (198) points out this
usage as an example of an omitted preposition after a verb
of motion. Cf. Appius and Virginia: "So great men should,
that aspire eminent place" (I.i.58).
    110. Policie . . . all/ i.e., /Farwell7 Policie and
and all.

Selby. The traitors fled, and Wallace thus supprest,

My sons bloud's paid, and his wrong'd ghost at rest--

Haslerig. And the whole land at quiet. Wher's Sir

John Graham?

Wee'l joyn him partner in Commission;

'Twill be a means to make our party strong,   115

And keep down mutinies. Search out old Wallace

And hang the Carle at his own door. Sir Jeffrey

Place tables in the streets, bonefires, and bels;

Since without cause they murmur, let 'um know   119

That with their knees wee'l make their proud harts bow.

---

111. The traitors . . . supprest/ In these two nominative absolutes, the participle "being" is implied (cf.
Abbott, 381); i.e., The traitors being fled, and Wallace
being thus suppressed..."

112-113. My . . . quiet/ The only real verb of the
sentence ("'s paid") provides the verb force for the latter
clauses in this conjunctional series; thus, ghost /is/ at
rest--And the whole land /is/ at quiet. Abbott (383) points
out that the Elizabethans disliked such repetition in
clauses connected by conjunctions.

112. wrong'd . . . rest/ Though probably not literally
accepted by most people of the Protestant English audiences
of the seventeenth century, folk tradition held that the
ghost of a murdered man pursued the murderer until revenged
(Eleanor Prosser, Hamlet and Revenge /Stanford: Stanford
Univ. Press, 1967/, p. 101). The audience understands that
Selby is not speaking of a real ghost, but metaphorically
summing up the results of his revenge.

114. partner/ i.e., as a partner.
    in Commission/ in the exercise of delegated au-
thority.

117. hang . . . door/ Buried in this cruel command is
the image of a signpost over the door of an inn. Haslerig
intends that Old Wallace be executed near his own home as a
sign to other potential rebels of inexorable English retribution.

Sir <u>Jeffrey</u>, be you Master of the Feast,

You keep the purse; if money fall out short,

Send out for more, you have commission for't.

<u>Exeunt.</u>

123. commission<u>7</u> delegated authority.

Act/us/ II. /Scena i/

Enter Grimsby, two or three followers,
Wallace bound and hoodwinkt.

Grimsby. What talk'st of Conscience? Th'art an
          apparant rebell.

Wallace. How can he be a rebell was nere subject?
     What right has Edward to the Crowne of Scotland
     (The sword except) more then my selfe, or Grymsbie?
Grimsby. What greater right then conquest?
Wallace.   Then what cause,   5
     Juster then mine? Respected Country-man,
     Thou hast beene nobly valued, and held ranke

II.i The place of the scene is the Scottish camp.
1. apparant/ evident, obvious.
2. he . . . was/ i.e., he be a rebel who was. The
omission of the relative pronoun was frequent in Elizabethan practice (Abbott, 244). The purpose here seems to
have been to avoid adding to the present eleven syllables
of the line.
4. sword/ symbol of war, thus the right to gain rule
by conquest.
        except/ excepted, excluded. The Elizabethans often
omitted "ed" endings after verbs ending in "t" for euphony
(Abbott, 341).
5. What . . . conquest/ For the legitimate right to
seize rule by conquest as opposed to illegitimate rebellion
against a lawful prince, see Introduction, pp. 95-98.
7-8. held . . . deservers/ i.e., maintained a position
among the most faithful Scots (those who have deserved most
from their country).

172

With best deservers. Look upon the wounds

And mortall stabs of that distressed breast

That gave thee suck; see thy poore brethren slaves,   10

Thy sisters ravisht, and all out-rages

That bloudy Conquest can give lycense to;

See this, and then aske Conscience if the man

That with his bloud seeks generall reformation

Deserves the name of Traitour.   15

Whither do'st leade me?

Grimsby.   To Northumberland

And Beaumont.

Wallace.   Butchers do your worst:

Torture, I spit defiance in thy face,

And death, embrace thee with as kinde an arme

As if thou wert--

8-12. Look . . . to/ The probable source of this speech
is 1 Henry VI: "Look on thy country, look on fertile
France, And see the cities and the towns defaced By wasting
ruin of the cruel foe. As looks the mother on her lowly
babe When death doth close his tender dying eyes, See, see
the pining malady of France! Behold the wounds, the most
unnatural wounds, Which thou thyself hast given her woeful
breast" (III.iii.44-51). For Blind Hary's expression of
the English ferocity in the conquest of Scotland, see
Wallace, (I.161-166).
   9-10. distressed . . . suck/ i.e., Scotland.
   17. Butchers/ Cf. I.ii.35.
   18. Torture . . . face/ Spitting often accompanied the
act of defying, or challenging, an opponent; cf. Measure
for Measure: "But as she spit in his face, so she defied
him" (II.i.86); also Richard II: "I do defy him, and I
spit at him" (I.i.60). A nearly exact parallel is found in
Heywood and Rowley's Fortune by Land and Sea: "Fortune I
spit defiance in thy face" (IV.v /Heywood's Works, VI, 418/).

Enter Old Wallace, Peggie, Graham, Friar /Gertrid7,
Coming, and Mentith.

Old Wallace.   Thy Father--

Peggie.   And thy waife.   20

                    /Wallace is released.7

Wallace. In heaven or in a slumber, who resolves me?

Speake: am I dead, or living? or asleep?

Or all, or both, or neither? Tell me fate.

Me thinks I see my Father, warlike Graham,

The Fryer-- What Peggie too? I prethee joye   25

Do not ore-flow my sences. Deerest friends,

Pegg, Father, Coming, Mentith, Graham, see

I am new moulded, and here stands the creature

That by a warrant granted from the Queene

Form'd me from out a second Chaos, breath'd   30

New life, new motions, new dimensions.

To tell the story were to shame the world,

And make all mankinde blush.

Peggie.   May luive--

Graham.
Friar.   }   Our prayers--

---

21. resolves7 frees from doubt or uncertainty.
28. moulded7 shaped from the "mould" of human flesh,
thus "created."
30. Chaos7 primitive strife of the elements from which
the universe was created.
33. May luive7 "My love."

<u>Coming</u>. And all our friendship like a coat of steele

    Stand betwixt him and danger.

<u>Wallace</u>.   All joyne hands;   35

    Thus like a mountaine Cedar <u>Wallace</u> stands

    Amongst a grove of friends, not to remove

    For <u>Edwards</u> thunder, nor the frowne of <u>Jove</u>;

    I'le hew the yoke from off my countries necke,

    Or never house. This religious Fryer   40

    Is a full witnesse to the sacred bond

    Twixt heaven and me, which on my part I'le keep,

    Or pay the forfeit with my bloud.

<u>Friar</u>.   Heaven shield!

    Many a tall wood oake beene fell'd

---

    36. Cedar⌐ Common in Elizabethan drama are references
to the cedar's strength despite the hostility of the elements. Cf. <u>Duchess of Malfi</u>: "the oft shaking of the
cedar-tree Fastens it more at root" (I.i.242-243). Dent
(p. 186) cites the classical source in Seneca, <u>De Providen-</u>
<u>tia</u> (IV.16), and indicates other Elizabethan parallels.
    40. house⌐ take shelter, as in a house.
    44-51. Many . . . dead⌐ The source for this prophecy
is Thomas the Rhymer's prediction in Hary's <u>Wallace</u>: "For-
suth, or he deces, Mony thousand in feild sall mak thar end.
Off this regioune he sall the Sothroun send, And Scotland
thris he sall bryng to the pes. So gud off hand agayne
sall neuir be kend" (II.346-350). Note that the Friar
speaks in iambic tetrameter couplets. This verse form was
conventional for prophecies, incantations, curses, etc.,
which led Alfred Harbage to speak of the "short, jingling
lines of incantations" (General Introduction to <u>William</u>
<u>Shakespeare, The Complete Works</u>, ⌐Baltimore: Penguin, 1969⌐,
p. 36). Cf. the chants of the witches in <u>Macbeth</u>, I.i. and
IV.i.
    44. beene⌐ "be," elsewhere spelled "bin"; cf. I.ii.16.
Use of this subjunctive form implies doubt or uncertainty
(Abbott, 299). The friar is here uttering a pious hope for

Ere Wallace stoope. Heed <u>Gertrid</u> sawe: 45

Theke sword shall keep in mickle aw

Fell Sotherne folk. Many a crie,

Fray cradled barns ere he shall flie;

Nurses sighes, and mothers tears

Shall swell the clouds. Till thy awne bloud   50

Prove false thilk Crag sall nere lig dead.

<u>Wallace</u>. Shall <u>Wallace</u> live till his owne bloud prove

       false?

Why, that can never be till palsey age

Hath thrust his icy fingers through my veins,

And frozen up the passages of bloud.   55

Wallace's survival before the prophecy proper which begins
with line 46.
   45. stoope⌐ subjunctive form of the verb.
      <u>Gertrid</u> sawe⌐ i.e., Gertrid's "saying" or "advice."
Though Abbot offers no exact parallel for this dropped
possessive ending, J.W.'s usage here conforms generally to
the Elizabethan practice of trying to avoid doubled sibi-
lants ("as in Gentrid's sawe"). See Abbott, 471.
   46-48. Theke . . . flie⌐ "This sword shall keep in
much awe cruel English folk. Many a cry ⌐shall come⌐ from
cradled children before he shall fly ⌐to Heaven⌐." Note
the lack of verb in the last sentence.
   46. Theke⌐ "This"; cf. "thick" in English Dialect Dic-
<u>tionary</u>. Another variant spelling is "thilke" of line 51
and elsewhere.
   48. flie⌐ apparently an image referring to the flight
of the sanctified soul after death.
   50-51. Till . . . dead⌐ "Until thy own blood prove
false, this neck shall never lie dead." Note the inconsistency between the dialect spelling "sall" in line 51 and
"shall" of line 50.
   53-55. palsey . . . bloud⌐ Cf. Dekker, <u>Old Fortunatus</u>:
"The frostie hand of age now nips your bloud" (II.1.138).

Coming. The town of <u>Lavercke</u>, peopled

    Only with English pride and overjoyed

    With thy surpriz, all are made drunk with mirth.

    Bonefires, bels, banquets, and the devill and all

    Invite our swords to their sad funerall.   60

<u>Wallace</u>. Close with advantage! Put your selves in Armes,

    And cease their forfeit lives. This holy Frier

    Shall first bestow a matrimoniall band

    Of our united love, and then my sword

    Like winged lightning shall prepare a way   65

    To Lavercks doom.

<u>Friar</u>.   Nea marry, stay a wheane;

---

56. town_7 As the referent of "all" in line 58, "town"
is apparently regarded as a collective term for all the in-
habitants of the city. Schmidt cites <u>Othello</u>: "The town
will rise" (II.iii.161), in which "town" means "townspeople"

56-60. The . . . funerall_7 Cf. <u>1 Henry VI</u>: "This
happy night the Frenchmen are secure, Having all day car-
oused and banqueted. Embrace we then this opportunity As
fitting best to quittance their deceit Contrived by art and
baleful sorcery" (II.i.11-15).

59. devill . . . all_7 A common expression meaning
"Devil and all others (anyone else)"; cf. Dekker, <u>Witch of
Edmonton</u> (III.i.16).

61. Close . . . advantage_7 attack; come to close quar-
ters when favorable opportunity offers.

62. cease_7 put an end to.

63. band_7 bond.

64. Of_7 i.e., on. Abbott (175) explains that "of" is
sometimes used in metaphorical expressions for "on." He
cites Falstaff's famous "A plague <u>of</u> all cowards!" (<u>1 Henry
IV</u>, II.iv.130-131).

66-77. Nea . . . fate_7 "Nay, marry, stay a while; do
not dip your sword /̄winyard'_7 in the womb of Laverck town,
for if you go, you'll work me /̄thy lives friend'_7 much
wrong: you'll come back safe, but child I fear I'll never
see you again. Kneel to crave your father's /̄Sier'_7

Dip not thy winyard in the weambe

Of <u>Lavercks</u> town, for giffe thou gange,

Thou'se weark thy lives friend mickle wrang;

Thou'se come back seafe, but barne I feare   70

I'se never blinck upon thee meare.

Kneel till thy Sier, his benuson crave;

Next duty bin till dig her grave.

Kisse, kisse thy <u>Peg</u>, for well a neer,

These amerous twins sall nere kisse mare,   75

Till in deaths armes they kisse. Thilke state

Stands writ in heaven and seal'd by fate.

<u>Wallace</u>. Then fate dissembles with mee, this the

        second time

---

blessing /⌐benuson'7; your next duty will be to dig his
grave. Kiss, kiss your Peg, for alas /⌐well-anear'7, these
amorous twins shall never more kiss until they kiss in
death's arms. This situation /⌐state'7 stands written in
heaven and sealed by fate."
     66. marry7 the name of the Virgin Mary used as an
exclamation.
              wheane7 The <u>English</u> <u>Dialect</u> <u>Dictionary</u> defines
"wheane" as "few." The meaning here is apparently "a short
while."
     73. her7 i.e., his. This pronoun refers to Wallace's
"Sier," his father. The female gender in pronouns referring to males was a standard form of Welsh dialect; however,
there is no reason why such should be the case in this
instance, especially as "his" is used properly in line 72.
     75. Thase7 As Wallace and Peggie embrace, the Friar
shifts his address from a command to Wallace to a general
comment on the touching sight.
     78-79. this . . . armes7 Wallace's comment may indicate
the intended acting style of a portion of this scene. As
no "vision" is suggested by stage directions or text, the
actor playing Wallace may have signified, by staring eyes,
stiff posture, and unworldly tones, that he was "trans-

She has by vision summon'd me to armes.

Exeunt.

ported" during his vow in lines 35-43 and during the Friar's prophecy. The mention of this as the second vision is unclear: possibly a passage in Act I was to be recited in such a way as to indicate a visionary experience, or perhaps this is an inconsistency in the play. There is the possibility that an earlier passage might have been cut.

/Actus II. Scena ii7

Alarum. Enter Haslerig one way; Selby,

and Sir Jeffrey with Friar,

Old Wallace, and Peggie.

Haslerig. Whom have you there?

Selby.   Seeking the cave for shelter,

See whom kind fate hath given us.

Haslerig.   Treacherous Wallace,

The doting wizzard, and dissembling woman

Chief cause of this Rebellion. Now revenge,

Clothe thee in crimson, and prepare to feast;   5

Wee'l tune such dismall musick as shall dint

Smiles in thy shallow cheeks.

Peggie.   Alas, for wae,

What gars this Fewde? What ill intend ye man?

8. Fewde7 Iewde Q.

II.ii. The place of this scene is the battlefield outside Lanark.
    6. tune7 play, make music.
        dint7 make a dint or impression.
    7-8. Alas . . . Fewde7 "Alas, for woe, what causes
this hostility?" No term similar to the Q form ("Iewde")
appears in OED. "Fewde" (Feud) fits the context perfectly,
with the primary meaning as "enmity, hostility." Moreover,
"Feud" was regarded in England after the sixteenth century
as a distinctly Scottish term.

Haslerig. To make rebellion fatherlesse, and murder

   A madding widdower.

Old Wallace.   Oh, spare mine age.   10

Peggie. Pitie my beauty--

Friar.   My religion.

Selby. Like pity, as thy barbarous sonne bestow'd

   On my boyes life, I'le print upon thy bosome.

Haslerig. Like pitie, as thy husband pitilesse

   Took on the widdows tears, and Orphans cryes   15

   That kist his, and hung about his knees

   At Lavercks massacre, I'le shew on thee.

Selby. Thus fell my sonne,

   And thus the father of his murtherer fals.

---

    9. rebellion, murder/ The substitution of Wallace's
crimes for his name is an instance of antonomasia.
    10. madding/ frenzied.
    10-23. Oh . . . dies/ This stylized scene of execution
owes much to the execution scenes in 3 Henry VI. From the
death of Rutland (I.iii.35-47), "J.W." takes the execution
of a relative for his kinsman's wrongs and the bitter answer
to the plea for pity. From the killing of York (I.iv.175-
180) and Prince Edward (V.v.38-40), the playwright takes
the multiple killers who stab in turns as they declaim
their hatred.
    14-17. Like . . . massacre/ This view of Wallace con-
flicts with Hary's Wallace, who makes a point of sparing
women, children, and priests. For the first of many references to his mercy, cf. Wallace: "He sparyt nane that
abill was to wer, Bot wemen and preystis he gart thaim ay
forber" (III.217-218).
    15-16. Orphans . . . kist/ i.e., cries of the orphans
that kissed.
    16. his . . . his/ It is unclear whether the initial
"his" was intended to modify a missing noun, or whether it
is an unusual form of repeated pronoun that anticipates the
pronoun of "his knees," the object of both "kist" and "hung."

／Selby stabs Old Wallace.7

Haslerig. Thus wither'd the pride of Laverck,   20

    And thus fades the flower that caus'd their ruine.

／Haslerig stabs Peggie and7 Exit.

Jeffrey. Thus religious cries

    Were stopt with steele, and thus religion dies.

／Jeffrey stabs the Friar.7

Old Wallace. Wallace, revenge me as thou art my sonne.

Peggie. Revenge thy waif.

Friar.   Revenge Religion.   25

    A Crie within, "Wallace and Conquest!"

    Enter Haslerig.

Haslerig. Thunderbolts and fire rampier your throats!

    The slave's growne infinite, and moves

    In every place at once. Shift for your selves:

    Proud Wallace reeking in the bloud of Lavercke,

    Like a fierce tiger nurst in humane spoyle,   30

---

    21. fades . . . ruine7 Hary reports that Wallace's
wife was killed after the street battle at Lanark: "Quhen
Sotheroun saw that chapyt wes Wallace Agayne thai turnyt,
the woman tuk on cace, Put hir to dede, I can nocht tell
yow how" (VI.191-193).
    fades . . . flower7 a commonplace conceit; cf.
Tilley (F386).
    26. rampier7 wall up, as with a rampart. This is a
curse cast at the prevailing Scots offstage.
    28. Shift7 manage, contrive.

Pursues the slaughter. The barren hills lye strewed

With mangled limbes; such as the gentle night

Rescue from death fall in the morning flight.

They flye or fall for company!

Flie from a rebell, but fate keep true course,   35

Wee'le ebbe like flouds, to flow with stronger force.

                                        Exeunt.

31. Pursues . . . slaughter⌐ Note the somewhat in-
artistic repetition of these words in II.iii.1 below.
Coincidence is surely stretched for us to believe both Haslerig and Wallace would use the same phrase within seven
lines.

33. Rescue⌐ Abbott (367) explains that the subjunctive
is used indefinitely in the relative clause following "such
as." He cites _Measure for Measure_: "in her youth There is
a prone and speechless dialect Such as move men" (I.ii.187-
189).

34. fall . . . company⌐ i.e., fall for company with
the dead on the hills.

36. Weele . . . force⌐ Ebb-flow comparisons are commonplace in Elizabethan drama; cf. Tilley (E56, F378, F381).

36.1. _Exeunt_⌐ Note that the bodies of Old Wallace,
Peggie, and the Friar remain in place as the stage is
cleared of "living" characters between Scenes ii and iii.

/Actus II. Scena iii_/

Enter Wallace all bloudy.

Wallace. Pursue the slaughter, whilst I-- Salvation

shield me!

Fryer Gertrid answer me, what barbarous hand

Has cast my friend into this cold dead sweat?

Resolve me gentle Father. Fellon death,

Tha'st acted sacrilegious burglary,   5

And told my-- Father!

Old Wallace.   Wallace.

Wallace.   No excuse.

Peggie. Ay, sea husband.

II.iii. The place of the scene is the same. The bodies
of Old Wallace, Peggie, and the Friar are still in place.
    1. Pursue . . . slaughter_/ Cf. II.ii.31.
    4. Resolve_/ Cf. II.i.21.
        gentle Father_/ Wallace has not yet noticed the
forms of Peggie and Old Wallace, and the epithet "gentle
Father" is directed to the Friar. That he does not mean
Old Wallace is clear from the adjectives "gentle" and
"sacrilegious."
    6. told_/ "Told" fits vaguely in the sense of "reckon
up the value of," as the burglar, Death, calculates his
booty. However, it is possible that the term is a corruption of "stole" ("stold") which would fit more closely with
the image of Death as a thief.
        Father_/ Wallace breaks off the previous sentence at
this point because he perceives the body of Old Wallace.
    7. Ay . . . husband_/ "Aye, so husband." The dialect
spelling "sea" for "so" has already been seen in I.vi.42.
Apparently Peggie's meaning is: "Yes, thus it is, husband."

184

Wallace. Intreat not, ye are guilty both,

And parties in the deerest robbery.

Then, though my wife and father (mercy, fate!),   10

Play not the tyrant with me, do not try

My sences 'bove their weake abilitie.

Cease to afflict me, or I shall turne Rebell,

And breathe invectives 'gainst thy power.

Peggie. O my deare Wallas for the luive waife,   15

12. 'bove⌐ bore Q.

─────────────────────────────

9. deerest⌐ Wallace puns on "dearest" as (1) most
loved, (2) most costly.
10-12. Then . . . power⌐ The meaning of this passage
is apparently: "Then, although you are dear relations,
don't play the role of tyrant with me by trying my senses
above their ability to endure affliction." It is, however,
possible that the parenthetical address to fate should
actually commence a new sentence, after the mention of wife
and father causes Wallace to break off: "Then though my
wife and father--Mercy, fate! Play not the tyrant with me."
11. Play . . . tyrant⌐ This theatrical image is drawn
from the ranting villain of the popular drama; cf. Dekker,
The Noble Spanish Soldier: "But who hath plaid the Tyrant
with me thus?" (I.ii.116). Cf. also II.iv.135-136: "what
Turke that murders his owne brethren Durst play the tyrant
thus?"
12. 'bove⌐ The Q reading ("bore") makes no sense in
this context, which seems to demand the present emendation.
The substitution of an "r" for a "v" would be a natural
mistake for a busy compositor in view of the similarity of
the two letters. McKerrow describes the "v" in terms of
the "r". The "v" "Resembles the form of r described above,
except that the 2 is simply carried upwards in a curve to
the left without being looped. It consequently does not
link with a following letter" (p. 348).
15. the . . . waife⌐ This seems an obvious corruption
as the line should end with a word rhyming with "waife,"
but which would refer to something valuable to Wallace
besides Peggie, Old Wallace, and the Friar, who are referred to ("awe sawles") in line 16. Did J.W. write, "O my
deare Wallas for the luive of laife"? It would fit the
meter perfectly.

For liuue of awe sawles, and thy daying waife,

List to my latter accens, and attend

Of all thy joyes the derne and dismawe end.

Wallace. Torture above indurance! King of dreams

Dissolve my vision.

Peggie.   Wallace is awake.   20

Wallace, O if I be, let my soule never sleepe,

In the blest bosome of my Ancestors,

Till I have drawne a sea of purple teares

From forth the bosomes of the murderers.

Deere Peggie, father, Gertrid, which way, where,   25

How, when what meanes, what cause shall I devise

16-18. For . . . end⌐ "For love of old souls, and
⌐for⌐ thy dying wife, listen to my last ⌐'latter,' see OED
3⌐ accens, and hear ⌐'attend' = listen to = hear, OED I.1⌐
the dark ⌐'derne'⌐ and dismal end of all your joys."

19. King of dreames⌐ The exact nature of the spirit
here invoked is unclear. Morpheus was the god of dreams;
however, Wallace is probably generally addressing any
spirit with power over dreams, possibly simply God in the
Christian sense.

23. sea . . . teares⌐ This image may be a combination
of two images from 3 Henry VI, "seas of tears" (II.v.106)
and "purple tears" (V.vi.64). Both of these images appear
later in The Valiant Scot, "purple teares" at II.iii.94,
and "sea of teares" at IV.1.23. The "sea of purple teares"
refers to the flow of blood anticipated by Wallace.
"Purple" was conventionally applied to the color of blood
and is thus appropriate to images of bloodshed and violent
death. As the traditional liturgical color for penitence,
purple is also associated with guilt (cf. especially II.iii.
93-95).

25-26. which . . . shall⌐ The rhetorical figure in
which a series of words or phrases is concluded by the
terms which give sense to them is hypozeugma (see Warren
Taylor, Tudor Figures of Rhetoric ⌐Chicago: Univ. of
Chicago, 1937⌐, p. 33.

To finde it out, and venge your tragedies?

Peggie. I'le teache ye how: Selby and Haslerigg

    Byn the fell blood-hounds whae have hunted laife

    Untill thilcke toyles of death.

Wallace.   Are they turn'd hangmen?   30

Peggie. Religious cryes, beauteous entreats,

    And reverend well-awayes could not winne

    Grace or favour. Wallas revenge my death,

    And for a favour keep my hindmost breath--

                        /Peggie7 dies.

Wallace. And house it here.

       Enter Grimsby, Coming, Mentith, and Graham.

Grimsby.   Where's Wallas? Never eye   35

    Saw such a ruthlesse massacre.

Wallace.   Yes Grimsby,

    Wallace can shewe a massacre will prove

    Thine but a may-game.

Grimsby.   Terrible and strange!

---

    27. it7 apparently refers to the identity of the mur-
derers.
    29-30. Byn . . . death7 "Be the cruel blood-hounds who
have hunted life unto these snares of death."
    30. toyles7 nets set where quarry is to be driven,
hence figurative for "snares."
    31-32. Religious . . . well-awayes7 This series refers
to the cries of Friar Gertrid, the entreaty of Peggie, and
the laments ("well-awayes") of Old Wallace.
    31. entreats7 entreaties.
    38. may-game7 Cf. I.ii.13.

Wallace. Dost start at this? Then see a spectacle

    Of force to stay the motion of the spheares,   40

    Or strike the Sun dead in the browe of heaven.

    Looke, and like men shott from the browe of thunder

    Fall senceles: death wounds not so deepe as wonder.

Graham. Whose bloody act was this?

Wallace.   The bloody act's

    Contriv'd and plotted by experienc'd villaines.   45

Grimsby. Who were the authors?

Wallace.   Judge, they all spake English,

    Death best becomes that Dialect.

    The first was bloody Hasleriggs, the second

    More villaine-like was Selbyes, but the third

    All had a hand in.   50

Trumpet. Enter Messenger.

---

    40. Of force⟩ strong enough.
          stay⟩ halt, arrest.
          spheares⟩ The concentric, transparent, hollow
globes imagined by the older astronomers as revolving
around the earth and carrying with them the heavenly bodies.
    42. browe⟩ As "browe" appears also in the preceding
line, its appearance here is questionable. It is possible
that the original reference was to the "bow of thunder"
from which lightning bolts flash like arrows to strike down
men. Such similar words could be easily confused in ad-
joining sentences by the compositor.
    44. act's⟩ As the exchange between Wallace and
Grimsby is in the past tense, "act's" may be an unusual
contraction of "act was." On the other hand, Wallace may
be using the historical present tense for immediacy.
    46-47. they . . . Dialect⟩ Throughout the following
forty lines, Wallace plays on the notion of English as the
language of cruelty. Cf. lines 61, 69, 85.

Messenger. English Embassadours.

<u>Exit</u> Messenger.

Wallace. They are welcome. /Aside7 Let not one sullen
       browe

Be seene in all this fiery firmament.

    <u>Enter</u> Mountford, Glascot, <u>and</u> Sebastian.

Wallace. Welcome, your businesse?

Sebastian. /Aside7 Farre more like a Prince,   55
    Then a base rebell looks the Northerne traytor.

Mountford. Thus to a rebell from a royall King:
    If <u>Wallace</u> will confesse himselfe a traytor
    And for his bloody outrages and thefts
    Crave mercy, and submit himselfe to <u>Edward</u>,   60
    There's hope of life.

Wallace.   Still charitable English.

Sebastian. /Aside7 'Tis not he sure;
    This looks not like a man shold shake a kingdome.

Mountford. This if he shall denie,

    51-142. English . . . Armes7 The visit of the English
heralds is drawn from Hary's <u>Wallace</u> (VI.349-426).
    57-61. Thus . . . life7 Cf. Hary's Wallace: "The
awfull king gert twa harroldis be brocht, Gaiff thaim com-
maund in all the haist thai mocht To charge Wallace, that
he sulde cum him till Witht-out promys and put him in his
will: 'Be-caus we wait he is a gentill man, Cum in my
grace and I sall saiff him than'" (VI.349-354).
    64. denie7 refuse.

Rape, murther, ruine, all the sonnes of warre   65

Stands striving for the prey, and once let loose,

Shall not be checkt, nor taken up, till rage

Be tyr'd with murther, and thy selfe in chaynes

Hang'd like a villaine.

Wallace.   This is all perfit English;

Have ye yet spoke?

Mountford.   We have.

Wallace.   Then we begin,   70

And to a tyrant thus sayes a loyall subject:

If Edward will confesse himselfe a tyrant

And kingly fellon, and make good such theft

As he and his have practis'd, sue his peace

By yeelding up his and himselfe to Wallace,   75

There's hope of life. This if he shall deny,

65-69. Rape . . . villaine/ Mountford's image of the
effects of war as hounds to be loosed upon Wallace may have
its source in Henry V: "and at his heels, Leashed in like
hounds, should famine, sword, and fire Crouch for employ-
ment" (Prologue, 6-8). Note the careful parallelism of
language between the two parts of Mountford's speech (lines
57-61 and 64-69) and Wallace's defiance of Edward in lines
70-80 below. Whereas Mountford characterizes the "sonnes
of warre" as hounds, Wallace images "the brood of warre" as
hawks, thus transcending the English threat; falconry was a
nobler sport than venery.
    66. striving/ struggling.
    67. checkt/ stopped by loss of scent.
         taken up/ restrained.
    68. tyr'd/ Cf. I.vi.86.
    68-69. thy . . . villaine/ Cf. Hary's Wallace: "To
this proffyr gaynstandand giff he be, Her I awow he sall be
hyngyt hye" (VI.361-362).
    74. sue/ appeal for.

190

Rape, murther, ruine, all the brood of warre

Shalbe let flie, and never be lur'd of

Till they be gorg'd, and bated with the heart

Of the proud King himselfe.

Sebastian.   Now speakes a man   80

Would thrust Jove from Olympus.

Glascot.   Calme your spleene,

For now speakes mercy: if your Countryes wrongs

Grow from abuse in Edwards substitutes,

You shall have equall hearing, and the wrongs

Punish't in the deservers.

Wallace.   /Aside7 This should not be

          English,   85

Or if it be King Edward is no tyrant.

Glascot. What answers Walace?

Wallace.   First pray pardon me

If like the working of a troubled sea

My bosome rose in billows, for though the windes

That rais'd the storme be downe, yet the deare ruines 90

Lye still in view, a father and a wife.

---

78. lur'd of7 recalled by means of a falconer's lure.
79. bated7 _fed.
81. spleene7 anger.
84. equall7 impartial.
89-90. windes . . . downe7 By "windes," Wallace may
mean the last sighs of his dead friends which threw him
into the emotional frenzy ("raised the storme") over which
he has regained control.
90. ruines7 i.e., remains, bodies.

191

Age, beauty, and religion, for thee

Thousands shall weep, as many wives

Shed purple teares for thee, as many Church-men

Offer their reeking soules in sacrifice;   95

Court, City, Church, the Chamber of your King,

The Chaire of State shall be no priviledge.

<u>Sebastian</u>. This was not <u>Edwards</u> act.

<u>Wallace</u>.   Yet such as <u>Edward</u>

Plac'd in commission. Oh 'twas a churlish storme,

And wretched I like a forlorne surviver   100

Left to interre their deare remembrances.

<u>Sebastian</u>. Good gentlemen--

<u>Wallace</u>.   But bid relentlesse <u>Edward</u>

92-97. Age . . . priviledge7 The source for this threat
is Wallace's vow after the murder of his wife in Hary's
<u>Wallace</u> (VI.213-222). It should be noted, however, that
Hary's hero specifically refrains from seeking vengeance
against women and priests: "Sichand he said, 'Sall neuir
man me se Rest in-till eys quhill this deid wrokyn be, The
saklace slauchtyr of hir blith and brycht. That I awow to
the makar off mycht, That off that nacioune I sall neuir
forber Yong nor ald that abill is to wer. Preystis no
wemen I think nocht for to sla In my defaut, bot thai me
causing ma. Schir Ihon', he said, 'lat all this murnyng be,
And for hir saik thar sall x M de.'"
    94. purple teares7 Cf. II.iii.23.
    95. reeking7 steaming, smoking.
    97. Chaire . . . State7 throne.
    99. in Commission7 Cf. I.vi.114.
    99-101. 'twas . . . left7 Abbott (383) explains that
the Elizabethans disliked repetition in the latter of two
clauses connected by a conjunction. In this case, "'twas"
provides the missing auxillary for the verb of the clause
following "and": "I . . . /was7 Left."
    101. remembrances7 souveniers, (here figurative for
"remains").

Send in the pyrats <u>Haslerigg</u> and <u>Selbye</u>,

And in their hands letters of Mart subscribed,

To make me Master of my owne revenge,   105

Or like a Ball wrapt in a cloud of fire,

Ruine shall fall upon his palace top,

Pierce through the roofe, and in his chayre of State

Sollicit Justice.   109

<u>Mountford.</u> Into his Princely eares I'le give your wrongs.

<u>Grimsby.</u> Will <u>Walace</u> here advise?

------

104. letters of Mar<u>t</u>/ letters of marque, a form of
license granted by a sovereign permitting a subject to make
reprisal on the subjects of an enemy state for injuries
received. Professor R. G. Howarth points out the English
adoption of letters of marque in February 1625 as evidence
for that year as the date of composition of <u>The Valiant
Scot</u>. As evidence for John Webster's hand in the composition of the play he points to a similar passage in Webster
and Rowley's <u>A Cure for a</u> Cuckold: "She carries a <u>Letter
of Mart</u> in her mouth too" (II.iv.150). For a discussion of
the significance of this allusion, see Introduction, pp.
36-37.
        subscribe<u>d</u>/ formally assented to as attested by
the royal signature.
    106-109. like . . . Justic<u>e</u>/ This threat echoes the
themes of such Biblical passages as Psalm XI.6: "Upon the
wicked he shall rain snares, fire and brimstone, and an
horrible tempest."
    106. Ball . . . fir<u>e</u>/ This image may refer to a lumi-
nous meteor (cf. "fire-ball," <u>OED</u> 1). It may also suggest
a cannon ball issuing from the smoky mouth of a gun.
    107. Ruin<u>e</u>/ For a similar example of "ruin" as the
agent of destruction, cf. <u>1 Henry VI</u>: "And see the cities
and the towns defaced By wasting ruin of the cruel foe"
(III.iii.45-46).
    111-113. Will . . . <u>Grymsby</u>/ Cf. Hary's <u>Wallace</u>: "Bot
Iop knew weyll the squier yong Fehew And tald Wallace, for
he was <u>euir</u> trew" (VI.397-398).
    111. here advis<u>e</u>/ i.e., hear advice.

Wallace. Yes.

Grimsby. Then be rul'd by Grymsby.

<u>Whispers.</u>

Wallace. Thanks for thy kindnesse. Lords Embassadors,

    Such we esteeme you, may we crave perusall   115

    Of your commission?

Mountford.   <u>Wallace</u> shall command it.

Wallace. Mountfort and Glascott, what third fellow's

          that?

           /Wallace points to Sebastian./

Mountford. One of our followers.

Wallace.   Good, his name

    Is not inserted. One call out a headsman.

Sebastian. Ambitious rebell, know I am a Prince,   120

    And nephew to the Queene.

Wallace.   Wert thou the King,

    Having no portion in the Embassie,

    I'de ha' thy head. Goe on, and strike it of,

    120-121. know . . . Queene/ Cf. Hary's <u>Wallace</u>: "A
yong squier, was brothir to Fehew, He thocht he wald dys-
gysit to persew Wallace to se, that tuk so hie a part.
Born sistir sone he was to king Eduuart" (VI.363-366).
    121-126. Wert . . . sword/ In this passage, Wallace
sentences Sebastian, Glascot, and Mountford for their
crimes against honor. His explanation of how the punishment
of each fits his crime is delayed until the maimed heralds
are returned before him after their punishment (see lines
131-142). In Hary's <u>Wallace</u>, however, the English heralds
are brought before Wallace one-at-a-time to receive the explanation for the sentence, the condemnation, and the
punishment.

A second cut his tongue out, ⌐Wallace <u>indicates</u>

       Mountford⌐ and a third

Thrust out his eyes, ⌐Wallace indicates Glascot⌐

      and put their followers   125

To the sword.

<u>Omnes</u>.   <u>Wallace</u> wilbe more milde.

              <u>Exeunt</u> ⌐<u>soldiers</u> <u>with</u> Mountford,

                  Glascot, <u>and</u> Sebastian.⌐

<u>Wallace</u>. <u>Wallace</u> wilbe more just then see the Law

125. hi<u>s</u>⌐ their Q.

123-126. I'de . . . sword⌐ Wallace's treatment of the
English ambassadors seems excessive in the light of contemporary international usage. Alberico Gentili, <u>De legationi-
bus libri tres</u> (Hanau, 1594), II, 73, reproduced in <u>The
Classics of International Law</u>, ed J. B. Scott, No. 12 (New
York: Oxford Univ. Press, 1924), suggests that an ambassador who has been proven a spy be held only if he has
completed a mission of espionage and possesses damaging
information; if newly arrived, he should be dismissed and
sent home unharmed. The 1541 execution of two disguised
ambassadors attempting to cross Imperial territory to their
stations at Venice and Turkey was an international <u>cause
celebre</u>; cf. Garrett Mattingly, <u>Renaissance Diplomacy</u> (1955;
London: Jonathan Cape, 1962), pp. 270-271. The prosecuting
ruler, realizing the weakness of his case under international usage, disavowed responsibility for the punishment,
unlike Wallace who glories in his act. We do notice, however, the justification of the deed by Clifford, one of the
disinterested "value bearers" of the play (cf. II.iv.163-
165). Yet the context of Clifford's defense of Wallace,
who is being condemned <u>in absentia</u>, may indicate that
Clifford speaks more from a desire for fair play and a
hatred of subterfuge, than from approval of the execution
of indiscreet diplomats.
    123. of⌐ off.
    125. hi<u>s</u>⌐ The Q reading ("their") appears to be a
memory error in anticipation of "their" appearing four words
later. As Glascot is the only Englishman blinded, "his"
alone makes sense in this context.

Of Armes disgrac'd. Sound Drums and drown their cries.

Revenge beats at heavens gates for tyrannies.

Enter again /_soldiers_ _with_ Mountford, _leading_ Glascot.

    Sebastian's _head_ _is_ _carried_ _in_ _a_ _wallet_/.

So now our tragick Muse ets on the stage.   130

/_To_ Glascot/ You that for seeing basenesse want

        your sight

Beare with this present our indeer'd commends

Back to the Queen, and say so much we tender

Her sacred honour, wee'd not see it wrong'd

Even in her Nephew. /_To_ Mountford/ You that for

        sparing speech   135

In honours cause are justly mute conduct

This eyelesse messenger; abuse not our intent

127-128. Law . . . Armes/ the recognized custom of professional soldiers.

128. Sound . . . cries/ Cf. **Appius** **and** **Virginia**: "Sound all the Drums and Trumpets in the camp, To drowne my utterance" (II.ii.24-25). A similar passage is found in **Richard III** (IV.iv.148-150).

130. So . . . stage/ Cf. Dekker, **Lust's** **Dominion**: "Murder be proud, and Tragedy laugh on, I'le seek a stage for thee to jett upon" (V.i.238-239).

      jet_s_/ struts, swaggers.

131-142. You . . . Armes/ The source for Wallace's comment on the nature of punishment has been discussed above, see note to lines 121-126. For Wallace's instructions to Mountford, cf. Hary's **Wallace**: "'To your fals king thi falow sall the leid. With my ansuer turs him his newois heid. Thus sar I drede thi king and all his bost'" (VI.413-415).

132. indeer'd commend_s_/ cordial regards.

133. tender/ cherish.

In the delivery. Make speedy haste,

Lest we be there before you. Share in like wrong,

Lend him your eyes, and borrow you his tongue.   140

If any question you about your harms,

Say <u>Wallace</u> did it in the right of Armes.

<u>Exeunt</u> <u>English</u>.

<u>Grimsby</u>. This will affright the English.

<u>Wallace</u>.   Honor'd <u>Grimsby</u>,

This and ten thousand, thousand more extremes

Cannot appease my anger. You that love me   145

See those I lov'd inhum'd; my selfe disguis'd

Will be their Convoy to the English Campe,

And see their usage.

<u>Grimsby</u>.   'Twill be an act of danger.

<u>Wallace</u>. The fitter him that undertakes it: <u>Wallace</u>

Would hold himself not worthy of his fate   150

137-138. abuse . . . delivery⌉ i.e., represent our
intentions accurately when you make this delivery to the
King.
139-140. Share . . . tongue⌉ Cf. Rowley's <u>All's</u> <u>Lost</u>
<u>by</u> <u>Lust</u>: "Pluck out his eyes and her exclaiming tongue;
She shall in silent sorrow then lead him; Her eyes shall
be his starres" (V.v.39-41).
142. right . . . Armes⌉ the cause of military honor.
146. inhum'd⌉ buried in the ground.
149. The . . . him⌉ Abbott (198-202) indicates a number of cases in which Shakespeare dropped the preposition,
though none of these examples precisely fits the present
case. However, the sense can easily be reconstructed:
"⌊A dangerous act is⌉ the fitter ⌊for⌉ him."

Should he bawke danger. Disswade not, I will on

Were certain death against my bosome bent;

There's gain in bloud it's honorably spent.

                        Exit /Wallace/.

Grimsby. And such I feare will thine be. Honor'd friends

See those remayns of honorable love   155

Cradled in earth; that once perform'd take Armes

To venge their deaths. Mentith, I attend

The comming of some speciall friends by oath

Bound to assist us. Hark! How their friendly drums

Chide them for loytring.

      Enter Douglas, Mackbeth, **and** Wintersdale.

                 Honor'd Douglas, welcome,   160

Welcome Mackbeth, and doughty Wintersdale,

Not unto men more driven in needfull want,

---

151. bawke/ balk, said of a horse stopping at an
obstacle.
      will on/ Abbott (405) explains that "I will"
followed by a preposition of motion means "I purpose
motion;" thus, in this case, "I intend to continue on."
     152. Were/ The subjunctive use of "were" after "if"
and "though" is examined by Abbott (301). In this case,
the subordinating conjunction is elided; therefore, the
sense is: "/though/ certain death were bent."
     153. it's/ As in the previous line, this sentence
appears to contain an elided subordinating conjunction,
i.e., if it's. This is clearly the meaning intended.
     154. thine be/ i.e., thy blood be spent.
     157. attend/ await.
     162. driven . . . want/ i.e., urged along in a condi-
tion of extreme hardship.

Could you have brought supply.

Douglas.   The better welcome;

   Gold to rich men, and treasure to the wealthy

   Are known companions. Wher's our Generall,   165

   The hopefull Wallace?

Grimsby.   Gone in quest of death,

   Firme as his fate. 'Cause he sees danger shuns him,

   He's gone to seek it in the English tents.

Mackbeth. So Hercules sought honour out in Hell.

   He not deserves the name of Generall   170

   Dares not face danger, and out-do the Devill.

Grimsby. And such a man is Wallace, yet least worth

   Bears him beyond his strength, bring up your powers

   For present charge. His thoughts are tragicall,

---

   163. The . . . welcome/ i.e., The better are we welcome.
   166. hopeful/ inspiring hope (because brave and
resourceful).
   169. Hercules . . . Hell/ The allusion is to Hercules'
journey to the underworld in order to capture Cerberus, the
last of his twelve labors.
   170. not deserves/ The auxiliary was not always used
by Elizabethan authors when "not" preceded the verb. Abbott
(305) cites The Tempest: "Whereof the ewe not bites" (V.1.
38).
   171. Dares/ i.e., /Who/ dares. Abbott (244) explains
that the relative pronoun is frequently omitted in Elizabethan usage, though generally the antecedent immediately
precedes the verb of the dropped pronoun; cf. Measure for
Measure: "I have a brother /who/ is condemned to die" (II.
ii.34). In line 172, the antecedent "He" is separated by
several words from the verb "Dares."
   173. powers/ forces.
   174. present charge/ ready action.

And full of bloud, active and violent all.   175

<u>Douglas</u>. You that best know 'em, feed 'em, all

that's ours,

For <u>Scotlands</u> good call <u>Wallaces</u> and yours.

<u>Exeunt</u>.

/Actus II. Scena iv7

Enter Wallace, like a halting Souldier on

wooden stumps, with Mountford dumbe, and

Glascot blinde.

Wallace. Whare man? Till the English Campe senu you?

Gad sides you gang as I ha' seene mony a your

Countrymen like ranck riders amble up westward;

you gang the wrang wey man, you sall luse and ye

play at shoola-groate.   5

II.iv. The place of this scene is a road near the English camp. The source for Wallace's disguised inspection
of the English camp is found in Hary's Wallace (VI.429-475).
    1-5. Whare . . . linckers7 "Where, man? To the English
camp, do you say? God's sides, you go as do many of your
countrymen whom I have seen amble up toward the west like
reckless /'rank'7 riders. You go the wrong way, man; you
shall lose if you play 'tiddly-winks' with coins. Have you
no eyes?"
    3. amble7 ride a gait in which both the horse's feet
on a side are moved at the same time. There may be a double
reference in this term: (1) to the English troops riding
by, (2) to Mountford and Glascot walking in step as the
blind man is guided by the dumb.
        westward7 (1) toward the west, (2) toward execution,
i.e., Tyburn (see OED, A2); cf. "they all go Westhod" (III.
i.49-50).
    4. sall luse7 There is the possibility that this term
should be "fall luse," in which case the meaning would be
"wander aimlessly." However, "sall luse" makes perfect
sense in context.
    5. shoola-groate7 shovel-groat, a game played by flip-
ping small coins onto a marked surface. It is here used in
the figurative sense to indicate random direction.

Ha' ye na linckers?

Glascot. Ahlas I want my eyes, but have a tongue;

He sees, but cannot speake.

Wallace. Blyncke at smaw faults then. Make me the

thridman, and here's a bunny noyse of Fidlers to   10

gang fra winehouse to winehouse, a blind harper, a

mute Cornet, and an old Scotch bagpipe worne toth'

stumps.

Glascot. Are you a Scotch man Sir?

Wallace. Ye marry am I, boddy and sawle. A true   15

Scotchman borne, but a true liegeman: hang him

that does not luife your King, and your Country-

man. What gude victales is that which thilke

---

6. linckers/ i.e., blinkers, eyes.
7. want/
9-13. Blyncke . . . stumps/ "Blink at small faults
then. Make me your partner and we will be a bonny company
of musicians to go from winehouse to winehouse, a blind
harper, a mute cornet-player, and an old Scotch piper worn
down to crutches."
9. Blyncke . . . faults/ a form of the common proverb,
"Wink at small faults" (Tilly /F123/).
11. a blind harper/ Traditionally, the handicapped in
Scotland and Ireland were trained as popular musicians.
Cf. note to Love's Labor's Lost.(Arden Edition, ed. Richard
David /London: Methuen, 1951/): "Nor woo in rhyme, like a
blind harper's song" (V.ii.405).
15-20. Ye . . . there/ "Yes, marry I am body and soul
a true Scotchman born, but a true subject /liegeman/; hang
him that does not love your King and your countrymen. What
good rations are those which this bonny man that has glazed
eyes has tied up in his knapsack /wallet/ there?"
18. victales is/ Abbott (333) explains that certain
terms were regarded by the Elizabethans as singular in
thought though the form of the terms was plural. "Victuals"
is apparently an example of this practice. Cf. (I.ii.60-
61); also Dekker, Sir Thomas Wyatt: "good victailes makes
good blood" (II.iii.70).

bonny man that haz glazen windows to his lindging

has tyed up in his wallet there?   20

Glascot. 'Tis the head of a young murder'd gentleman.

Wallace. What senn you man! A mans scalpe? I doubt

ye be three fawse knaves liggand yare heads together

about na gudenes; a traytors head is't not?

Glascot. No, but we ha' met with villaynes worse   25

then traytors. Walace your countryman, that bloody

hangman mangled us all three thus.

Wallace. Walas my Countryman, ay fay upon him. Sawe

lymmerlike wad I had his head here, too; I'zed

beare it by my sawle toth' English Campe or neere   30

gang farder.

Glascot. 'Twold be a glorious sight there.

Wallace. And you could see it ye sulled sea so man.

---

19. lindging/ lodging; cf. line 57. The image is of
the head as a house with eyes as the windows.
    22-24. What . . . not/ "What do you say, man! A man's
scalp? I fear you were three false knaves laying your
heads together about no goodness. A traytor's head, is it
not?"
    28-31. Walas . . . farder/ "Wallace my countryman!
Aye, fie upon him. So like a rogue /'lymmerlike'/ I wish
that I had his head here too; by my soul, I'd bear it to
the English camp or never go further."
    29. too/ The disguised Wallace persists in his grim
jokes on Sebastian's head. In an irony which he shares
with the audience, he wishes that he had both his own and
Sebastian's heads to carry to the English camp. Somewhat
similar is King Edward's jest on Bruce's head at V.iv.120-
121. Cf. also Ferdinand's equivocation in Webster's The
Duchess of Malfi: "Send Antonio to me; I want his head in
a business" (III.v.28).

Wallace cut of my shancks too, 'cause I ran away

from him to serve your gude Prince. Harke man,   35

I weare na shooen but wodden clampers.

Glascot. Of charity leade us to th' English Campe.

Ye shall besides thanks be most royally payd.

Wallace. Gang alang man, 'tis hard by now. A mans

head-- I deempt the pure man had gangand lang   40

to lawe and sae was thrust out of dores by head

and shoulders.

Glascot. No lawe was ere so cruell as Wallas is.

Wallace. Ne marry? Na law sa cruell? Fay man fay,

I luick'd upon a man a lawe not lang since that   45

sent an awde man and his wife, and many barnes a

begging. He had better a slizand theire weazond

34-36. And . . . clampers⁊ "If you should see it, you
should say so, man. Wallace cut off my shanks, too, 'cause
I ran away from him to serve your good prince. Hark, man,
I wear no shoes but wooden clogs ∠'clampers'⊓."

39-42. Gang . . . shoulders⊓ "Go along, man, it is
close by ∠hard by⊓ now. A man's head-- I suspect ∠deempt⊓
the poor man had gone a long time into lawsuits and so was
violently thrust outside."

41-42. by . . . shoulders⊓ violently, by force. Cf.
Thomas Heywood and Rowley, Fortune by Land and Sea: "the
least he can do is to thrust us out of doors by head and
shoulders" (III.ii ∠Heywood's Works, VI.398⊓).

44-49. Ne . . . ye⊓ "Nay, marry? No law so cruel?
Fie, man, fie, I saw a lawyer not long since that sent an
old man and his wife and many children a-begging. He would
have done better to have slit their windpipes, and cut
their heads off, but why was he so bloody minded, do you
think?"

47. weazond⊓ weasand, windpipe; cf. The Tempest: "Or
cut his weasand with thy knife" (III.ii.99).

pipes, and cut theire heads off; but whay was a

sa bludy mynded, thinke ye?

Glascot. I cannot judge.   50

Wallace. Marry man, to get possession of the pure

mans house, but there was a cat ganged beyond

the man a lawe.

Glascot. A cat goe beyond a lawyer? How?

Wallace. I'le tell you how: the man a lawe being   55

got in, the Cat outreach'd him, and leaped toth'

top o'th' lindging, and standand on the tyles.

The man a lawe scoarning any ane to be abuife

him, offer to fling and dingand downe the poore

51-53. Marry . . . lawe⟋ "Marry, man, to get possession of the poor man's house, but there was a cat that outsmarted the lawyer."
   54. cat . . . beyond⟋ There are two difficulties in
this phrase: (1) the omission of the relative pronoun
"that" (i.e., cat that went beyond) which is not specifically mentioned by Abbott, though he gives a number of
examples of other omitted relatives; (2) the idiom "went
beyond" ⟋gangand beyond'⟋ which means "passed ⟋someone's⟋
comprehension" or "outsmarted"; cf. OED 5b.
   55-64. I'le . . . souldiers⟋ "I'll tell you how: the
lawyer having entered, the cat outreached him and leaped to
the top of the lodging and stood on the tiles. The lawyer,
scorning anyone to be above him, attempted to knock down
the poor pussycat, but she miaowed at him, and cried,
'Hold, you foul loon, hold! As you thrust out this poor
man and his children, so there is one above who shall
thrust out you--' Stay, blind man, here come soldiers."
   57. lindging⟋ cf. line 19 above.
   59. offer⟋ attempt to use force; see OED 5. The
present tense of this verb is inconsistent with the past
tense of the rest of the passage.
        fling and dingang⟋ throw violently about. See
English Dialect Dictionary II.i for a definition of "ding"
as "to dash down with violence."

puscatt, but she meawed at him, and cryed, hawd,   60

thou foule lowne, hawd! As thou thrusts out this

poore man and his barnes, sa there is ane abuife

sall thrust out thee. Stay blind man, here comes

souldiers.

Enter Bolt with three or foure tattar'd Souldiers.

Omnes. Stand, que voula! Spyes about our trenches?   65

Bolt. And see they have knock'd some man downe.

   Sirra, you that carry two faces under a hood,

   what are you?

1 Soldier. He must be prest, he will not speake.

61-63. As . . . thee⌐ The moral of the fable teaches
the familiar Christian theme that the sins of the earth
shall be requited in the afterlife. The "ane abuife" is,
of course, God, who will thrust out the grasping lawyer
from Heaven, as the lawyer has thrust out the poor family
from their home on earth.
   65. Stand . . . voula⌐ The usual formula for a sentry's
challenge to intruders. "Stand" has the same meaning as
our modern "Halt." "Qui va là?" means "who goes there?"
Cf. Henry V (IV.i.35). For other forms of the French watch-
word, cf. 1 Henry VI: "Qui est là?" (III.ii.13) and The
Works of Thomas Nashe, "Cheuela" (I, 359) and "Queuela"
(II,223).
   66. knock'd . . . downe⌐ This comment perhaps refers
to the head in the wallet. If Glascot is kneeling or
seated with the wallet beside him, the bulge in his cloak
may appear to be a prone figure.
   67. carry . . . hood⌐ A common expression for a hypo-
crite; cf. Tilley (F20). Here the phrase also refers to
Sebastian's head carried by Glascot.
   69. prest⌐ The punishment of pressing to death by
weights (peine forte et dure) was executed upon alleged
felons who stood mute and refused to plead in order to save
their property from confiscation by the Crown.

Bolt. What art thou I charge thee? Hast thou   70

   neere a tongue in thy head? Give the word.

Glascot. He has no tongue indeed sir.

Bolt. Two heads and neere a tongue? What are you

   that like a blinde asse stand still, and cannot

   tell us so?   75

Glascot. I'm blind indeed.

   Conduct us to the Lords i'th' English Campe.

2 Soldier. How, Lords? Are you Ladyes that you

   long for Lords?

Bolt. Do you take us for gulls to goe tell the   80

   Lords here's a dumbe man would speake with 'em?

   What are you sirra? Come halt not; let's not

   find you in two tales y'are best.

70-71. Hast . . . head7 This question is similar to a
number of expressions quoted by Tilley (T402); cf. The
Merchant of Venice: "I have ne're a tongue in my head"
(II.ii.165-166).

71. word7 password.

74-75. like . . . so7 The exact meaning of this line
is unclear. The "blind asse" appears to refer to some proverbial expression, such as "that which thou knowest not,
peraduenture thy Asse can tell thee" (The Works of Thomas
Nashe, I.43). But the sense of Hashe's paradox is unclear
(McKerrow could find no "proverbs of Chrysippus"), for the
connection between the blindness of the ass and its wisdom
remains obscure.

78-79. Ladyes . . . Lords7 verbal play on the common
pairing of "lords and ladies."

80. gulls7 dupes.

82. halt7 hesitate, as in making up a lie.

83. in . . . tales7 telling contradictory stories,
thus lying.

Wallace. I'ze a <u>Scotch</u> man sir, ye shall neere find

me in two tales. 85

Bolt. A <u>Scotch</u> man sir, do you know where you are

sir, your blew bonnet on before an <u>English</u> scull?

Where's your leg sir, when an Officer speaks to you?

Wallace. My leg sir is not in my galligaskin and

slop as yours is; I'ze a pure <u>Scotch</u> souldier 90

out at heeles, and am glad to bestirr my stumps.

Guide these gude men, y'are wranged Countrymen,

84-85. I'ze . . . tales₇ "I'm a Scotchman, sir. You
shall never find me in two tales." To be caught in two
tales was to be caught in a lie (<u>OED</u>, 3d). This comment
may pun on "tales" and "tails," i.e., unpaid bills. It may
refer to the common belief that Scotchmen are parsimonious
and thus are not likely to acquire debts. On the other
hand, <u>The English Dialect Dictionary</u> mentions the phrase
"proud as a dog with two tails," meaning to be very proud.
Wallace may be referring to this phrase with the intended
meaning that, as a Scot, he will not be caught in false
pride.
  87. blew bonnet₇ Blue bonnets were distinctive Scotch
garb.
      scull₇ the armored skullcap of English soldiers.
  88. leg₇ the bow of an inferior to his superior.
Wallace takes up another meaning of the term, the physical
limb, which he is supposedly lacking.
  89. galligaskin₇ wide hose or breeches worn in the
sixteenth and seventeenth centuries.
  90-94. I'ze . . . wise₇ "I'm a poor Scotch soldier out
at heels, and am glad to bestir my stumps. Guide these
good men, your wronged countrymen, whom that false traitor,
Wallace, has misused in such manner /'wise'₇."
  91. out . . . heeles₇ This phrase has here a double
meaning: (1) worn through the heels of his stockings,
hence, shabby; (2) minus his normal supply of heels because
he is missing his legs.
      bestirr . . . stumps₇ figurative expression for
acting briskly; cf. Tilley (S946). The grim joke here is
on the actual stumps of the disguised Wallace.

wha that fawse traytor <u>Wallace</u> has misusand in sike wise.

<u>Omnes</u>. <u>Wallas</u>, oh slave!

<u>Bolt</u>. I shall live (fellows in armes out at Elbows)   95

    to give fire to my peece with a burnt ynch of

    match made of that rascals fat of mawegut.

<u>Wallace</u>. By my sawle sir, wad I might come toth'

    making of sike a match.

<u>Bolt</u>. Here's my hand, because thou sayest so.   100

    Thou shalt be by when I make him give fire to

    my touch-hole.

<u>Enter</u> Queen Elinor, Clifford, Percy

Beaumont, <u>and</u> <u>others</u>.

<u>Omnes</u>. The Lords are going to view the trenches.

<u>Bolt</u>. Every man to his parrapet! To your trenches

    you tatter'd roagues!   105

---

    95. out . . . Elbows/ worn through garments at the
elbows. This phrase plays on the secondary meaning of
"arms" in "fellows in armes" which here not only means the
military profession, but the physical limb.
    96. give fire/ set fire to the powder in the touch-
hole to discharge the weapon. Cf. Massinger, <u>The</u> <u>Picture</u>:
"I'll give fire With mine own linstock; if the powder be
dank, The devil rend the touch-hole!" (III.i /<u>Works</u>, p.
224/).
    peece/ firearm, here a matchlock. See Claude
Blair, <u>European</u> <u>and</u> <u>American</u> <u>Arms</u>, <u>c</u>. <u>1100-1850</u> (New York:
Crown Publishers, 1962), Plate CCLIII, for matchlock musket,
c. 1630, by English gunsmith, "J.W."
    97. mawegut/ portion of stomach.
    102. touch-hole/ vent through which the charge of a
matchlock is ignited.
    104. parrapet/ breastwork, portion of a fortification.

<u>/Soldiers perform military exercise</u>./

<u>Clifford</u>. It's well done fellowes.

<u>Bolt</u>. Cry your Lordship mercy, this blind buzzard

here cannot see. Whither will you march headlong

my friend?

<u>Percy</u>. What men are these?   110

<u>Bolt</u>. I leave them to your Honors sifting, I have

fortifications to look too.

<u>Clifford</u>. There's drinking money. Hence to your works.

<u>Bolt</u>. Blesse your honours.

<u>Exeunt</u> Bolt <u>and</u> Souldiers.

<u>Percy</u>. What men are these? I aske, will no man speak? 115

<u>Glascot</u>. Heare and in hearing wish the sound unheard.

Youthfull <u>Sebastian</u>, nephew to the Queene,

---

107. Cry . . . mercy/ polite expression, equivalent to
"I beg your pardon;" see Robert Nares, <u>A</u> <u>Glossary</u> <u>of</u> <u>Words</u>,
revised by J. O. Halliwell and T. Wright (1905; Detroit:
Gale Research Co., 1966).
      blind buzzard/ commonplace expression for the
inobservant; cf. Tilley (B792).
111. sifting/ scrutiny, examination.
112. too/ to
116-121. Heare . . . presence/ This garbled passage
may suffer from corruption, such as the possible misreading
of "wish" for "with" in line 116. There is also evident a
strained attempt at wit in the repeated play on the ideas
of hearing and seeing. A close approximation of the meaning
of the passage in its present state (with the above mentioned substitution of "with") is" "We /Glascot and Mount-
ford/ are here and listening, although one of us is mute.
Perceiving that he was not included in the honorable
embassy, Sebastian, the young nephew to the Queen, who
longed to see Wallace (the man famous for both excessive
virtue and vice), attempted in disguise to enter the presence
of the rebel, Wallace."

Longing to see the man fam'd for th'excesse

Of goodnes and of badnes, seeing unjoyned

In honored Embassie, disguis'd, attempted   120

The rebell <u>Wallaces</u> presence.

<u>Omnes</u>. <u>Glascot</u> and <u>Mountford</u>!

<u>Clifford</u>. Who did this damned villany?

<u>Glascot</u>.   Our message told,

The traytor newly set on fire with madnes,

Showing the mangled bodies of a Fryer,   125

His wife and father, burst out into flames

Hye, hot and violent (in which fierce rage

Revolted <u>Grimsby</u> knew <u>Sebastian</u>

Tho Herald-like he went disguis'd) and seazed

Him and us for three intelligencing spies;   130

Cut off his head, his tongue, and <u>Glascots</u> eyes.

<u>Percy</u>. Hang up this /Percy <u>indicates</u> Wallace7;

provide for these. Trusse him up. /<u>They</u> <u>seize</u>

Wallace <u>who</u> <u>struggles.</u>7

                          <u>Exeunt</u> Mountford <u>and</u> Glascot.

<u>Wallace</u>. What sen ye man?

<u>Percy</u>. What slave, what Turke that murders his owne

---

130. intelligencing7 cunning and full of secrets; cf.
The <u>Winter's</u> <u>Tale</u>: "A most intelligencing bawd!" (II.iii.
68).
   134. sen7 say.
   135-139. What . . . first7 In Hary's <u>Wallace</u>, the
maimed ambassadors are brought before King Edward who
explodes in a furious outburst: "A lang quhill he stud

brethren

Durst play the tyrant thus? Hang all the Nation

Whom we have tane to mercy. I'le not spare

Fathers, nor mothers, nor their bawling barnes.

Fire their houses! Hang up this tike first.

<u>Wallace</u>. Ah bonny men, I met 'um playeand at bo-   140

peep, and gangand out a their way, and sall I

---

wrythand in a rage. On loud he said, 'This is a fell owtrage. This deid to Scottis full der it sall be bo<u>cht</u>. Sa
dispitfull in warld was neu<u>ir</u> wro<u>cht</u>. Off this regioun I
think no<u>cht</u> for to gang Quh<u>i</u>ll tyme that I sall see th<u>at</u>
Rybald hang'" (VI.421-426).
    135. Turke . . . brethren7 The Turkish practice of
fratricide was well known to the Elizabethans. Cf. Peele,
The Battle of Alcazar: "That Muly Mahamet the traiter
holdes . . . .That murthered his younger brethren both"
(I.i.137-139 /The Dramatic Works, ed John Yoklavich (New
Haven and London: Yale Univ. Press, 1961), I7). A discus-
sion of the practice of fratricide may be found in A. D.
Alderson, The Structure of the Ottoman Dynasty (Oxford:
The Clarendon Press, 1956), pp. 25-29.
    136. play_. . . tyrant7 Cf. II.iii.11.
    137. tane7 taken. Note that the dialectal style of
Wallace's speech carries over into Percy's standard English.
"Barnes" in line 138 may be another example; however, a
touch of irony may be intended by the use of the Scottish
idiom.
    139. tike7 dog, cur (used as a term of reproach).
    140-149. Ah . . . heaven7 "Ah, bonny men, I met them
losing themselves, and going out of their way, and shall I
be hanged for my charitable good deeds? I am a poor
Scotch soldier, and have run away from that rebel, Wallace,
to fight for your good Prince. Ah, he's a good king, and
you /Englishmen7 are all bonny men; I'll follow you all to
the death, and to the Devil, if any man dares go so far.
For all my crutches, if I seize Wallace, he'll conquer only
after his death, when he wins hell or heaven."
    140-141. playeand . . . bo-peep7 losing themselves;
figuratively from the nursery rhyme. Cf. Dekker, <u>Satiro-</u>
<u>mastix</u>: "our vnhansome-fac'd Poet does play at bo-peepes
with your Grace, and cryes all-hidde as boyes doe" (V.ii.
153-154).

be hanged for my good deeds of charrity? I'ze

a poor Scutch souldier, and am ron away from that

Rebell <u>Wallas</u>, to feight and for your gude Prince.

Ah he's a gude King, and y'are all bonny men; I'ze   145

follow ye all to thè death, and to the Devill, and

ony man dare gang so far. For all my crutches,

giffe I clutch Wallace, he's neer carry it till

hell nor heaven.

<u>Percy</u>. If he do, may <u>Percies</u> name be crost   150

Out of the roll of men.

<u>Clifford</u>.   So much swears <u>Clifford</u>.

<u>Percy</u>. Sneak not away sirra; y'are not gone yet.

<u>Wallace</u>. I ken it vary weèl. I'ze not gangan to

147.   crutche_s_7   clutches Q.

146-147. and on_y_7 if any; see Abbott (101).
147.   crutches_7 The Q reading "clutches" is probably a
compositorial memory error in anticipation of the "clutch"
appearing three words later. "Crutches" alone makes sense
in this context, in which the disguised Wallace affirms his
service, despite his lost legs.
148-149. he's . . . heaven_7 This passage is uncertain
because of the ambiguity of "till," which normally means
"to" in dialect. However, in this line it seems to have
its normal significance, with the meaning that Wallace will
never be victorious ("carry it," see <u>OED</u>, 15b) until after
his death, when he wins heaven or hell.
151.   roll . . . men_7 (1) list of the living, or (2)
list of those deserving to be considered manly.
153-154. I . . . yet_7 "I understand /ken_7 it very well.
I'm not going to hang /?_7 yet." I can find no Elizabethan
usage that satisfactorily accounts for this use of "hanging."
It could be a noun acting as the object of the preposition
"to" with the possessive pronoun omitted /to my hanging_7, a
dialect spelling of the infinitive "to hang," or perhaps
simply a gerund.

to hanging yet.

Clifford. Yet though a traitour, thus much let me speak 155

    For absent Wallace: were the case your own,

    Or one that's baser having any spirit,

    A murder'd father and a bleeding wife

    Mangled before him, would strike fire in snow,

    Make loyalty turn traitor, and obedience   160

    Forget all duty.

Elinor.   But our Nephews death

    And the disgrace done our Embassadours?

Clifford. They then put off their title, and put on

    The name of spies, when in their companies

    They take disguis'd observers.   165

Wallace. /Aside7 By my sawle, the English are

        gallant men.

Percy. No snare to intrap this Wolfe?

---

    156. were . . . case7 i.e., if the case were. Cf.
Abbott (301) for the use of the subjunctive.
    157. Or one7 an elliptical expression: "or the case
of one." This elision may be explained by the Elizabethan
dislike of repetition after a conjunction; cf. Abbott (382
and 388a).
    159. would strike7 This image refers back to "the
case" of line 156, i.e., it /the case7 would strike.
    159-161. would . . . duty7 The association of contra-
dictory notions appearing in these predicate expressions is
a form of oxymoron.
    163. then7 i.e., at that time.
        title7 the title of ambassador, which confers the
right to protection.
    166. sawle7 soul.
    167. No . . . Wolfe7 The conception of Percy as pre-
ferring policy to honorable battle is opposite to Hary's

Clifford.   How Northumberland,

   Intrap a fo? Sure 'tis no English word,

   Clifford at least was ne're acquainted with't.

   Give him fair summons, dare him to the field,   170

   And trap him then.

Wallace. /Aside/ Ah bony man!

Percy. His being a traitour warrants it. Dispatch

   A second message with acknowledgment

   Of former wrongs to our Embassadours,   175

   With promise of a friendly enterview

   Early to morrow, impartially to heare

   Their wrongs, and mildely minister redresse.

---

view of Persye as one of the few honorable Englishmen; cf.
Wallace: "The Sothroun /Percy and his followers/ wist that
it was wicht Wallace Had thaim ourset in-to that sodand
cas. Thair trewis for this thai wald nocht brek adeill"
(III.417-419). In the planning of the "Barns of Ayr" atrocity (Wallace VII.15-38), which is the source for Clifford's
refusal to countenance treachery, it is Percy who refuses
to take part in dishonorable duplicity: "'Thai men to me
has kepit treuth so lang Desaitfully I may nocht se thaim
hang. I am thar fa and warn thaim will I nocht. Sa I be
quytt I rek nocht quhat yhe wrocht'" (VIII.33-36).
    168. Intrap . . . word/ There are several Shakespearian
parallels to this refusal to admit unworthy terms as be-
longing to the language. Cf. 1 Henry VI, "Submission,
Dauphin! 'Tis a mere French word. We English warriors wot
not what it means" (IV.vii.54-55). Cf. also 1 Henry IV
(IV.i.84-85) and Richard II (V.iii.123-124). Webster
employs a similar device in The White Devil: "my jealousy?
I am to learn what the Italian means" (II.i.160-161).
    175. wrongs . . . Embassadours/ Abbott (185) points
out that "to" can mean "in addition to"; therefore, Percy
may be acknowledging both former wrongs and the wrongs com-
mitted by the illegitimate embassy, i.e., former wrongs
in addition to /those of/ our ambassadors.

Clifford. Insnare him so and spare not, for you'le finde

    I feare, that <u>Selby</u>, <u>Haslerig</u>, and the rest   180

    Lay yokes too heavy on the Nations neck.

Elinor. If they do, punish 'em--

Clifford. Punish 'em! 'Sdeath, hang 'em.

Percy. Shall we agree to have such message sent

    To allure this bloudy Tygre into th' net   185

    And waking then or sleeping kill him.

Clifford.   No.

Percy. All stratagems are lawfull 'gainst a fo.

Clifford. Do what you will, but my consent is no.

Beaumont. I'le venture to the Rebell.

Percy.   Do good <u>Beaumont</u>

    <u>Scotchman</u> dar'st thou conduct him as his guide?   190

Clifford. But return sirra, or the next time

    We take yee y'are Crag shall pay for't.

Wallace. I'ze not run away fra yee; giffe I do hang

    mee and drae mee. Cum bully <u>Joe</u>. I dare not

---

    179. Insnare . . . no<u>t</u>⁄ "so" here means "as you have
just suggested," i.e., "Insnare Wallace by redressing his
legitimate complaints and spare not the truly guilty."
    183. 'Sdeath⁄ God's death, an exclamation.
    188. consent⁄ counsel; Schmidt cites <u>1 Henry VI</u>: "By
my consent, we'll even let them alone" (I.ii.44).
    192. y'are Crag⁄ Your neck. Note the Scotch flavor
picked up as Clifford addresses Wallace.
    193-197. I'ze . . . <u>Wallace</u>⁄ "I'll not run away from
you, if I do hang me and draw me. Come, stout friend
⌈bully <u>Joe</u>'⌉, I dare not go to the Scottish camp. They'll
so fly upon me I'd never come back again, but I'll bring
you ⌈to⌉ where you shall see that Rogue, Wallace."
    194. Joe⁄ Cf. I.ii.45.

gang to the Scottis Campe. They'le sa flay upon   195

me, I'se near cum back agen, but I'ze bring you

where yee shall see that Lowne Wallace.

Beaumont. That's all I wish; lead on.

Wallace. Marry sall I. Luke to your selfe, I'se

thrust you into the Dewles chops.   200

Beaumont. For getting out let me scuffle.

                    Exeunt Beaumont and Wallace.

Elinor. Consult for present execution.

            /Percy and others consult with Queen,

            while Clifford speaks aside./

Clifford. What is, what should, what can this Wallace be,

Whom fame limbs out for such a gallant peece,

And is so curious in her workmanship,   205

No part deforms him?

Yet Wallace is a Rebell. His chief scandall

199-200. Marry . . . chops/ "Marry, I shall; look out
for yourself. I'll thrust you into the Devil's jaws."
    202. present execution/ action to be taken immediately.
    203. What . . . be/ The series of clauses completed by
the single term "be" is an example of hypozeugma.
    204. limbs/ limns, portrays.
        peece/ piece of craftsmanship.
    205. curious/ careful; cf. Shakespeare, Sonnet 38.13:
"If my slight Muse do please these curious days, The pain
be mine, but thine shall be the praise."
    207. scandall/ shame, disgrace. Clifford's meaning is
that Wallace's lack of rank /"poverty of Gentry"/ drives him
into rebellion as a means of gaining the recognition due
his noble nature.

Is poverty of Gentry; by my sword

Wer't no impeach to my deare Ancestors,

I well could spare him some of my unus'd titles,   210

Or would at martiall gaming so I might lose

And Wallace winne so much of Cliffords honour

Our stocks might be alike. But I exceed,

This night he is betray'd. He shall not!

I'le turn traitor first, he shall not!--   215

Call Beaumont back, or else by Cliffords honor,

An oath which I esteem above my life,

I will turn traitor, and reveal your plots.

Call him back.

Percy.   Is Clifford mad?

Clifford.   No.

Percie's lunatick; suppose he be a traitor   220

---

209. impeach/ reproach.
210. unus'd titles/ unemployed titles of honor. The
historical Baron Robert de Clifford inherited only the
Hereditary Shrievalty of Westmorland; he was himself
created the first Lord Clifford. Thus the idea of Clifford
as possessing subsidiary titles which he might grant to
Wallace is J.W.'s invention.
211. would . . . gaming/ Abbott (405) discusses elipses
after auxiliary verbs, citing Richard II: "I must /go/ to
Coventry" (I.ii.56). In this case, the preposition of
motion has the effect of completing the action initiated by
"must." Closer to the case of line 211 is Henry V: "He is
very sick, and would /desires to go/ to bed" (II.i.86-87).
Thus, Clifford's meaning is that he desires to gamble
through combat with Wallace.
213. stocks/ endowments, capital supplies.
      exceed/ exaggerated, go too far.

And discipline of the field allow the act,

What honour is it for a herd of yours

To worry a sleeping Beare? Goe call him back.

Enter Beaumont <u>with</u> <u>a</u> <u>wooden</u> <u>stump</u>.

<u>Percy</u>. See he comes uncall'd.

<u>Clifford</u>. The news?

<u>Beaumont</u>.   News call you it? Let no <u>Scot</u>   225

Come neer your tents. <u>Wallace</u> sends you this token.

<u>Clifford</u>. Ha, how, <u>Wallace</u>?

<u>Percy</u>.   Was that the traitor?

<u>Clifford</u>. By <u>Mars</u> his helme, a compleat Warrior!

I so love his worth, I'le court it with my sword.   229

<u>Beaumont</u>. Had you but stood in distance of his thunder,

For, we parted just where our trenches ended,

You'de ha' sworn the God of War had spoke.

Quoth he, tell <u>Percy</u>, he shall not need

To hunt me in my tent, I'le rouse him in's own;

---

221. discipline . . . ac<u>t</u>/ i.e., military law permit
the trapping of Wallace.
228. <u>Mars</u> . . . helm<u>e</u>/ Cf. I.vi.95.
        complеate/ perfect.
229. court i<u>t</u>/ "to court it" is an expression meaning
to play or act the courtier; cf. <u>OED</u> 2. In this case, Clifford means that he will acknowledge Wallace's worth by
seeking him out in battle as a courtier seeks out his lord
or lady.
232. spoke/ Abbott (343) uses "I have spoke" as his
general example of the common Elizabethan practice of dropping the "en" inflection from participles.
234. rouse/ a hunting term meaning to frighten the
quarry from his cover or lair.

And bids me give you this wooden stumpe,   235

And sweares to make you weare it, if you dare

Stand him in the field.

Percy.   Base Rebell,

Why durst he not stand here?

Clifford.   None pray'd him stay;

'Twas manners being not welcom'd to get away.   239

Beaumont. He sends commends to Clifford, with this wish:

That if at this great match of life and death,

He chance to lose the smallest part of honour

His sword may joyn't, he knows best how to use it.

At my return from France, quoth he, this vow

Which I have promis'd shall be surely payed.   245

Our Country overtopt with tyranny,

Makes us flie thither for succour; Aeolus,

Let favourable winds and tydes assist me.

---

237. stand/ confront.

238-239. None . . . away/ For a parallel to this
ironic use of "manners," cf. Beaumont and Fletcher, The
Maid in the Mill; "'Tis manners to fall to When grace is
said." (IV.i /Works, VII, 50/).

240. commends/ remembrances, compliments.

243. joyn't/ join it; be increased by it, annex it.
The meaning is that if Wallace chances to lose the smallest
part of his honor as a fighting man, he hopes that Clifford
may gain it.

244. vow/ refers to the threat of lines 236-237.

246-247. Our . . . succour/ In Hary's Wallace, it is
the King of France who seeks Wallace's aid against his
English enemies (see IX.1-32). It is during Wallace's
repeated absences from Scotland to fight the English in
France that Edward reconquers Scotland. In the play, it is
a weak Scotland that seeks French aid.

That spoak, revolted <u>Grimsby</u> and his powers

Met him in Armes. What further he intends,   250

Harke their Drum tels. Here my Commission ends.

<u>Clifford</u>. Lets send him commendations too, beat ours.

/Drums.7   <u>Exeunt</u>.

252. commendations7 respects sent to those at a dis-
tance.

<u>Act/us</u> III. /Scena i/

<u>Enter</u> Sir Jeffrey <u>and</u> Bolt <u>with</u> <u>a</u> <u>Trunke</u>.

<u>Jeffrey</u>. Set downe Bolt, I can beare with thee no
            longer.

<u>Bolt</u>. No more can I beare any longer with you, Sir
       <u>Jeffry</u>. But what a reeling drunken sot is this
       sea, that casts up such gobbets as this. Is this   5
       a windfall or no now Sir <u>Jeffery</u>? Your Worship
       knows both the tags and points of the law.

<u>Jeffrey</u>. Yes sure it is a windfall, for as we
       walk'd upon the shore, we saw the ship split;
       this fell out, the winds were the cause, therefore   10

III.i. The place of this scene is a seashore in English
occupied Scotland. From the change in Selby and Haslerig's
condition (see lines 294 ff.) Carver (p. 103) infers that
several months have elapsed since the close of Act II.
    1-3. beare . . . beare/ Bolt puns on a second sense of
"bear with": (1) to carry together, (2) to put up with.
Cf. <u>Richard</u> <u>III</u>: PRINCE. Uncle, your Grace knows how to
bear with him. YORK. You mean to bear me, not to bear
with me" (III.i.127-128).
    4-5. But . . . this/ Cf. <u>Pericles</u>: "What a drunken
knave was the sea to cast thee in our way!" (II.i.61-62).
    5. gobbets/ lumps of half-digested food.
    6. windfall/ The exchange with Sir Jeffrey, covering
lines 6-11, plays on two meanings of "windfall": (1) something blown down by the wind, (2) an unexpected acquisition.
    7. tags . . . points/ Points were the laces used to
tie clothing together before buttons, tags the metal coverings at their ends. In this figurative usage, the phrase
means "intimate knowledge of the law."

222

it must needs be a windfall.

Bolt. Well some body has had but a bad fish-dinner

to day.

Jeffrey. The Seas have crost them that sought to

crosse the Seas, and therefore for my part I'le   15

never meddle with these water-works.

Bolt. Nor I, lets be more wise then a number of

gallants, and keep the land that's left us. Did

you ever see such gambols as the waves made us

Sir Jeffrey?   20

Jeffrey. Never since I wore the nightcap of Justice,

and that this her dudgeon dagger was a' my side.

Bolt. Did you note what puffing the winds made till

they got great bellies, and then how sorely the

ship fell in labour.   25

---

14. crost . . . crosse7 This pun plays on two meanings
of "cross": (1) to thwart, (2) to transverse.
    17-18. lets . . . us7 There are many allusions in
seventeenth-century drama to gallants selling the family
estates to keep up with extravagant court life. See L. C.
Knights, Drama and Society in the Age of Jonson (New York:
George W. Stewart, 1936), pp. 124, 261-262.
    21. nightcap7 black cap, the covering assumed by a
judge before pronouncing sentence of death.
    22. dudgeon dagger7 This allusion is to the sword
traditionally borne by Justice. "Dudgeon" is the type of
wood used for dagger hilts.
    23-25. what . . . labour7 This passage refers to the
action of the winds billowing out the sails. Cf. A Midsummer's Night's Dream: "When we have laughed to see the
sails conceive And grow big-bellied with the wanton wind"
(II.i.128-129).

223

<u>Jeffrey</u>. Didst heare what a dolefull cry they made,

when their maine yard was split?

<u>Bolt</u>. Alas sir, would it not make any man roare

that had but an inch of feeling or compassion in

his belly to have his mayne yard split, and how   30

the marriners hung by the ropes like Saint <u>Thomas</u>

Onyons.

<u>Jeffrey</u>. I saw it <u>Bolt</u> with salt eyes.

<u>Bolt</u>. So that you may see at sea however the winde

blowes, if a man be well hung, hee's cocke sure.   35

<u>Jeffrey</u>. But <u>Boult</u> what dost thou thinke this to be?

<u>Bolt</u>. A matter of some weight as I take it.

26-27. Didst . . . split7 Cf. <u>Pericles</u>: "Alas, poor
souls, it grieved my heart to hear what pitiful cries they
made to us to help them" (II.i.21-22).
    27. maine yard7 spar from which the mainsail is hung.
    30. mayne yard7 Bolt twists "main yard," which means a
spar in line 27, into a sexual innuendo.
    31-32. Saint . . . Onyons7 The sailors hanging from
the ropes or "lines" of the ship are compared to round,
white onions, strung together by their stems in a "rope."
Cf. Barnabe Rich's <u>Farewell</u> <u>to</u> <u>Military</u> <u>Profession</u>, ed.
Thomas M. Cranfill (Austin: Univ. of Texas Press, 1959),
p. 205: "In their Hoose so many fashions as I can not describe . . . sometymes rounde like to Saincte Thomas Onions."
Cf. also G. F. Northall, <u>English</u> <u>Folk-Rhymes</u> (London: Kegan
Paul, Trench, Trubner & Co., 1892), p. 116: "Buy my rope
of onions, White St. Thomas's onions."
    33. salt7 (1) with teares, (2) with seawater, blown by
the storm.
    35. well hung7 (1) well supported by ropes, as the
sailors in the lines, (2) having large sexual organs.
        cocke sure7 (1) secure, (2) having a reliable
sexual organ, this sense being partially derived from the
connection with "well hung."
    37. matter . . . weight7 (1) a heavy matter, (2) an
important matter, (3) a weighty sexual organ.

Jeffrey. I hope 'tis gold, 'tis so heavy, and 'twas

    going out of the Land.

Bolt. Like enough, for gold goes now very heavily   40

    from us, and silver too. Both red chincks, and

    white chincks flie away; but Sir Jeffrey, if this

    be gold, how rich is the sea, thinke ye, that has

    innumerable such sands?

Jeffrey. More rich then the land, and more fat.   45

Bolt. So it had need, for the land looks with a

    leane payre of cheeks, yet it has an excellent

    stomach: it digests any thing.

Jeffrey. Then 'tis like the sea, for all's fish

    that comes to net there.   50

Bolt. I'le tell you the mystery of that: looke

---

40. heavily̲/ burdensomely (continuing the idea of
"weight" in line 37).
41. red̲/ as a conventional, poetic epithet for gold
(OED, 3).
       chincks̲/ coins.
45. fat̲/ rich, fertile.
4 -4 . looks . . . cheeks̲/ i.e., looks hungrily.
49-50. all's . . . net̲/ a commonplace expression (cf.
Apperson, p. 6).
51-54. looke . . . fishes̲/ Cf. Pericles: "Why, /the
fish live̲/ as men do a-land; the great ones eat up the
little ones. I can compare our rich misers to nothing so
fitly as to a whale: A' plays and tumbles, driving the
poor fry before him, and at last devours them all at a
mouthful. Such whales have I heard on o' the land, who
never leave gaping till they've swallowed the whole parish,
church, steeple, bells, and all" (III.i.31-38). This speech
may also be reflected in Selby's comment: "How many beggars
does a rich man eate at his table at one meale" (III.i.221-
223). However, cf. also, Philip Stubbes, Anatomy of Abuses,
Part I: "rich men eat vp poore men, as beasts doo eat

what mouthes gape at land, the selfe same gape at

sea; all the land is one kingdome, and all the

sea another.

Jeffrey. And people in't.   55

Bolt. And people in't (right worshipful) but they

all go Westhod. As there are good and bad here,

so there are good and bad there; gulls here,

gulls there; as great men here eate up the little

men, so Whales feed upon the lesser fishes.   60

Jeffrey. Belike then the watry common wealth are

ill govern'd.

---

grasse" (ed. F. J. Furnivall, New Shakespeare Society Publications, ser. 6, no. 6 /London: N. Trübner & Co., 1877/,
p. 117).
    57. Westhod/ Westward. See II.iv.3.
    58. gulls/ dupes.
    61. Belike/ I suppose, it seems.
    are/ Although there is no example in Shakespeare
of "belike" taking the subjunctive mood, it may be that the
apparently incorrect "are" was regarded by the author as a
subjunctive construction. "Belike"does introduce a statement of probability, rather than actual fact.
    61-94. watry . . . Clyents/ Although word-play on
fish names is common in Elizabethan drama, Bolt's fanciful
commonwealth of fishes is worked out at greater length than
any example seen. The suggestion for the comparison may
stem from Pericles: "How from the finny subject of the sea
These fishers tell the infirmities of men, And from their
watery empire recollect All that may men approve or men
detect!" (II.i.52-55). Possibly derived from The Valiant
Scot is a brief conceit from 1639: "In the Common-wealth
of Fishes are many officers; Herring the King, Swordfish
his guard; Lobsters are Aldermen, Crabs are Constables, and
poor Johns the common sort of people" (Conceits, Clinches,
Flashes, and Whimzies, reprinted in Shakespeare Jest-Books,
ed. W. C. Hazlitt, /London: Willis & Sotheran, 1864/, III,
40).

Bolt. No bravely, for heroicall <u>Hector</u> <u>Herring</u> is

    King of fishes.

<u>Jeffrey</u>. So.   65

<u>Bolt</u>. Rich cobs his good subjects, who at Yarmouth

    lay downe their lives in his quarrell; sword-

    fish and Pike are his guard.

<u>Jeffrey</u>. On.

<u>Bolt</u>. Fresh Cods the gallants, and sweet slipper   70

    the Knights; whiting-mopps the Ladies, and

    Lillie-white-mussels the wayting-gentlewomen.

<u>Jeffrey</u>. Dangerous meat to take too much of.

<u>Bolt</u>. But who the pages?

<u>Jeffrey</u>. Shrimps.   75

---

63. <u>Hector</u>/ Schmidt explains that the name of the Tro-
jan hero is used appellatively to denote highest valor.
66. cobs/ fish called otherwise "Miller's Thumbs" (cf.
<u>OED</u> 3). This term was also associated with herring, as the
head of the red herring was called "cob"; cf. Jonson, <u>Every</u>
<u>Man</u> <u>in</u> <u>his</u> <u>Humour</u>, (the character Cob speaking): "Mine
anc'trie came from a Kings belly...<u>Herring</u> the King of fish"
(I.iv.10-13).
       Yarmouth/ an important fishing port in Norfolk.
70. sweet slipper/ In an 1885 reference, the <u>OED</u>, 6b
lists "slipper" as a fish-name for a slimy eel-like fish.
It is doubtful if this is the same fish mentioned by Bolt,
but I have discovered no other fish with a similar name.
71. whiting-mopps/ young whitings; the name is elsewhere used figuratively for young girls; cf. Massinger, <u>The</u>
<u>Guardian</u>: "I have a stomach, and would content myself With
this pretty whiting-mop" (IV.ii /Works, p. 358/).
72. Lillie-white-mussels/ The association between this
mussel and the gentlewomen is the elegantly white complex-
ions of the ladies.
75. Shrimps/ Jocular comparisons between shrimps and
small people--as youthful pages--are quite common; cf. 1

Bolt. No, no sir, perriwinckles are the pages,

perriwinckles.

Jeffrey. No Justices among them?

Bolt. Yes Sir Jeffery, Thornebacks are the Justices;

Crabs the Constables, whom if you butter with   80

good words, 'tis passing meat at midnight.

Jeffrey. Ah, ha.

Bolt. Dogfish are Jaylors, and Stockfish the poore

common people.

Jeffrey. Indeed they live hardly.   85

Henry VI: "It cannot be this weak and writhled shrimp
Should strike such terror to his enemies" (II.iii.23-24).
    76. perriwinckles/ periwinkles, small molluscs with
spiral shells.
    79. Thornebacks/ fish with sharp spines along the back
and tail. The name was applied to sharp, censorious people;
cf. Nashe, Lenten Stuff: "to bee helde a flat thornebacke
or sharp pricking dog-fish to the weale publique" (Works,
III, 218).
    80. Crabs/ As the term "crab" was applied to ill-
tempered people, Bolt assigns to these crustacea the thank-
less job of constables.
        butter/ (1) "butter up," flatter, (2) season with
butter.
    81. passing/ (1) surpassing, exceedingly, (2) "passing"
in the sense of being allowed to continue past the watch
without detention.
    83. Dogfish/ As the term "dogfish" was applied oppro-
briously to persons (see OED 2, and the note to line 79
above), Bolt assigns to this fish the ignominious profession
of jailor.
        Stockfish/ dried fish. The term is often used
humorously with reference to the beating of the fish before
cooking. Cf. The Tempest: "by this hand, I'll...make a
stockfish of thee" (III.ii.77-79).
    85. hardly/ with difficulty.

<u>Bolt</u>. But sir they are beaten too't. Then have you

wet Eeles for whores, and great Oysters for Bawds.

<u>Jeffrey</u>. Why great Oysters Bawds?

<u>Bolt</u>. Because for the most part they are stewed.

<u>Jeffrey</u>. Very good.   90

<u>Bolt</u>. Lastly, because no Kingdome can stand without

laws, and where law has her eyne, there Lawyers

and Pettifoggers swarme; therefore the Lawyers

here are sharks, and gudgeons the poore Clyents.

Wallace <u>within</u>.

<u>Wallace</u>. Wa ho ro sol fa, sol fa.   95

---

86. too't7 to it; Abbott (185) **points out that** "to"
can mean "in addition to"; cf. <u>Macbeth</u>: "'Tis much he
dares, And to that dauntless temper of his mind, He hath a
wisdom" (III.i.51-53). The meaning is that the common
people are beaten in addition to living "hardly."

87. Eeles7 Partridge cites <u>Pericles</u>: "I warrant you,
mistress, thunder shall not so awake the beds of eels as my
giving out her beauty stir up the lewdly inclined" (IV.ii.
154-156) to indicate the suggestions of penis contained in
"eels." Associated masculine sexual puns are connected
with the conger (see Partridge), lamprey (cf. <u>The Duchess
of Malfi</u>, I.i.336), and snake (see Partridge under "eel").

88. Oysters7 Oysters are especially appropriate to be
designated bawds because of their use as aphrodisiacs which
dates back to antiquity (cf. Juvenal, <u>Satire</u> VI.302).

89. stewed7 (1) cooked in a stew, (2) kept in a brothel.

92. law . . . eyne7 Justice is traditionally depicted
as blindfolded. In Bolt's comment, the law has eyes and is
thus biased and prejudiced.

93. Pettifoggers7 lawyers employing mean, petty
practices.

94. gudgeons7 small fish used as bait. The term is
used figuratively for credulous, gullible people.

95-100. Wa . . . pricksong7 Wallace's calling out for
help is mistaken by Bolt as a falconer calling to his bird

Bolt. Harke.

Jeffrey. Peace Bolt.

Bolt. Nay peace you, good Sir Jeffrey, peace, peace.

Wallace. Sol la, sol la sol la sol la.

Bolt. Some Faulconer's teaching his Hawke pricksong.   * 100

    Shall I mocke him in's owne key?

Jeffrey. Do.

Bolt. Sol fa sol fa, here boy.

               Enter Wallace.

Wallace. Here boy, wa ha ho ho. All haile to you two.

Bolt. And all snow to you sir.   105

Jeffrey. Sirra what are thou that wishest all the

    haile to light upon us two.

---

either to encourage her hunting or to call her back to him;
see "The Treatise of Falconry of Albertus Magnus," trans.
George Kotsiopoulos in The Art and Sport of Falconry
(Chicago: Argonaut, 1969), pp. 57 and 64.

    100. pricksong/ written music. Bolt may also include
a sexual reference in "prick--" as puns on this euphemism
for penis were common; cf. Romeo and Juliet: "the bawdy
hand of the dial is now upon the prick of noon" (II.iv.118-
119).

    101-104. Shall . . . ho/ The shouting between Bolt on
stage and Wallace off-stage is similar to an exchange in
William Rowley's The Birth of Merlin: "Clown. So ho, boy,
so ho, so so. /Within/ Prince Vter. So ho, boy, so ho,
illo ho, illo ho. Clown. Hark, hark, sister, there's one
hollows to us" (II.i.45-47). Cf. also Hamlet's exchange
with Marcellus (Hamlet, I.v.115-116).

    104-105. haile . . . snow/ Bolt picks up the term
"haile," which Wallace intends in the sense of "greetings,"
and turns it to its other sense of "ice crystals." In lines
106-107, Sir Jeffrey rather laboriously carries on the
jest.

Bolt. Answer wisely to my master, for hee's a Justice

of peace, and you'l be smelt out.

Wallace. I am a drown'd rat. 110

Jeffrey. A Rat?

Bolt. Do you take Sir **Jeffrey** for a Rat-catcher?

You'le tell a sweet tale for your selfe anon.

Wallace. Pox rot you, I am shipwrack't. Give me

some meate. 115

Bolt. Shall I make his **Mittimus**? He begs sir.

Wallace. I ha' met more then my match. **Neptune**

---

109. smelt out/ proverbial expression meaning to be
searched out, detected (cf. Tilley, S558).
110. a . . . rat/ figuratively a miserable castaway;
cf. Dekker, The Honest Whore, Part I: "if you fal into
this whirlpoole where I am, y'are drownd: y'are a drownd
rat" (V.ii.190-191).
114-151. Give . . . Wisacres/ The theme of the hungry
Wallace taking food from the English derives from Hary's
Wallace (XII.554-646). The connections are slight, but
clear. Note especially the verbal parallel in line 179).
116. Shall . . . begs/ Bolt's mocking Wallace as a
beggar is taken from Pericles, II.i.66-97.
Mittimus/ warrant ordering imprisonment as for
unauthorized begging in the streets. The term derives from
the first words of the warrant, which are Latin for "We
send..."
117-120. I ha . . . soundly/ J.W. has skillfully woven
together elements from Pericles and from Hary's Wallace in
this passage. The initial source was Wallace's complaint
against the cold water after saving his life by a long swim
across the Firth of Forth: "So bett I am with strakis sad
and sar. The cheyle wattir vrned me mekill mar" (V.383-
384). Line 119 closely reflects Hary's ideas and some of
his language. However, this is fit into a sporting image
similar to that in Pericles: "A man whom both the waters
and the wind In that vast tennis court have made the ball
For them to play upon" (II.i.63-65). Shakespeare's image
is changed along the lines suggested by Hary's term "bett."

231

and I, Wrastling for fals, he got the masterie;

I'me with his beating bruis'd, weary, cold, weak,

Liquor'd soundly.   120

Bolt. He's drunk.

Wallace.   Yet so thirstie scarce can speak;

If ye be men, help me to food and fire.

Jeffrey. What Countryman art thou sirra?

Wallace. A Scot. Give me some victuals, pray.

Bolt. No minde but of thy belly.   125

Jeffrey. Sirra, sirra, you are a Scot, and I a true

English justice.

Bolt. Not a word of Latine, neither Justice, nor Clarke.

Jeffrey. Peace Bolt. In the Kings name, I charge

thee: if you will eat bread earn bread; take up   130

this luggage, sirra, follow me home to my house.

Thou shalt have good bread, good drink, and good

fire. Up, I command thee.

Wallace. I am necessities slave, and now must beare.

Bolt. Must! Nay, shall: are not the English your   135

good Lords and Masters?

Wallace is made the loser in the sport of wrestling, where
he was physically "beaten" by Neptune, the personification
of the waters and the wind that played upon Pericles.
    121. scarce . . . speak/ i.e., I scarce can speak.
Abbott (399) explains that nominative elements were sometimes omitted by Elizabethan writers if the omission created
no doubt as to the meaning; cf. Hamlet: "Nor do we find
him forward to be sounded, But, with a crafty madness /he/
keeps aloof" (III.i.7-8).

Wallace. Well they are.

Bolt. Do you grumble sir? On Sir <u>Jeffrey</u>.

Jeffrey. Have an eye to him <u>Bolt</u>, lest he give us

the slip. And were you in this terrible storm   140

at Sea say you?

Wallace. Over head and eares, sir.

Bolt. If th'execution had been upon the land Sir

<u>Jeffrey</u>, as 'twas upon the Sea, your worship had

been in a worse pickle then he.   145

Jeffrey. Why Knave? Why?

Bolt. Because he that has a bad name is half-hang'd,

and your worship knowes, ye have but an ill name.

Jeffrey. Thou Varlet is not wise good?

Bolt. Yes passing good.   150

Jeffrey. Why should <u>Wiseacre</u> being put together

be nought then?

Bolt. Is not Plumb-porridge good, Sir <u>Jeffrey</u>?

Jeffrey. Yes.

Wallace. Would I had this trunk full of 'em.   155

---

142. Over . . . eares/ completely immersed.
143. th'execution/ The exact significance of "execution" is not clear. Schmidt points out the use of the term
for "any deed of hostility and violence,...destruction;"
however, he preserves no Shakespearean example in reference
to a storm.
145. been . . . pickle/ common expression for one in a
sorry condition (cf. Tilley, P276).
147. he . . . half-hang'd/ common proverb (cf. Tilley,
N25).
150. passing/ surpassingly, exceedingly.

Bolt. Peace Greedi-gut. Plum-porridge is good, and

    Bag-pudding is good, but put them together, and

    they are filthy meat.

Jeffrey. Well, that's true.

Wallace. Right sir.   160

                       Sets down the Trunk.

Jeffrey. How now?

Wallace. Hunger is good, and two Woodcocks are

    good, but the feathers of those two Woodcocks

    must be pluck'd first.

Jeffrey. Hold, I charge thee.   165

Wallace. Y'are a scurvy Justice, yare man's an

    Asse, and you another with a velvet foot-cloth

    on your back; I ken ye vary weel, and I'se knock

    156-158. Plum . . . meat⌐ The meaning of this bawdy
passage is contained in the hyphenated words, the first
term of which would be stressed by the actor. Partridge
glosses "plum" as the female genitals and "bag" as the
male scrotum.
    162. Woodcocks⌐ proverbial for foolish birds, or men
compared to the birds. Cf. "A Roaring Boy," The Overburian
Characters: "He cheates young Guls that are newly come to
Towne; and when the Keeper of the Ordinary blames him for't,
answeres...That a Woodcock must bee pluckt ere he be drest"
(ed. W. J. Paylor, The Percy Reprints, No. 13 ⌐Oxford;
Blackwell, 1936⌐, p. 58).
    166-169. Y'are . . . here⌐ Wallace slips into Scots
dialect in this speech.
    166-167. yare . . . back⌐ A footcloth is a rich hanging
laid over the back of a horse, a caparison. In this expression, it figures worthlessness gilded; cf. The White
Devil: "Merely an ass in's foot-cloth" (I.ii.51).
    168. I'se⌐ I'll.

ye vary weele. If any thing be worth victales,

it goes down here.   170

Bolt. The Devill choake you, if you be a man of

your word.

Wallace. Wiseacres, if you would fain know who has

got this trash from yee, 'tis I, Wallace the Scot.

Jeffrey. ⎫
          ⎬ Wallace!   175
Bolt. ⎭

Bolt. Flie Sir Jeffrey! He calls us Woodcocks,

let's flie and raise the Country.

Wallace. D'ye grumble? Raise the Devill and spare not.

                    ⎾Sir Jeffrey and Bolt⏌ Exeunt.

Wert thou a chest of gold, I'de give thee all

            for victuals.

Hunger, they say, will break stone wals;   180

Your chops are not so hard,

---

173. fain⏌ willingly.
174. 'tis . . . Scot⏌ Cf. Hary's Wallace: "Off Scotland
born my rycht name is Wallace." (IX.375).
176-177. Flie . . . flie⏌ Bolt alludes to the woodcock's burst into the air in its attempt to escape after
being flushed from a brake, i.e., Since he calls us "woodcocks," let us speed away as does the bird.
177. raise . . . Country⏌ i.e., stir up the district
for defense.
178. D'ye grumble⏌ As the English flee, Wallace ironically repeats Bolt's scornful question of line 138.
179. Wert . . . victuals⏌ Cf. Hary's Wallace: "Meit
in this tym is fer better than gold" (XII.639).
180. Hunger... wals⏌ A common proverb (Cf. Tilley, H811).
181. Your . . . hard⏌ i.e., Your jaws are not so hard
(as are stone walls).

Ye shall burst tho with iron ribs ye were bar'd.

Victuals--wine too--few justices doe feed the hungry

thus. O these Wiseacres are the bravest fellowes,

specially English Wiseacres.   185

                Enter Selby, miserably poore,
                 /a rope in his hands./

Selby. I'le now be my own carver; misery and age

    Want and despaire have brought me to deaths doore,

    And shall I not enter? Yes I will, this key

    Shall doo't. Is death so surly, may a poore man

    Speake sooner with a King then speake with him   190

    When he has most need of him? Ugly leane slave,

    So I may see him, no matter for a grave.

Wallace. How now, what do'st looke for?

Selby. For that which a quarter of the world wants,

    a tree to be hang'd upon.   195

Wallace. Art weary of thy life?

---

    184. Wiseacres/ Wallace puns on the standard meaning of
"Wiseacres," a foolish person affecting wisdom.
    185.2. rope/ A rope is a traditional emblem of despair;
cf. Despayre in Spenser's Faerie Queen, I.ix.22 and I.ix.54.
    191. leane/ refers to the traditional personification
of Death as a skeleton.
    193. do'st/ Abbott (241) explains that the Elizabethans
sometimes omitted the "thou" in questions after a second
person singular verb. He cites Othello: "Didst /thou/ not
mark that?" (II.i.260). Cf. line 196.
    194. wants/ lacks.
    196. Art/ Cf. line 193.

Selby. Yes all men are of their old wives. My life

 has gone up and downe with me this threescore and

 odde yeares; 'tis time to be weary on't, I thinke now.

Wallace. And when tha'st hang's thy selfe, whither   200

 do'st thinke to go then?

Selby. To the Linnen-draper.

Wallace. What Linnen-draper?

Selby. The richest in the world, my old Grandmother

 the Earth. How many pairs of sheets has she had,   205

 thinke ye, since Adam and Eve lay together?

 It's the best Inne to lye at, a man shall be

 sure of good linnen.

Wallace. Who dwels hereabouts?

---

 197. all⁊ Though "all" makes some sort of sense in
this line, it is quite possible that the original reading
was: "as men are of their old wives." This comparison is
continued into lines 197-199, in which the tenor of Selby's
life is compared to the sexual motion ("up and downe"). As
line 197 now stands, "wives" may be a metaphor for lingering
life, i.e., you can't get rid of them when you're tired
with them.

 198-199. and odde⁊ and more.

 199. on't⁊ of it; see Abbott (182).

 202-208. To . . . linnen⁊ Webster plays on the idea of
the linen of shrouds in his "Character of a Sexton":
"Though one would take him to be a sloven, yet hee loves
clean linnen extreamely, and for that reason takes an order
that fine holland sheets be not made wormes meate" (Lucas,
IV, 41-42).

 202. Linnen-draper⁊ Linen merchant.

 205. sheets⁊ The reference is to "sheets" used as
shrouds; cf. Othello: "prithee shroud me In one of those
same sheets" (IV.iii.24-25).

 207. lye⁊ (1) stay, as at an inn, (2) recline, as in a
grave.

Selby. One upon whom all the poore in the Countrey   210

   cryes out.

Wallace. Whose that?

Selby. Scarcity, dearth, penurie, famine, hunger;

   I have not knowne that man lives by food these

   four dayes, and therefore I'le descend to   215

   th'Antipodes, because I'le kicke at this world.

Wallace. Stay, famine shall not kill thee; sit

                     and eate

   Thy belly full, thy cares in good wine drowne.

   By my owne fall I pitty others downe.

   Is't not good cheere?   220

Selby. Brave, I thanke you for it. How many

   beggers does a rich man eate at his table at

   one meale, when those few crummes are able to

   save a mans life. How came you sir into this

   fearefull nest of Screech-owles and Ravens?   225

215-216. I'le . . . world/ Selby plays on the literal
meaning of "Antipodes": "opposite-foot," thus "kick." "To
kick against the world" is an expression for a foolish or
bitter rejection of one's position in life; cf. Ford, The
Broken Heart: "You intend not To kick against the world,
turn cynic, stoic?" (I.i.5-6).
     21 . th'Antipodes/ place on the opposite surface of
the world.
     219. By . . . downe/ Cf. Hamlet: "For by the image of
my cause I see The portraiture of his" (V.ii.77-78).
     221-223. How . . . meale/ Cf. lines 59-68.
     225. Screech-owles . . . Ravens/ Because of the noctur-
nal habits of owls, the black hue of the raven, and the
harsh cries of both birds, owls and ravens were traditionally associated with darkness, sickness, and death. Cf.

Wallace. Cast up by the Sea; I was shipwrack'd

   and lost all my company.

Selby. Would I had beene one of 'em. I have lost

   more then you have done; I ha' lost all that I

   had but my sinnes, and they hang so heavy on my   230

   eye-lids, I can scarce look so high as the

   brimmes of my hatt to heaven. I have such a

   minde downwards, I have almost forgot who dwels

   over my head.

Wallace. Looke up, be not afraid, there raignes   235

   no tyrant. Wud thou hadst beene with me at sea.

Selby. So wud I.

Wallace. Hadst thou an Atheist been, and God not known,

   Th'adst found him in the deepe, there hee's best showne.

   He that at Sea is shipwrackt, and denyes   240

   A Deity (being there sav'd) damn'd lives and dyes.

Marlowe, The Jew of Malta: "Thus like the sad presaging
raven that tolls The sick man's passport in her hollow beak"
(II.i.1-2) and Othello: "oh, it comes o'er my memory, As
doth the raven o'er the infected house" (IV.i.20-21). Cf.
also 3 Henry VI: "Bring forth that fatal screech owl to
our house That nothing sung but death to us and ours" (II.
vi.56-57) and A Midsummer Night's Dream: "Whilst the
screech owl, screeching loud, Puts the wretch that lies in
woe In remembrance of a shroud" (V.i.383-385).
   235. Looke up/ i.e., look toward Heaven. Cf. The
Devil's Law-Case: "Oh looke upwards rather, Their deliver-
ance must come thence" (V.iv.213-214). Very ironically,
Wallace here acts as Christian minister to the despairing
Selby. This is the first step in Wallace's relinquishing
revenge in favor of the providential justice that strikes
down Selby and Haslerig.

Man no where in the twinckling of an eye

Is throwne so neare to hell, or rais'd so high

Towards heaven, then when hee's toss'd upon the waves;

It must be a hand omnipotent there that saves.   245

But how came you sir hither?

Selby. I was banish'd from England (but that

         grieves me not)

But I kill'd an old man, he was call'd Wallace.

Wallace. Ha?   249

Selby. Wallace, and me thinks hee's still at mine elbow.

Wallace. Elbowe? /Aside/ Idle: Selby my fathers

         murderer?

    Thinke not upon it.-- Sit, eat heartily

    /Aside/ Thy last.-- Sit downe, I say, /aside/

         never to rise.--

    Drinke wine. /Aside/ Drinke deepe, let thy soule

---

242. Man . . . heaven/ This passage echoes 1 Corinthians XV.52: "In a moment, in the twinkling of an eye, at
the last trump: for the trumpet shall sound, and the dead
shall be raised incorruptible, and we shall be changed."
   251. Idle/ Although the Q text for lines 251-254
appears questionable, Wallace may here be casting doubt
upon his own sanity. "Idle" means "light-headed, delirious"
(OED 2b). The sudden appearance of the broken-down Selby
may momentarily make Wallace uncertain as to whether the
beating of the storm may not have disturbed his reason.
   254. let . . . hell/ This common image derives from
the late medieval and renaissance concept of the Dance of
Death; cf. The Revenger's Tragedy: "let him reel to hell"
(V.i.49). Cf. also Dekker, The Noble Spanish Soldier: "to
goe reeling to damnation" (II.ii.68).

reele to hell.

Selby. I am almost dead with cold.

⎾Selby dozes off.⏋

Wallace.   I'le fetch dry sticks,   255

And with two flints kindle fire, beat out his braines:

O that physicke had the power to make thee yong,

I'de fetch thee drugs from th'utmost of the world,

And then would arme thee, or, into thy veines   259

Halfe my owne bloud I'de power, to lend thee strength,

That I might kill thee nobly.

⎾Selby starts up.⏋

Selby. Be quiet, I'le pay thee.

Wallace. How now?

Selby. A slumber took me, and me thought old Wallace

Clapt me upon the shoulder with one hand   265

And with the other pointed to his wounds,

At which I started, spake, but know not what.

I'me cold at heart.

Wallace. I'le seeke for fire.

Selby.   I thanke ye. If what I utter

Ye tell to any, I am a dead man.   270

---

256. fire⏋ The comma is ambiguous. Wallace could mean
(1)"kindle fire and beat out" or (2) "kindle fire ⎾of Hell⏋
by beating out."
258. th'utmost . . . world⏋ the most remote regions.
A similar use of "utmost" as a noun appears in The White
Devil: "I'll know the utmost of my fate" (V.iv.116).

You have me at your mercy, and may betray me.

<u>Wallace</u>. Not I. Eate and get strength, I'le

        seek for fire.

Unlesse I be a devill (tho I have cause

To kill thee) yet my quicke hand shall eschew it;

Thy carelesse confidence does bind me to it.   275

This mercy which I show now is for Gods sake,

In part of payment of his showne to me.

If I should kill thee now, thou owest me nothing;

Live, and be still my debter; I shall do thee   279

More harme to give thee life, then take it from thee.

Heaven in my fathers bloud who is chiefe sharer,

Shall strike for me a revenge more just and fairer.

       <u>Enter</u> Haslerig, <u>poore as th'other</u>,

            <u>with Apples</u>.

<u>Haslerig</u>. <u>Selby</u>, <u>Selby</u>!

  /To himself/ How like a Churle thou feed'st alone,

    273-282. Unlesse . . . fairer/ See Introduction, pp. 92-
94, for a discussion of the traditions behind Wallace's
relinquishment of revenge.
    274. quicke/ hasty, impatient.
    275. to it/ i.e., against killing thee. Abbott (197)
explains that "to" may mean "against"; cf. <u>Much Ado About
Nothing</u>: "The Lady Beatrice hath a quarrell to you" (II.i.
243-244).
    277. part of/ partial.
    281. Heaven . . . sharer/ i.e., God (see "Heaven," <u>OED</u>
6) whose liability in my father's death ("bloud") is
greater than any other.
        sharer/ stockholder (as in a company of actors).

And greedy art to fatten misery.-- 285

Selby!

Selby. Here.

Haslerig. Look I ha' found a jenniting tree.

Selby. Where stands it? 290

Haslerig. I'le not tell thee; see brave food.

Selby. Lets taste it.

Haslerig. Not a paring. What hast there?

Selby. The dole of plenty.

Haslerig. Good old Rogue I thank thee; 295

I have a stomacke like a Lawyer.

Lets eat fruit when we have fill'd our bellies.

Selby. Not a bitt.

Haslerig. Ha?

Selby. Not a paring of cheese. 300

Haslerig. I must.

Selby. Thou shalt not, I pay thee in thy own coyne.

Haslerig. Thy doting age is almost at her journies end;

My youth having far to go needs more provision,

---

289. jenniting/ a kind of apple tree.
293. paring/ Cf. line 300.
294. dole/ charitable distribution.
296. stomacke/ appetite.
300. paring . . . cheese/ "Cheeseparing" was used by
the Elizabethans to indicate the humblest bit of food. Cf.
Massinger, A New Way to Pay Old Debts: "Durst wish but
cheeseparings, and brown bread on Sundays" (II.ii.60).

And I'le have this--

Selby.   Hands off!   305

                         /Haslerig/ kils him.

Haslerig. You Dog, you old Devill.

Selby. I thank thee; thou hast cut the threed in two

   Of all my woes. Heaven pardon us both. Adue.

Haslerig. Selby, no water from the hallowed Fount

   Toucht thee, thou art so fatall. Selby dead!   310

   Gods building which has stood this threescore yeeres,

   This has defac'd; would it were up agen

   With ruine of mine own. I never knew

   Partners but one still th'other overthrew.

   Thou and I did set up with one stock of care;   315

   I have undone thee, and now all's my share.

   'Tis not so sinfull, nor so base a stroke

   To spoile a Willow as an old reverend Oke.

_____

   307. threed/ thread. The course of life was represented in classical mythology as thread spun by the Fates; cf.
Pericles: "till the Destinies do cut his thread of life"
(I.ii.108).
   309. hallowed Fount/ Haslerig's meaning may derive
from Psalm XXXVI.9: "For with thee is the fountain of
life," which speaks of the blessings of those that trust in
God. Unlike the faithful, Selby has trusted in the Devil
(cf. line 306); thus, his life has been "fatall."
   311. Gods building/ The idea of the body as the temple
of God goes back to Lucretius, De Rerum Natura, II, 554.
It also has Biblical precedent (cf. 1 Corinthians, III.9):
"ye are God's building"). Cf. also The White Devil: "your
body, Which is the goodly palace of the soul" (V.vi.56-57).
   312. This/ indicates his weapon, probably a dagger.

From me th'art gone, but I'le from hence nere fly,

But sit by thee, and sigh, and weep, and die.   320

Enter Sir Jeffrey, Bolt, Souldiers.

Bolt. Stand, that's he who turns his taile to us,

which is as much as to say, a fart for your Worship.

Omnes. Down with him.

Sir Jeffrey. Peace, it's a wilde Bull we come to set

upon, and therfore let those Dogs that can fasten   325

bite soundly.

Bolt. My harts, we come not to bait an Asse in a

Beares skin, but a Lion in his own skin. He's a

traitour.

Omnes. How know we that?   330

Bolt. Thus, he hides his face, and wee are not to

back a traitor. Sir Jeffrey, you'le get between

mee and the Gallows, if I strike him down?

324-325. set upon/ attack; cf. 1 Henry IV: "we'll set
upon them" (I.ii.194).

325. fasten/ bite firmly.

327-328. bait . . . own skin/ The bating of asses and
horses by dogs was occasionally practiced, but was never
genuinely popular. Assse, in particular, made poor sport
and were therefore seldom used (Strutt, p. 204). Cf. the
proverb, "An ass in a lion's skin" (Tilley, A351).

332. back/ a poor pun that turns on two meanings of
"back": (1) the rear of a man, (2) to give aid and support
to. Cf. Appius and Virginia: "1. I know no man more
valiant then we are, for wee back Knights and Gentlemen
daily. 2. Right, we have them by the back hourely" (III.
ii.17-19).

245

Jeffrey. I'le enter into a Recognizance to hang

    before thou shalt hang.   335

Bolt. If you see my heart begin to faint, knock

    mee down to put life into me.

Jeffrey. Feare nothing.

                 Bolt strikes him down.

Haslerig. Be damn'd! Both gods and men the act detest.

    Oh heaven, wipe this sinne out for all the rest.   340

                      /Dies/.

Bolt. Your sins are wip'd out sir, your Scottish

    score is paid sir.

Jeffrey. Is he down?

Bolt. He sprawles. Stay, there's one asleep by him;

    shall I kill the lice in his head too?   345

Jeffrey. No, wake not a sleeping Mastive. The

    King's in the field, lets post to him. Bolt,

    thou shalt be a Knight as deep as my selfe for

    this manly deed. As ye go through the Country,

    cry aloud, the traitor's dead.   350

---

    334. Recognizance/ an obligation of record, an official
bond to perform an act.
    339. act/ i.e., murder.
    342. score/ account, bill. Apparently Bolt means the
score for Haslerig's sins, mentioned in line 340.
    346. wake . . . Mastive/ a version of the common pro-
verb, "It is evil waking of a sleeping dog" (cf. Tilley, W7).
    347. post/ hasten.
    348. Knight . . . deep/ Wisacres associates with
"Knight" the common adjective for an intensely dark "night."
His meaning is: "as much a knight as myself."

<u>Bolt</u>. Cry it out at the Crosse, and at the old Palace,

 That <u>Bolt</u> was the man that brain'd lusty <u>Wallace</u>.

<u>Omnes</u>. The traitor's dead, the traitor's dead, etc.

/Exit./

351. Crosse/ A cross, erected at a central position in
towns and villages, was the location for meetings and
proclamations. <u>OED</u>, 7b, cites Cotgrave: "Thou hast not
cried it at the <u>cro</u>sse."
        old Palace/ Westminster Palace, the meeting place
of Parliament. <u>OED</u> cites <u>Hay any work</u>: "Going to the old
pallas at Westminster."

/Actus III. Scena ii7

Enter Wallace, with dry sticks and straw,
beating two flints.

Wallace. Thou shalt have fire anon old man--
            Ha', murdred?

  What shouldst thou be? The face of Haslerig,

  'Tis he! Just heavens ye have bestow'd my office

  Upon some other; I thank ye that my bloud

  Stains not my hand. However both did die   5

  (In love or hate) both shall together lie:

  The Coffin you must sleep in is this Cave,

  Whole heaven your winding sheet, all earth your grave;

  The early Lark shall sadly ring your Knell,

  Your Dirge be sung by mournfull Philomell.   10

  III.ii. The place of this scene is the same. The
bodies of Selby and Haslerig remain in place.
  3. office/ duty.
  5-13. However . . . adue7 For a comparison of this
dirge with similar passages in Webster and Shakespeare, see
Introduction, pp. 44-46.
  7. Cave7 As there is no provision made for removal of
the bodies after this scene, Wallace apparently drags them
into the "enclosure" where they can be curtained off at the
close of the scene (see Bernard Beckerman. Shakespeare at
the Globe /New York: MacMillan, 19627, pp. 73-74, 82-88,
for a discussion of the "enclosure."
  8. Whole7 i.e., the entirety of.
  10. Philomell7 the nightingale, after the myth of Philo-
mela metamorphosed into the bird (Ovid, Metamorphosis, VI.
412-716).

248

Instead of flowres and strewing herbs take these,

/Wallace <u>scatters</u> <u>sticks</u> <u>and</u> <u>straw</u> <u>over</u> <u>bodies.</u>/

And what my charity now fails to do,

Poor Robin-redbrest shall. My last adue.

I have other streames to swim. Tho rough, or calme, 14

Venture: 'tis brave when danger's crown'd with palme.

Exit.

14. Tho roug<u>h</u>/ through <u>Q</u>.

---

13. Robin-redbrest/ Cf. <u>The</u> <u>White</u> <u>Devil</u>: "<u>Call</u> <u>for</u>
<u>the</u> <u>robin-red-breast</u> . . . <u>Since</u> <u>o'er</u> <u>shady</u> <u>groves</u> <u>they</u>
<u>hover</u>, <u>And</u> <u>with</u> <u>leaves</u> <u>and</u> <u>flow'rs</u> <u>do</u> <u>cover</u> <u>The</u> <u>friendlesse</u>
<u>bodies</u> <u>of</u> <u>unburied</u> <u>men</u>" (V.iv.95-98). Lucas's note to this
passage discusses the tradition of Robin Redbreast as sexton
for the friendless dead. See also Dent on the same passage
(p. 159).
14. Tho roug<u>h</u>/ The <u>Q</u> reading, "through," appears a misprint, possibly caused by compositorial misreading, or by a
proofreader's "correction" of "thorough." The sense
requires "rough" as an antithesis for "calme."

/Actus IV, Scena i7

Enter with Drum and Colours, the Generall of
Scotland, with Grimsby, Mentith, Coming,
and Souldiers with blew Caps.

General. Upon this field-bed will we lodge this night;

The earth's a souldiers pillow. Here pitch our tents.

Omnes. Up with our tents.

General. To councell, beat a Drum.

/Drum.7

Grimsby. Beat it for action then, and not for words.   5

IV.i. The place of this scene is a field near Falkirk.
The action of Act IV is thematically continuous and concerns
only the Battle of Falkirk and its aftermath. In Q the act
division comes after line 27, where Wallace enters upon an
already populated stage. Since there is no break in the
action at this point, Q's division is clearly meaningless.
The present edition shifts the division backward to the
opening of the action where the Scots are presented as en-
camping and marshalling their forces. This arrangement
possesses a certain logic, for it has the effect of balancing two different aspects of the play's title character.
It marks a formal separation between the scenes which present the shipwrecked and isolated Wallace and emphasizes
his personal dilemma in addressing the moral conflict
between revenge and honor (Act III) from those that show
the hero confronting a similar problem--the respective
claims of power and honor--in a more political and public
context (Act IV). So far as there are sources for Act III,
they are Shakespearean; Act IV stems from Hary's Wallace
(XI.88-546).
    1. field-bed7 bed upon the ground; cf. Appius and Vir-
ginia: "never bedded But in the cold field-beds" (I.iv. 9-10).

Upon our Speare points our best counsell sits:

Follow that (noble Generall). Up with no tents,

If you dare hold me worthy to advise,

But with an easie march move gently on.

General. You speak against the Scholership of war.   10

Grimsby. Now their Beef-pots, and their Cans,

Are toss'd in stead of Pikes. Their Armes are thrown

About their Wenches middles; there's their close feight.

Let us not lose the forelock in our hands:

Of us they dream not, yet we are as free-born   15

---

7. that/_ i.e., our best counsel.
9. easie/ quiet.
10. Scholership . . . war/ traditions and conventions
of war are reflected in such texts as Caesar's Commentaries.
11. Cans/ vessels for holding liquor.
12. toss'd/ This term is used in a double sense:
(1) throwing food and drink down the throat, (2) wielding
the long thrusting spear--the pike--that was the standard
weapon of footsoldiers.
13. close feight/ hand-to-hand combat, here used in
both military and sexual senses. For a parallel to the
sexual use, cf. Marston, Sophonisba: "thinke not but kisse,
The florish fore loves fight is Venus blisse" (III.i /Plays,
II,33/). Partridge (p. 42) lists many military terms used
as sexual images in Shakespeare. For example, cf. All's
Well That Ends Well: "When you have conquered my yet maiden
bed" (IV.ii.57) and 2 Henry IV: "FAL. Do you discharge
upon mine hostess. PIST. I will discharge upon her, Sir
John, with two bullets" (II.iv.121-124). Cf. also Marston's
Antonio and Mellida: "Troth, one that will besiege thy
maidenhead, Enter the walls, i'faith, sweet Mellida, If
that thy flankers be not cannonproof" (I.i.101-103).
14. Let . . . hands/ This refers to the common proverb:
"Take occasion by the forelock, for she is bald behind"
(Tilley, T311).
15-16. free-born . . . slaves/ These lines are developed around the antithesis between "free-born" and "slaves."
For a similar passage, see The Telltale: "I am as free
borne as any prince, and ere Ile liue slaue to a stranger"
(I. /p. 107/).

As th'<u>English</u> King himself. Be not their slaves;

Free <u>Scotland</u>, or in <u>England</u> dig our graves.

/Cryes/ within, "<u>A</u> Wallace,

<u>A</u> Wallace, <u>A</u> Wallace!"

<u>Enter</u> Ruge-crosse, <u>a</u> <u>Scottish</u> <u>Herald</u>.

<u>General</u>. Rugcrosse, what cry is this?

<u>Ruge-crosse</u>.   Of the whole Army,

Grown wild twixt joy and admiration,

At the sight of <u>Wallace</u>.   20

<u>Omnes</u>. Ha.

<u>Ruge-crosse</u>. That dreadlesse Souldier,

For whom all <u>Scotland</u> shed a sea of teares

As deep as that in which men thought him dead,

Sets with his presence all their hearts on fire,   25

That have but sight of him.

/Cryes/ within, "<u>A</u> Wallace, <u>A</u> Wallace!"

17.3. Ruge-crosse/ The name of the Scottish herald is
probably drawn from <u>Rouge Croix</u>, the title of one of the
Pursuivants of the English College of Arms.
    19. admiration/ (1) wonder, astonishment, (2) hero-
worship.
    22. dreadlesse/ fearless.
    23. sea . . . teares/ CF. II.iii.23.
    26.1. <u>A</u> Wallace/ The "<u>A</u>" of the battle cry represents
the French "à". The note to 2 Henry VI (IV.viii.53), ed A.
S. Cairncrosse, 3rd Arden ed. (London: Methuen, 1957) cites
Gösta Langenfelt, in <u>Studier</u> <u>i</u> Modern Språkvetenskap, 18

<u>Grimsby</u>. Intreat him hither.

<u>Enter</u> Wallace <u>with</u> <u>Drum</u>, <u>Colours</u>, <u>and</u> <u>Souldiers</u>.

<u>They</u> <u>all</u> <u>imbrace</u> <u>him</u>.

<u>Coming</u>. D'ee heare th'<u>English</u> march? They are at hand.

<u>General</u>. Now <u>Grimsby</u>, they for Pikes are tossing Cans.

<u>Grimsby</u>. I am glad our thunder wakes 'em.   30

<u>Mentith</u>. Shall we on?

<u>General</u>. Whether is't best, to stop 'em in their march,

   Or here to make a stand and front 'em?

<u>Omnes</u>.   Stand.

<u>General</u>. Or else retire back to the spacious Plaine

(1953), 55-64, who presents the case for "<u>à</u>". These cries
were used in combat to assemble the troops of various com-
manders. See William Patton, <u>The</u> <u>Expedition</u> <u>into</u> <u>Scotland</u>
<u>in</u> <u>1547</u>, who comments on these cries continuing into the
night after a battle: "our Northern prickers /light caval-
ry/, the Borderers, notwithstanding (with great enormity,
as me thought me, and not unlike, to be plain, a masterless
hound howling in a highway, when he hath lost him he waited
on) some "hoop"ing, some whistling, and most with crying,
"A Berwick! A Berwick!" "A Fenwick! A Fenwick!" "A Bulmer! A Bulmer!" or so otherwise as their Captains' name
were, never ceased their troublous and dangerous noises all
the night long. They said they did it to find out their
captains and fellows..." (<u>Tudor</u> <u>Tracts</u>, in <u>An</u> <u>English</u>
<u>Garner</u>, ed. Edward Arber, rev. ed., 6 /1877-1890: West-
minster: Archibald Constable, 1903), 134.
    27. In <u>Q</u> Act III ends with this line. See note on IV.i
above for a discussion of this division.
    29. Pikes . . . Cans/ Line 29 refers back to lines 11-
12.
    32-33. Whether . . . 'em/ i.e., Which is best, to
intercept them or to wait to fight until they reach here?
    33. front/ confront.

For battaile far more advantagious.

<u>Wallace</u>. And so retiring be held runawayes.

Here stands my body, and ere this <u>English</u> Wolves

Stretch their jaws ne're so wide, from hence shall drive

I'le rather lie here fifty fathome deep,

Now at this minute, then by giving back   40

One foot, prolong my life a thousand yeers.

<u>General</u>. Then let us die or live here.

<u>Omnes</u>. Arme, arme.

<u>Wallace</u>. Fall back? Not I. Death of my selfe is part;

I'le never flie my self, here's no false heart: 45

Lets in our rising be, or in our falls,

---

37. this⁄ i.e., these.
38. drive⁄ There is an elided indirect object after
this verb, i.e., shall drive ⁄me⁄.
39. fathome⁄ The use of the singular inflection for
distances marked by fathoms is quite common; cf. <u>Henry VIII</u>:
"Wish him ten fathom deep" (II.i.51).
40. giving back⁄ giving ground, retreating.
44-45. Death . . . my self⁄ These lines may contain an
echo of Richard III's raving before the Battle of Bosworth
Field; cf. <u>Richard III</u>: "Is there a murderer here? No.
Yes, I am. Then fly. What, from myself?" (V.iii.184-185).
46-48. Lets . . . Coronations⁄ Professor Haworth feels
that this image indicates evidence for John Webster's authorship of <u>The Valiant Scot</u> since it parallels <u>The White Devil</u>:
"They are those flattering bells have all one tune, At wed-
dings, and at funerals" (III.ii.92-93); cf. Introduction,
pp. 21-24. In his note to the passage in <u>The White Devil</u>,
Dent points out parallels in <u>Sir Thomas Wyatt</u>: "The flattering belles that shrilly sound At the Kings funerall,
with hollow heartes Will cowardly call thee Soueraigne"
(I.ii.21-12). See also <u>The White Devil</u> (V.vi.275).
46-49. Lets . . . crown'd⁄ Cotgrave quotes these lines
as one of the "beauties" of the play: "Let's in our rising
be, as in our falls, Like Bells which ring alike at
funerals, As at Coronations, each man met his wound. With
self same joy as Kings go to be Crown'd" (p. 282).

Like bels which ring alike at Funerals

As at Coronations; each man meet his wound

With self-same joy as Kings go to be crown'd.

Where charge you?

General.   In the battaile.   50

Valiant Grimsby is Generall of our Horse;

The infantry by Comming is commanded;

Mentith and you shall come up in the Reare.

Wallace. The Reare.

General.   Yes.

Wallace.   No, sir. Let Mentith;

Wallace shall not.

General.   He may choose.   55

Wallace. Were I to hunt within a Wildernesse

A herd of Tigres, I would scorn to cheat

My glories from the sweat of others brows,

By encountring the fierce beasts at second hand,

50-74. Where . . . pleasure⌐ In Hary's account of the
division between the Scots leaders (Wallace, XI.94-162),
Coming's envy at Wallace's reputation caused him to suggest
to the General, Sir John Stewart, that Wallace should not
be given precedence over him.

50. battaile⌐ main body of troops. The customary
order of battle for Renaissance armies was a three-part
division into the vanguard, battle, and rearguard; see Sir
John Smithe, Instrvctions, Obseruations, and Orders Myli-
tarie (London: R. Johnes, 1594), p. 86.

56-57. Were . . . indignation⌐ This passage is the
first of several instances of hunting imagery used effectively in Act IV to express the emotions and the characters
of the warriors (see also ii.65; iii.20-21; iii.27-28;
iii.35; iii.51-52).

When others strength had tam'd him. Let me meet   60

The Lion being new rowz'd, and when his eyes

Sparkle with flames of indignation.

I ha' not in the Academe of War

So oft read Lectures chief, now to com lag.

'le ha' the leading of the Van or none.   65

General. Then none. You wrong us all: men now

                  are plac'd,

And must not be dishonour'd.

Wallace.   So, dishonour'd.

General. Charge in the Reare for Gods sake; now to stand

On terms of worth hazards the fate of all.   69

Wallace. Well, be't so then, the Reare. See you yon hill?

Yonder I'le stand, and tho I should see Butchers

64. Lectures chief,7 Lectures, chief

---

60 him7 i.e., them. There seems no reason for this
lack of agreement unless the author was thinking ahead to
the lion of the next line.
  61. rowz'd7 a hunting term for flushing large animals,
especially deer; cf. 1 Henry IV: "Oh, the blood more stirs
To rouse a lion than to start a hare!" (I.iii.197-198).
  63. Academe7 school.
  64. Lectures chief7 Cf. Abbott (419) for constructions
in which the adjective is transposed with the noun for the
sake of emphasis. Here the adjective is stressed because
of the interplay between the terms "chief" and "lag."
  64. Van7 Vanguard, foremost body of troops, thus the
position of greatest honor (cf. line 50 above).
  68-69. stand . . . worth7 insist on conditions appropriate to his merit or rank.
  71-73. Yonder . . . my selfe7 Cf. Hary's Wallace: "For
thi ogart othir thow sall de, Or in presoun byd, or cowart
lik to fle. Reskew off me thow sall get nane this day"
(XI.155-157).

Cut all your throats like sheep, I will not stirre

Till I see time my selfe.

<u>General</u>.   Your pleasure.   On!

Each leader spend his best direction.

<u>Exeunt</u>.

73. See time7 i.e., see the proper time (<u>OED</u>, II, 16).
74. spend7 employ (<u>OED</u>, 3).

<u>/A</u><u>ctus</u> IV, <u>Scena</u> ii/

<u>Enter</u> King, Percy, <u>and</u> Bruce, Hertford,

Sir Jeffrey, <u>and</u> Bolt, <u>with</u> <u>Drums</u> <u>and</u>

<u>Colours</u>.

<u>King</u>. Which is the fellow?

<u>Bolt</u>. I am the party sir.

<u>Percy</u>. Stand forth before the King.

/Percy <u>pushes</u> Bolt./

<u>Jeffrey</u>. Nay, he's no sheep-biter.

<u>King</u>. Didst thou kill <u>Wallace</u>?   5

<u>Bolt</u>. Yes marry did I sir; if I should be hang'd here

before yee, I would not deny it.

<u>King</u>. How didst thou kill him? Hand to hand?

<u>Bolt</u>. Hand to hand, as Dog-killers kill dogs; so I

IV.ii. The place of this scene is the battlefield at
Falkirk.
0.1. Hertford/ This name should probably be "Hereford"
to conform to the stage direction at V.iv.46.3, where
"Herefor/d/ enters. The Earl of Hereford and Essex,
Humphrey de Bohun (1276-1322), is mentioned twice by Hary
as an important English leader at the Battle of Falkirk
(<u>Wallace</u>, XI.179 and XI.662).
4. sheep-biter/ a dog that worries sheep.
9-10. Dog-killers . . . brains/ Clubbing was the common
method of killing stray dogs; cf. Massinger and Field, <u>The</u>
<u>Fatal</u> <u>Dowry</u>: "Whose braynes should be knockt out, like
dogs in July" (II.i.159) /ed. T. A. Dunn, Fountainwell
Drama Texts (Edinburgh: Oliver & Boyd, 1969)/).

beat out his brains I'me sure.   10

King.   Me thinks, thou shouldst not look him in the face.

Bolt.   No more I did; I came behind his back and

    fell'd him.

King.   Art thou a Gentleman?

Bolt.   I am no gentleman borne. My Father was a

  poore Fletcher in Grubstreet, but I am a   15

  gentleman by my place.

King.   What place?

Bolt.   A Justices Clarke, Sir Jeffery Wiseacres.

Jeffrey.   My man, if it please your Majesty, an

  honest true Knave.   20

King.   Give to Sir Wiseacres Clark an hundred pounds.

Jeffrey.   I thank your grace.

Bolt.   God confound all your foes at the same rate.

King.   But if this Wallace, sirra, be alive now,

  You and your hundred pounds shall both be hang'd.   25

Bolt.   Nay I will be hang'd ere I part from my money.

  Who payes, who payes?

---

  11. shouldst/ Schmidt ("shall," 6) points out that
"should" can express doubt or uncertainty. In this case
the King is presenting an opinion on an uncertain issue,
i.e., I don't think you could look him in the face.
  12. No more/ i.e., As little as you expect it of me
did I do it (cf. Schmidt, 5, on "no more").
  15. Fletcher/ dealer in bows and arrows (hence the
name, "Bolt").
  17. place/ occupational position.
  23. rate/ charge.

Enter Clifford.

Clifford. Charge, charge!

King. The news brave Clifford.

Clifford. The daring Scot fuller of insolence   30

Then strength stand forth to bid us battel.

King.   Throw

Defiance back downe their throats, and of our Heralds

Northumberland the honor shall be thine.

Tell 'um

We come to scourge their pride with whips of steele;   35

Their City hath from Justice snatch'd her sword

---

30. Scot7 As a collective term for the entire Scottish
forces, "Scot" may be regarded as plural, hence the plural
verb, "stand."
35. scourge . . . steele7 a common image, possibly
drawn from the mythical whips of the Furies; cf. Massinger,
A New Way to Pay Old Debts: "And do appear like furies,
with steel whips To scourge my ulcerous soul" (V.i.368-369).
Cf. also The Thracian Wonder: "He'd lash you from his land
with whips of steel" (III.i. /The Dramatic Works of John
Webster, ed. William Hazlitt (London: John Russell Smith,
1857), IV, 161/). Cf. also IV.iv.96-97: "we bring whips
of steele To scourge Rebellion."
36. City7 As far as can be determined, this use of
"City" is unique. Figurative usages of this term generally
refer to an area of defense or refuge. Here, however,
"City" is an active agent. Were there reason to think of
the Scots collectively as the citizens of some town, the
term might be explained as meaning such a body. But there
is no association of the Scots with any geographical unit
other than Scotland herself.
          Justice . . . sword7 Cf. III.i.22.
36-38. sword . . . breasts7 Cf. Ford, Perkin Warbeck:
"their swords could have wrought wonders On their king's
part, who faintly were unsheath'd Against their prince, but
wounded their own breasts" (III.i.85-87).

To strike their Soveraigne, who has turn'd the point

Upon their own breasts: tell 'em this.

Percy.   I shall.

                         Exit /Percy7.

Clifford. Where's noble Bruce?

Bruce.   Here.

Clifford.   I have a message.

But 'tis more honorable, sent to you too: 40

The Herald saies that Wallace dares ye;

His spite is all at you, and if your spirit

Be great as his, you finde him in the reare.

King. Hang up that wiseacres, and the fool his man.

Bolt. My master, not me sir; I have a Recognizance   45

of him to stand betwixt me and the gallows.

King. A Kings word must be kept; hang 'em both.

Bolt. One word more good Sir, before I go to this

geere, if a Kings word must be kept, why was it

not kept when he gave me the 100 pounds. Wipe   50

out one, I'le wipe out the other.

---

42. spirit7 mettle, courage. Cf. line 58 below. Cf.
also Measure for Measure: "I have spirit to do any thing
that appears not foul" (III.i.212-213).
    45-46. I . . . gallows7 Cf. III.i.332-335.
    48-52. One . . . lives7 For a parallel example in which
punishment is waived in response to a lame jest, cf. Beaumont and Fletcher, A King and No King: "2. Sword-man. My
lord this is foule play ifaith, to put a fresh man upon us;
Men, are but men. Bacurius. That jest shall save your
bones" (V.iii.84-86).
    geere7 matter, business.

King. That jest hath sav'd your lives. Let me see you

    Fight to day.

Jeffrey. Bravely like Cocks.

Bolt. Now Wallace look to your coxcombe.   55

Omnes. Move on.

             Enter to them the Scottish Army, and are

                     beaten off.

King. We have flesh'd them soundly.

Clifford. I would not wish to meet with braver spirits.

King. Stay, Bruce, what's yonder on the hill?

Bruce. They are Collors.   60

King. Why do they mangle thus their Armies limbes?

    What's that so farre off?

Bruce.   Sure 'tis the Reare,

    Where burns the black brand kindles all this fire,

    I meane the Traytor Wallace.

King.   What? Turn'd Coward?

---

    57. flesh'd/ initiated into bloodshed.
    58. spirits/ brave men. Cf. King John: "a braver
choice of dauntless spirits" (II.i.72).
    59. what's . . . hill/ Wallace and his supporters are
visible on a "hill" to the rear of the battlefield. They
have climbed to the upper stage of the theater from which
they view the fortunes of the armies.
    61. Why . . . limbes/ i.e., Why do they weaken the
fighting strength of their army by such a division of
forces?

A dogge of so good mouth, and stand at bay?   65

If in this heat of fight we breake their ranks,

Presse through, and charge that devill, <u>Bruce</u>

      thy selfe.

<u>Bruce</u>. To hell if I can chase him.

<u>King</u>.   Charge up strong!

  Harke, brave,

Let now our hands be warriors, not our tongues.   70

                    <u>Exeunt</u>.

---

    65. A dogge . . . ba<u>y</u>7 "Good mouth" means a dog with a
loud and eager bark. It was not unusual for such a dog to
bark bravely but to chase poorly; cf. <u>Troilus</u> <u>and</u> <u>Cressida</u>:
"He will spend his mouth and promise, like Brabbler the
hound, but when he performs, astronomers foretell it" (V.i,
90-100). The meaning of line 65 is: /"Can Wallace be like7
a dog with such a fierce bark that we would expect him to
have an aggressive nature, yet who weakly awaits our attack
/like a hunted deer that can run no longer7."
    69. brave7 It is possible that "brave" is a verb com-
manding the English to defy the Scots: "Harke! Brave!"
However, it is also possible that line 69 is incomplete.
"Brave" may be an adjective hanging without a noun to
modify. The missing words may include a rhyme with "tongue,"
as the practice in the play is to end scenes with couplets.
    70. Let . . . tongues7 Variations on this expression
are common; cf. <u>Richard</u> <u>III</u>: "We come to use our hands and
not our tongues" (I.iii.353). For variations in which
"swords" are used instead of "hands," cf. Massinger, <u>The</u>
<u>Maid</u> <u>of</u> <u>Honour</u> (II.iv.29-30) and Dekker, <u>The</u> <u>Noble</u> <u>Spanish</u>
<u>Soldier</u> (II.i.231-232).

/Actus IV. Scena iii7

Enter the Scottish Army, Generall, Grimsby,
Coming, Mentith. /Wallace remains above.7

A cry within: "They flye, they flie!"

General. The English shrink!

  Knit all our nerves and fasten Fortunes offer.

Grimsby. Keep steedy footing; the daye is lost

           if you stir.

  Stirre not, but stand the tempest.

Coming.   I cry on.

General. And I.

Grimsby.   So do not I. This starting backe   5

  Is but an English earth-quake, which to dust

  Shakes rotten towers, but builds the sound more strong.

General. Lets on, and dare death in the thickest throng.

     Enter the English Army, and encompasse them.

Grimsby. Did I not give you warning of this whirpoole

  IV.iii. The place of this scene is the battlefield at
Falkirk. Wallace has been in place on the upper stage
during the clearing of the lower stage.
     2. Knit . . . nerves7 i.e., Arouse all our resolution.
Cf. Rowley, A Shoemaker a Gentleman: "Knit all our Nerves
in one? (III.iv.sig. F4v).
     4. tempest7 i.e., onslaught, battle.

264

For going too farre?

Mentith.   We are all dead men,   10

    Yet fight so long as legges and Armes last.

King. In how quicke time

    Have we about you built a wall of brasse?

    Had he whom here you call your Generall

    A Souldier beene remarkable of great breeding,   15

    And now to be caught with lyme-twigs?

General.   Keepe our ground.

Grimsby. If we must fall, fall bravely.

Mentith.   Wound for wound.

    Alarum. Exeunt King and Bruce pursuing the Scots.

    Clifford, Percy, Grimsby, and Generall stay.

---

11. Armes/ (1) the physical members, (2) weapons.
13. wall . . . brasse/ The image of a "wall of brass"
for an encircling army is unusual. The phrase is commonly
used to figure a stout defense. Cf. Richard II: "As if
this flesh which walls about our life Were brass impreg-
nable" (III.ii.167-168). Cf. Massinger, The Bashful Lover:
"innocence is a wall of brass (V.i. /Works, p. 410/).
14-16. Had . . . lyme-twigs/ King Edward's ironic
question borrows interrogative direction from the "how" of
line 12. The sense is, "How had he . . . previously been
distinguished as an accomplished soldier, when now he is
caught by a simple ruse?"
15. remarkable/ worthy of remark, distinguished.
    breeding/ education; hence, those accomplishments
in the sense of both training and experience that make a
complete soldier.
16. lyme-twigs/ twigs smeared with bird-lime, a sticky
substance to catch small birds. Here the expression means
"a simple ruse."

Clifford. Take breath. I would not have the world rob'd

    Of two such spirits. /To Messenger7 Poast to

        the King,

    And tell him that the noblest Harts   20

    Of the whole heard are hunted to the toyle;

    Aske whether they shall fall, or live for gaine.

Messinger. I shall.

                            Exit.

          A cry within: "Charge!"

      Enter Mentith at another doore. /Speaks to

             Wallace above.7

Mentith. For honours sake come downe, and save thy

          Countrey.

Wallace. Whose is the day?

Mentith.   'Tis Edwards. Come rescue.   25

    Our Generall, and the noble Grimsby.

---

    18. I . . . rob'd7 "Would" is often used to indicate
desire (Abbott, 329), i.e., I do not desire that the world
be robbed.
    19. spirits7 (1) brave men (cf. IV.ii.58), (2) souls.
        Poast7 Post, hasten (literally, "ride").
    21. toyle7 net for wild beasts, snare.
    24-32. For . . . againe7 Hary portrays the discussion
as to whether or not Wallace should aid the Scots as an
internal debate between Kindness and Will, Wallace (XI.217-
240). Through Bruce's leadership, the English forces defeat
the Scots after the cowardly Comyn flees. Wallace and his
men are eventually encompassed, but they break through
Bruce's lines to the safety of the Tor Wood.

Wallace.   Who?

Mentith. Our Generall and stout Grimsby are enclos'd

   With quick-sets made of steele. Come fetch them off,

   Or all is lost.

Wallace.   Is the day lost?

Mentith.   Lost, lost.   29

Wallace. Unlesse the day be quite lost, I'le not stirre.

Mentith. 'Tis quite lost.

Wallace.   Why then descend amaine.

   Art sure 'tis lost?

Mentith.   Yes.

Wallace.   Then wee'e winne it againe.

       /Wallace and soldiers exit from above./

Enter Messenger.

Clifford. How now?

Messenger.   The King proclaimes that man a traytor

   That saves when he may kill.

Clifford.   Charge them! Blacke day,

   The Lyon hunts a Lyon for his prey.   35

A fight.

---

   28. quick-sets/ Quickset hedges may have been used as
sections of the enclosures or traps into which deer were
driven.
   35. The Lyon . . . prey/ Cf. Wallace's comment about
Bruce: "The rycht lyon agayne his awn kynryk" (Hary's
Wallace, XI.209).

Enter Wallace <u>and</u> <u>Souldiers</u>, <u>beat</u> <u>off</u> <u>the</u> English

/<u>to</u> <u>find</u>/ <u>the</u> Generall, <u>and</u> Grimsby

<u>slaine</u>. /<u>Enter</u> Bruce <u>alone</u>./

<u>General</u>. Too late.

<u>Wallace</u>. Why then farewell; I'le make what haste I can

To follow thee. <u>Bruce</u>, <u>Bruce</u>, I am here.

'Tis <u>Wallace</u> calls thee, dares thee--

<u>Bruce</u>. Tho I nere stoopt unto a traitors lure!   40

I scorne thine; thy do'st thou single me,

Yet turnst thy weapon downward to the earth?

<u>Wallace</u>. Lets breathe and talke.

<u>Bruce</u>. I'le parly with no traytor but with blows.

<u>Wallace</u>. Ye shall have blows your guts full; I

am no traytor.   45

―――――――――

35.3. Grimsby/ The death of Grimsby indicated in this
stage direction is an obvious mistake, for Grimsby appears
again in V.ii. From Hary's <u>Wallace</u>, we learn that it was
Graham, not Grimsby, who was killed at Falkirk (XI.392-395).
The similarity in the names doubtless accounts for the confusion.
    38-67. Bruce . . . Soveraigntie/ In Hary's account of
the meeting between Wallace and Bruce (<u>Wallace</u>, XI.442-527),
it is Bruce who initiates the conference and who arranges
the later rendezvous.
    40. stoopt . . . lure/ An image from falconry refer-
ring to the pounce of the hawk upon the lure (the feathered
decoy used to recall the hawk). The expression here means
"responded to a traitor's enticement."
    41. single/ i.e., single out, separate from others.
    44. parly/ confer with enemies; cf. Rowley, <u>The</u> <u>Birth</u>
<u>of</u> <u>Merlin</u>: "We'l here no parly now but by our swords" (IV.
ii.39). Cf. also Marlowe, <u>Edward</u> <u>II</u> (I.i.125-126).

Bruce. Why 'gainst thy Soveraigne lifts thou then

        thy sword?

Wallace. You see I lift it not.

Bruce.   Tell Edward so, thy King.

Wallace. Longshanks was never Soveraigne of mine,

    Nor shall whilst Bruce lives. Bruce is my Soveraigne:

    Thou art but bastard English, Scotch true borne.   50

    Th'art made a mastive 'mongst a heard of wolves,

    45-49. I . . . Soveraigne⎦ This exchange parallels a
scene in Thomas Heywood, 1 Edward IV:
    Capt. Submit, and ask forgiveness of thy King.
    Fal. What king?
    Mor. Why Edward, of the house of Yorke.
    Fal. He is no king of mine. He does vsurp;
And, if the destinies had giuen me leaue,
I would have told him so before this time,
And pull'd the diadem from off his head.
    Mor. Thou art a traitor. Stop thy traitor's mouth.
    Fal. I am no traitor: Lancaster is King. (I ⎡Works,
I, 54-55⎦).
    46. lifts⎦ liftest (see Abbott, 340).
    49. Nor shall⎦ This elliptical clause omits both the
subject and main verb, i.e., Nor shall ⎡he be⎦.
    51-52. Th'art . . .of⎦ This image of the mastiff
running with the wolves is the only bit of evidence that
J.W. consulted John Major's Historia Brittanniae Iam Angliae
quam Scotiae (Paris, 1521). Speaking of the retreat after
the battle of Falkirk, Major says of Wallace that "He drove
his army before him as if it had been a flock of sheep, and
himself the shepherd, who in his slow retreat should keep a
watchful eye upon the wolves in pursuit" (John Major's
History of Greater Britain, trans. and ed. by Archibald
Constable, Publications of the Scottish History Society. 10
⎡Edinburgh: Univ. of Edinburgh Press, 1892⎦, 200). Though
the image has been changed slightly from that of the faithful shepherd to that of an unfaithful sheepdog, the image
is similar in subject, language, and application. However,
as references to sheep, wolves, and shepherds were quite
common because of the large number of Biblical references
to them, this single parallel is not sufficient to prove
that J.W. used Major's History. Shakespeare's dramas,
especially the history plays, are full of such references.

To weary those thou shouldst be shepherd of.

The fury of the battell now declines,

And take my counsell, though I seeme thy foe:

Wash both thy hands in bloud, and when anon   55

The English in their Tents their deeds do boast,

Life thou thy bloudy hands up, and boast thine,

And with a sharpe eye note but with what scorne

The English pay thy merit.

Bruce.   This I'le try.

Wallace. Dar'st thou alone meet me in Glasco-moore,   60

And there I'le tell thee more?

Bruce. Thou hast no treason towards me?

Wallace.   Here's my hand,

I am cleare as innocence. Had I meant treason

Here could I worke it on thee; I have none.

Bruce. In Glasco-moore I'le meet thee, fare thee well. 65

Wallace. The time.

Bruce.   Some two houres hence.

Wallace.   There I will untie

---

55. Wash . . . bloud/ By making Wallace advise Bruce
to ensanguine himself, J.W. softens the pro-English side of
Bruce. In the Wallace, Bruce is covered with the blood of
Scots whom he has actually killed: "Bludyt was all his
wapynnys and his weid" (XI.534).
  59. pay/ i.e., repay.
  60-65. Dar'st . . . meet thee/ J.W. combines the
meeting between Wallace and Bruce at Falkirk with the
arrangement for the later rendezvous at Glasgow Moor. In
the Wallace, the later meeting is arranged by a letter from
Bruce to Wallace (XII.979-982).

270

A knot, at which hangs death or Soveraigntie.

                                        <u>Exeunt.</u>

66-67. There . . . Soveraigntie7 i.e., There I will
explain this puzzling situation which may lead you to death
or to rule over Scotland.

Enter the English Army /except for Bruce./

King. We have swet hard to day.

Clifford.   'Twas a brave hunting.

            Bolt offers to lay his Coat under the King.

King. Sit, some wine. Away in the field all fellows!

   Whose is this?

Bolt. It was my Coat at Armes, but now 'tis yours

                 at legges.

King. Away! Why givest thou me a cushion?   5

Bolt. Because of the two, I take you to be the better man.

King. A souldiers coat shall never be so base

   To lye beneath my heele. Th'art in this place

   IV.iv. The place of this scene is the English camp at
Falkirk.
   1. brave/ gallant.
   2. fellows/ J.W. employs two distinct meanings of
"fellow" in lines 2 and 9. Here it means "inferiors, subordinates" (cf. Schmidt 3). In line 9, "fellow" means
"companions, comrads" (cf. Schmidt, 1).
   4. It . . . legges/ Cf. Love's Labor's Lost: "And lay
my arms before the legs of this sweet lass" (V.ii.558).
   6. two/ i.e., two of us.
   7-9. A souldiers . . . companion/ This idea of the
equality of comrads-in-arms parallels the great speech in
Henry V: "We few, we happy few, we band of brothers. For
he today that sheds his blood with me Shall be my brother.
Be he ne'er so vile, This day shall gentle his condition"
(IV.iii.60-63).
   7. base/ (1) plebian, inferior, (2) low, without height.

My fellow, and companion.

A health to all in <u>England</u>.

<u>Omnes</u>.   Let it come.   10

<u>Clifford</u>. Is not this he that kill'd <u>Wallace</u>?

<u>Bolt</u>. No sir, I am onely he that said so. As you

sit, so did I lye.

<u>King</u>. Sirra, where's your master?

<u>Bolt</u>. My master is shot.   15

<u>King</u>. How, shot, where?

<u>Bolt</u>. I'th' backe.

<u>Clifford</u>. Oh he ranne away.

<u>Bolt</u>. No, my Lord, but his harnesse Cap was blowne

off, and he running after it to catch it, was   20

shot betweene necke and shoulders, and when he

stood upright he had two heads.

<u>King</u>. Two heads, how?

<u>Bolt</u>. Yes truly, his own head and the arrow head.

It was twenty to one that I had not beene shot   25

---

9. fellow⁊ Cf. line 2 above.
10. Let . . . come⁊ A conventional response to a toast,
i.e., let the toast come to pass; cf. line 76 below.
13. lye⁊ (1) tell a falsehood, (2) recline. The second
sense of "lye" plays off the "sit" of line 13.
19. harnesse Cap⁊ Bolt could refer to a helmet or cap
of fence as "harness Cap," except that a helmet would not
be likely to blow off.
25-26. It . . . him⁊ Bolt must mean: "The chances
were twenty to one that I had been shot before Sir Jeffrey
was shot." However, his use of "not" seems to give his
statement the opposite meaning.

273

before him.

King. Why prethee?

Bolt. Because my Knights name being Wiseacres, and

mine Bolt, and you know a fooles bolt is soon shot.

Clifford. He has pin'd the foole upon his masters   30

shoulder very handsomly.

King. Sirra, go seek your master, and bid him

Take order for burying of the dead.

Bolt. I shall Sir, and whilst he takes order for

the burials of the dead, I'le take order for   35

the stomacks of the living.

/Exit Bolt./

King. How fought to day our English?

Percy.   Bravely.

King. How the Scots?

Clifford. The pangs of war are like to child-bed throwes,

29.. a fooles . . . shot/ Bolt puns on his name being
the same as the "bolt," or arrow launched by a crossbow.
He mentions the common proverb, "A fool's bolt is soon shot"
(Tilley, F515), which refers to foolish soldiers who shoot
their arrow before the enemy enters range.

30-31. pin's . . . shoulder/ i.e., attached the name
of fool to Sir Jeffrey (OED, 4). Cf. Middleton, Women
Beware Women: "Though you were pleased of late to pin an
error upon me" (III.i.297 /ed. Roma Gill, The New Mermaid
Series (London: Ernest Benn Ltd., 1968/).

33. Take order/ Take measures; cf. Othello: "Honest
Iago hath ta'en order for 't" (V.ii.72).

39-41. The pangs . . . taste/ Cotgrave reprints this
passage as one of the "beauties" of the play: "The Pangs
of War are like to Child-bed Throes, Bitter in suffering,
but the storm being past, The talk, as of 'scap'd shipwrack, sweet doth tast" (p. 289). Cf. The White Devil:

274

Bitter in suffering, but the storme being past,   40

The talk, as of scap't shipwrack, sweet doth taste.

The death of the <u>Scotch</u> Generall went to my heart;

He had in him of man as much as any,

And for ought I think, his bloud was poorly sold

By his own Countrymen, rather then bought by us.   45

Had not the Reare where <u>Wallace</u> did command

Stood and given ayme, it had bin a day

Bloudy and dismall, and whose hard to say.

Sir, you shall give me leave to drink a health

44. bough_t_7 sought Q.

"Lovers' oaths are like mariners' prayers, uttered in ex-
tremity; but when the tempest is o'er, and that the vessel
leaves tumbling, they fall from protesting to drinking" (V.
i. 176-179).
   43. man_7 i.e., masculine virtues.
   44-45. his . . . us_7 i.e., the Scottish General died
because his fellow Scots fought poorly, rather than because
we overwhelmed him.
   45. bough_t_7 Q's "sought" fails to make sense, for the
English most certainly did seek the blood of the Scottish
General. Clifford's attempt to save this General was
thwarted by Edward's direct order to put to death all of
the rebels. As Clifford is here accusing Wallace of betray-
ing the General by withdrawing from the battle, the common
expression for betrayal "bought and sold" obviously fits
the context; cf. <u>Richard III</u>: "Dickon thy master is bought
and sold" (V.iii.305). A compositor might easily misread
the initial letter of "bought" for the long "s" of "sought,"
especially inasmuch as "sought" does appear to fit the
sense.
   47. given ayme_7 guided the English in their aim by in-
forming them of the results of previous shots; cf. <u>The</u>
<u>White Devil</u>: "I am at the mark, sir, I'll give aim to you,
And tell you how near you shoot" (III.ii.24-25).

To all the valiant <u>Scots</u>.   50

<u>King</u>. <u>Clifford</u>, I'le pledge thee; give me my bowle.

<u>Clifford</u>. Sir, I remembred <u>Wallace</u> in my draught.

<u>King</u>. I did not. So this cup were <u>Wallace</u> Skull,

   I'de drinke it full with bloud, for it would save

   The lives of thousands.   55

<u>Clifford</u>. I for your Kingdoms would not pledge it so.

<u>Percy</u>. I would. No matter how a traitor falls.

<u>King</u>. <u>Percy</u>,

   Ten thousand Crowns should buy that traitors head,

   If I could hav't for money.

<u>Clifford</u>.   I would give   60

   Twice twenty thousand Crowns to have his head

   On my swords point cut from him with this arme--

---

50. the valiant <u>Scots</u>/ The title of the play may be
drawn from Clifford's epithet, which could be played so as
to include a compliment to the Scotch courtiers in the
audience. The title may be parallel intentionally to the
earlier chronicle play on British history, <u>The Valiant
Welshman</u>, by R. A. (1615).

53-55. So . . . thousands/ The theme of blood-drinking
is introduced here. Note that King Edward would willingly
drink the lives of his Scots subjects, the barbarism that
Bruce is accused of in lines 75ff. Edward claims to accept
harsh measures to bring a quick end to the war; however,
his early decree denying quarter to prisoners indicates a
desire for revenge rather than peace. For a parallel to
Edward's speech, cf. Marston, <u>Antonio and Mellida</u>: "I'll
drink carouse unto your country's health, Even in Antonio's
skull" (III.ii.228-229).

59. Crowns . . . head/ There may be a word play in-
tended between "Crowns" and "head," especially as King
Edward's jest at V.iv.120-122 likewise concerns a crown and
Bruce's head.

But how?

I'th' field, nobly, hand to hand. Not this straw

To a hangman that should bring it me.   65

King. Let that passe.

Wher's Bruce, our noble Earle of Carrick?

Percy. I saw him not to day.

Clifford.   I did.

And saw his sword like to a Reapers Sithe,

Mow down the Scots.

Enter Bruce.

Here he comes.

King.   Brave Armory,   70

A rampant Lion within a field all Gules.

---

64. No_t_7 The elliptical opening to this sentence seems
to have the intended meaning: "I would not pay...!" Though
Abbott does not mention this case, the ellipsis is probably
due to the exclamatory nature of the sentence. The omission
of subject and verb adds emphasis, as in the common expression, "Not again!"

69-70. sword . . . Mow_7 Cf. Rowley, A Shoemaker A
Gentleman: "Let your Swords worke like Sithes" (III.iii.
sig. F4). Cf. also Massinger, The Maid of Honour: "'tis
their swordes, Sir, Must sow and reape their harvest" (I.i.
219-220).

70-87. Brave . . . Peace_7 The source for this exchange
is Hary's Wallace (XI.528-544).

71. A rampant . . . Gules_7 heraldic description of a
rearing lion against a red background. King Edward's description may contain an allusion to the Royal Coat of Arms
of Scotland that includes a rampant lion gules on a gold
field. This allusion may be one of the few suggestions to
prepare the audience for Edward's apparently sudden decision
to restore the Crown of Scotland to Bruce in Act V.

Where hast been Bruce?

Bruce.   Following the execution

Which we held three English miles in length.

King. Give him some wine. Art not thirsty?

Bruce.   Yes

For Scottish bloud, I never shall have enough on't.   75

The Kings health.

Omnes.   Let come.

Percy. How greedily yon Scot drinks his own bloud!

Omnes. Ha, ha, ha.

King. If he should taste your bitternesse, 'twere

            not well.

Bruce. What's that ye all laugh't at?

Clifford.   Nothing but a jest. 80

Bruce. Hay, good Sir tell me.

King.   An idle jest;

More wine for Bruce.

Bruce.   No more, I have drunk too much

Wallace and I did parlee.

Percy.   How, in words?

---

73. English miles7 English miles are distinguished
from the old Scottish miles (1976 yards).
75. on't7 i.e., of it (cf. Abbott, 181).
77-79. How . . . well7 Cf. Hary's Wallace: "Sotheroun
lordys scornyt him in termys rud. Ane said, "Behald, yon
Scot ettis his awn blud'" (XI.535-536).
83. parlee7 parley (cf. IV.iii.44).

Bruce. No <u>Percy</u>, I'me no prater; 'twas with swords.

   Your laughing jest was not at me?

Omnes.   Sir, no.   85

King. <u>Bruce</u> would fain quarrell.

Bruce.   I ha' done sir.

King. Peace. What Trumpet's that?

Clifford.   From the enemy sure.

King. Go learn.

      Enter Ruge-crosse <u>a</u> Scottish Herald.

Ruge-crosse. I come from <u>Wallace</u>.

King.   So Sir, what of him?

Ruge-crosse. Thus he speaks: 90

   He bids me dare you to a fresh battaile.

   By to morrowes sunne, Army to Army,

   Troup to troup, he challenges; or to save bloud,

   Fifty to fifty shall the strife decide,

   Or one to one.

King.   A Herald to the traitor.   95

                         /Messenger **advances.**/

   Go and thus speak: we bring whips of steele

---

84. prater/ chatterer.
86. fain/ willingly, gladly.
93. Troup/ A "troop" of horse is comparable in size to
a company of foot.
96-97. whips . . . scourge/ Cf. IV.ii.35).

279

To scourge Rebellion, not to stand the braves

Of a base daring vassall. Bid him ere that Sun

Which he calls up be risen, pay it and save

His Country and himselfe from ruine. Charge him   100

On his head, to make his quick submission;

If he slow the minutes, wee'le proclaime in thunder

His and his Countries ruine. Go be gon.

/Exit Messenger./

Arme!

Omnes. Arme, Arme!   105

King. A Land that's sick at heart must take sharp pils,

For dangerous physick best cures dangerous ils.

Exeunt.

97. stand . . . braves/ i.e., endure the boasts.
99. it/ There appears to be no antecedent to this pronoun, unless there is some expression "to pay the sun"
which I have not discovered.
102. slow . . . minutes/ i.e., delay. "Slow" is a
subjunctive verb form following "If" (cf. Abbott, 361).
106-107. A Land . . . ils/ Cf. Ford, The Broken Heart:
"Diseases desperate must find cures alike" (III.ii.200).
Cotgrave quotes this couplet as: "A Land that's sick at
heart, must take sharp pills, For dangerous Physick best
cures dangerous Ills" (p. 70).

Actus V. /Scena i7

Enter Bruce and Clifford.

Bruce. As you are a souldier, as y'are noble,

    I charge you and conjure you to unclaspe

    A book in which I am gravel'd.

Clifford.   Perhaps I cannot.

Bruce. Yes, if you dare you can.

                    Dare? Clifford dares

    Do any thing but wrong and what's not just.   5

Bruce. Then tell me sir, what was that bitter scorn,

    Which I like poyson tasted in my wine?

Clifford. I care not if I doe, because I love

    Vertue even in my enemy. The bowle

    Of wine kissing your lip, behold, quoth one,   10

    How eagerly yon Scot drinks his own bloud.

Bruce. Yon Scot drinks his own bloud, which Scot?

    V.i. The place of this scene is the English camp at
Falkirk.
    2. conjure7 solemnly entreat.
    3. gravel'd7 perplexed.
    8-9. I love . . . enemy7 Cf. Massinger, The Maid of
Honour: "I must praise Vertue, though in an enemy" (I.i.
135-136). Cf. also Massinger's The Virgin Martyr: "such
is The power of noble valour, that we love it Even in our
enemies" (I.i. /Works, p. 3/).
    10. kissing7 i.e., touching.

Clifford.   Best wake

  Some Oracle.

Bruce.   Who brake the jest upon me?

Clifford. Pray pardon me.

                            Exit Clifford.

Bruce. The Oracle I'le wake is here. Oh Wallace,   15

   I ne're had eyes till now; they were clos'd up

   By braving English witchcraft. Drinks his own bloud!

   England my stepdame take my bitter curse:

   Thy own nails teare thy own bowels. Oh my parent

   Dear Scotland, I no more will be a goad   20

   Pricking thy sides, but if ere I draw a sword,

   It shall be double-edg'd with bloud and fire,

   To burn and drown this Kingdome and this King.

                Enter a Gentleman.

Gentleman. My Generall charg'd me in privacie

---

13. brake . . . jest⫽ ridiculed with a joke; cf. The
Duchess of Malfi: "And of a jest she broke, of a captain
she met" (I.i.107-108).

15. here⫽ Bruce may display the bloodstains on his
garments at this word for his mind turns to the absent
Wallace.

17. braving⫽ threatening, boasting.

19-21. Oh . . . sides⫽ Cf. Hary's Wallace: "Bot off
a thing I hecht to god and the, That contrar Scottis agayn
I sall nocht be. In-till a feild with wapynnys that I ber
In thi purpos I sall the neuir der" (XI.607-610).

24-34. My . . . right⫽ The source for this incident is
Holinshed: "The Erle of Glocester immediately after that
Robert Bruce was departed from the kings presence, sent to

To give you these.

Bruce.   Thanks noble <u>Clifford</u>;   25

What did he bid thee say?

                    Nothing but so.

                         <u>Exit</u> /Gentleman./

<u>Bruce</u>. A pair of Spurs, <u>Bruce</u> nere was runaway!

Twelve silver pence! Oh bitter scorn, with <u>Judas</u>

I have betray'd my Master, my dear Country,

And here's the embleme of my treachery,   30

To hasten to some tree, and desperate die:

Twelve sterling silver pence. Sterling, ha sterling,

'Tis a limbe of <u>Scotland</u>. Spurs for flight--

<u>Clifford</u>, I'le thither, comment I wrong or right.

                         <u>Exit</u>.

---

him .xii. sterling pennies, wyth two sharpe spurres, whereby
he coniectured his meaning to be, that the best shift was
to auoyde out of the waye in moste speedy wyse" (I, 310).
Cf. Introduction pp. 70-72 for a discussion of J.W.'s use
of Holinshed.
  25. Thank<u>s</u>/ i.e., M<u>y</u> thanks to.
  26. Nothing . . . s<u>o</u>/ i.e., Nothing but what I have
just said.
  28. <u>Judas</u>/ According to the account in <u>Matthew</u>, XXVI.
14-16, Judas betrayed Christ for thirty silver pieces. In
remorse Judas hanged himself (<u>Matthew</u>, XXVII.3-5) to which
action Bruce alludes in line 31.
  32-33. Sterling. . . . <u>Scotland</u>/ Bruce refers both to
"sterling" as a measure of silver, and to Stirling, the
county in central Scotland ("limbe of <u>Scotland</u>") where
William Wallace defeated the English in 1297 at Stirling
Bridge and in 1314 at Bannockburn.
  34. comment/ A very confusing usage. The text may be
corrupt at this point, for <u>OED</u> shows no sense for "comment"
that would fit this context. The phrase seems to mean
"whether I be wrong or right." Could this be a phonetic

approximation of the French <u>quand</u> <u>même</u>? We note the awkward
reproduction of "<u>Qui va la</u>" (<u>que voula</u>) at II.iv.65. Or it
could possibly be: "/I/ care not..."

/Actus V. Scena ii/

Enter Grimsby, Mentith, Coming, English

Herald and Ruge-crosse.

Mentith. Stay noble Grimsby, ere he further passe

One of us certifie our Generall.

Perhaps hee'l not admit him to his presence.

Grimsby. 'Tis like so; stay him here, that pains be mine.

Coming. Let Ruge-crosse bring his pleasure.

Grimsby.   Come; agreed.   5

                    Exeunt Grimsby, and Ruge-crosse.

Mentith. You bring from Longshanks some strange

                message now.

Coming. At least he sends his Gauntlet.

Mentith.   Gauntlet? No,

    The English fight not two dayes together;

V.ii. The place of this scene is the Scottish camp near
Glasgot Moor.
  1. he/ i.e., the English herald.
  2. certifie/ notify
  4. like so/ i.e., likely as you say.
      stay/ arrest, stop.
      that . . . mine/ i.e., Let the responsibility be mine.
      pains/ "Pains" is often viewed as a singular collec-
tive noun to be modified by a singular demonstrative
adjective; cf. Anthony and Cleopatra: "For this pains"
(IV.vi.15).
      be/ The subjunctive "be" is demanded by the imperative
mood (cf. Abbott, 364).
  5. bring . . . pleasure/ i.e., report to us whether
Wallace desires to see the Herald.
  7. Gauntlet/ mailed glove, thus a challenge.
                        285

The English fight not two dayes together;

But like swaggerers, a fray being made up

With a wound or so, the man whose throat   10

Before should have been cut is a sworn brother.

Now we have mall'd your Nation, they'le fawn on us

Like Spaniels. Will they not?

Coming. And that's thy errand, is't not?

Mentith.   Commonly,

When English see at cuffs they are too weak,   15

They fall to fishing, and then bait the hook

With mercie, and the Kings pardon, at which

Who bites has his swallowing spoiled for ever.

There's no Scot but scorns to hang his hope

On your Kings promises, be it nere so   20

Smoothly gilded.

Herald.   He gilds none sir.

Mentith. I warrant he would pawn half his Dominions

To shake hands with Wallace, and be friends.

Coming. Had he but him in's Court, he would out-shine

His capring gallants. He would dote on him,   25

8-14. The English . . . not⌐ Cf. I.ii.86-90.
9. made up⌐ settled.
12-13. fawn . . . Spaniels⌐ A common expression for
toadying (cf. Tilley, S704).
15. cuffs⌐ fighting.
20. it⌐ I have discovered no example of "promises"
used as a singular collective noun, but the word seems to
be the antecedent of "it" in the same line.
25. capring⌐ capering, prancing.

As <u>Jupiter</u> did on <u>Ganymede</u>, and make him

His chief Minion.

<u>Herald</u>.   Hee does already

So really dote upon him, 'tis not yet

The age of one houre since my Master sware

To give ten thousand Crowns to <u>Scot</u> or <u>English</u>,   30

That were so bold to bring him <u>Wallace's</u> head.

<u>Enter</u> Ruge-crosse.

<u>Ruge-crosse</u>. The <u>English</u> Herald.

                    <u>Exeunt</u> Ruge-crosse <u>and</u> Herald.

<u>Mentith</u>. Ten thousand Crowns.

<u>Coming</u>. Would make a faire shew in our purses <u>Jack</u>.

<u>Mentith</u>. I could pick out five thousand heads,   35

That I durst boldly sell him at that rate.

<u>Coming</u>. Ten thousand Crowns.

<u>Mentith</u>.   I and Court wind-falls too,

---

26. As . . . <u>Ganymede</u>/ In Greek mythology, Zeus carried off the beautiful boy, Ganymede, to be his cupbearer. The God is here given his Roman name, perhaps after the popular account of the story in Ovid, <u>Metamorphosis</u> (X.155-161). Cf. Marlowe, <u>Edward II</u>: "For never doted Jove on Ganymede So much as he on cursed Gaveston" (I.iv.180-181).

27. Minion/ favorite.

31. so bold/ Abbott (281) explains that "as" was often omitted after "so," i.e., so bold as.

35-36. heads . . . rate/ Cf. IV.ii.25.

36. durst/ i.e., would dare. The <u>OED</u> cites William Crashaw, <u>Roman Forgeries</u>: "Do but promise that you will iudge without partialitie, and I durst make you iudge in this case."

37. wind-falls/ Cf. III.i.8.

287

Some English Earldome or so. Here is none

But friends: should you betray the conference

I care not; I would deny it, and I   40

Would oresway your proofs tho neere so massie.

Coming. It shall not need, beleeve me worthy Mentith;

What here you locke is safe.

Mentith. Shall we earne this English gold, ten

thousand crownes?

Coming. My hand.

Mentith.   They are ours; hee's dead.

Coming.   No more,   45

He comes.

Enter Wallace, Grimsby, Herald.

Wallace. I am to him no vassal, hee's a tyrant;

So tell him, ere his frowne shall bend my knee,

This shall be hang'd upon the gallow tree.

For my appearance tell him this, I'le dyne   50

---

42. It . . . need/ a future form of the common impersonal "It need not." This expression means, "It shall
not be necessary."
43. What . . . safe/ Cf. Massinger, The Great Duke of
Florence: "What you deliver to me, shall be lock'd up In a
strong cabinet" (III.i. /Works, p. 176/).
        here/ i.e., in my heart.
48. bend/ i.e., cause to bend.
50-57. For . . . slaves/ The germ of this speech is
found in Holinshed: "he willed the Englishe ambassadors to
declare from hym unto king Edward, that he purposed to hold
his Easter in Englande (if God fortuned him lyfe) and that
in despite of king Edward and al such as would bear armour

On Christmas day next in his English Court,

And in his great Hall at Westminster, at's owne

     boord

Wee'le drink Scotch healths in his standing cups

     of gold.

His blacke Jackes hand in hand about his Court

Shall march with our blew bonnets. We'le eat

     nothing   55

But what our swords shall carve, so tell his

     Souldiers;

Wee'le sit like Lords there whilst they rayle

     like slaves.

Go with Scotch threats, pay backe your English braves.

                    Exit Herald.

Grimsby. You'le make the English mad.

Omnes.   A brave defiance.

Wallace. Defiance!   60

Lets mad them more. They shall not sleep to night.

Good Grimsbie beat a drum. Let bon-fires shine

Through all our Army, as if our Tents were burnt,

And we dislodg'd; but recollect our troops

---

against him" (I, 304). See Introduction, p. 72.
53. standing cups/ cups with bases on which to stand.
54. blacke Jackes/ leather mugs coated with tar.
58. braves/ i.e., boasts.
61. mad/ make mad, madden.
64. recollect/ re-collect, reassemble.

Into an ordered body. Some thing wee'le do   65

To make our Chronicles swell with English rue.

Grimsby. A Drum! Call a Drum.

Exit Grimsby.

Wallace. Oh Sir John Mentith I have crackt the Ice

To a designe, which if it will succeed,

England no more shall strike, nor Scotland bleed.   70

Coming. ⎫
         ⎬ Lets be partakers, deare sir.
Mentith. ⎭

Wallace. What will you say, if I winne Bruce from

the English?

Mentith. The happiest day that ever shone on Scotland.

Coming. And crowne him King?

Wallace. That's the up-shot must crowne all. I'm

to meet him   75

Before one houre grow old in Glasco-moore.

Mentith. How meet him?

---

65. Some . . . do/ A standard phrase for a threat in
which the exact nature is left vague; cf. Cymbeline: "Oh,
that I had her here to tear her limb-meal! I will go there
and do 't, i' the Court, before Her father. I'll do some-
thing--" (II.iv.147-149). Cf. also Rowley and Middleton,
The Changling: "Methinks I should do something too" (I.i.
89).

68. crackt . . . Ice/ i.e., opened the way; cf. Dekker,
The Honest Whore: "you were the first Gaue money for my
soule; you brake the Ice" (III.iii.94-95).

72-75. What . . . all/ Cf. Hary's Wallace: "For Men-
teth tald thai thoucht to mak Bruce king. All trew Scottis
wald be plessyd off that thing" (XI.1003-1004).

75. up-shot/ the final arrow shot in an archery
contest, thus, the conclusion.

Wallace.   As I am; both come alone.

   No words to any.

Mentith.   Our lips are seal'd.

Coming. Will you ride, or go on foot?

Wallace. No more, I'le ride.

                 /Aside/ Wee'le passe the wood

     on foot.   80

Wallace. Jack Mentith, I do laugh to think what face

   Longshancks wil make, when he shall heare what guests

   Will dine with him in's Court on Christmas day.

Mentith. What face? He'le kill the Herald sure.

Wallace.   Oh!

   Some charme for me to be invisible there,   85

   And see him.

Mentith.   For my part of ten thousand crownes

   By this hand, I do wish you there.

Coming. For as many of mine, I sweare.

Mentith.   Time may come,

   In his Exchequer we may share twice that summe.   89

Wallace. Hence. Hye you before, keep close in the wood.

   Breake forth if you spie treason, if not, not.

Coming. ⎫
        ⎬ Good.
Mentith. ⎭

---

89. Exchequer/ Treasury.
90. close/ quiet.
91. Breake forth/ Shout out.

Exeunt /Mentith and Coming./

Enter the Friar's Ghost.

Wallace. Ha, if what thou seem'st thou art, step

   forward.

Speake. I have fac'd more horrid terror.

Friar. Where do'st gang?   95

Wallace. What's that to thee?

Friar.   Thou'se not lestand lang,

Twa wolves will suike thy bluide. By the third night,

I charge thy sawle meete mine; thy death is dight.

92-125. Ha . . . feare/ J.W. has constructed this scene
from suggestions of supernatural activity scattered throughout the Wallace. A number of visions appeared to Hary's
hero (see Carver, p. 81). The only hint we have had that
Wallace was a visionary was II.i.78-79. The germ of the
present scene may have been Hary's account of Wallace's
dream of being captured and sold to the English: "In my
sleping a fell visioun me tauld, Till Inglishmen that thou
suld me haiff sauld" (XII.361-362). Huck notes the traditional nature of the ghosts and their resemblances to
popular ballads in their language and in the details of
their messages (p. 11). In his suspicions as to the in-
fernal nature of the spirits Wallace expresses a standard
viewpoint on ghosts (see John Dover Wilson, What Happens in
Hamlet /1935; Cambridge: Univ. of Cambridge Press, 1951/.
pp. 62-63), though Wallace's doubts may have come from a
false spirit seen by Wallace earlier in Hary's book (V.221-
222): "gif the man endyt in ewill entent, Sum wikkit
spreit agayne for him present."
    96-98. Thou'se . . . dight/ "You'll not last long; two
wolves will suck your blood. By the third night from now I
command your soul /to/ meet mine; your death is ordained
/'dight'/.
    96. lestand/ "last"; cf. Carver (p. 100) for a discus-
sion of the various uses of the suffix "-and".

Wallace. Thou art a lying spirit.

Friar.   Bruce byn thy bane;

Gif on thou gang luke not turne backe againe.   100

Wallace beweere, me thinks it thee should irke,

Mare need hast thou to serve God in the Kirke.

Wallace. Stay! If thou hast a voyce th'art bloud

         and bone,

As I am. Let me feele thee, else I'le thinke thee

A sorcerous imaginarie sound.   105

Stand me! Th'art some English damned witch,

99-102. Bruce . . . Kirke͡/ "Bruce is your bane; if you
go on, look not to turn back again. Wallace, beware! Methinks this prophecy should disturb you /for/ you have more
need to serve God in the Church."

101-102. me . . . Kirke͡/ Cf. Hary's Wallace: "For as
off wer he was in sumpart yrk, He purpost than to serue god
and the kyrk" (XII.961-962). Note that the meaning of the
Scots "yrk" is changed somewhat when transferred to the
drama. "Yrk" means "weary"; however, from the context it
seems "irk" is meant to mean "disturb" or "upset."

104-108. Let . . . me͡/ Cf. William Rowley, All's Lost
by Lust: "Where borrowed you those bodies, you damn'd
theeves? In your owne shapes you are not visible: Or are
you yet but fancies imaginarie?" (V.ii.9-11).

105. sound͡/ Wallace apparently believes that the
illusion of the spirits could be produced by some form of
ventriloquism. Cf. Reginald Scot, The Discoverie of Witchcraft, ed. Hugh Ross Williamson (Carbondale: Southern
Illinois Press, 1964), p. 120: "the Pythonists spake
hollowe; as in the bottome of their bellies, whereby they
are aptlie in Latine called Ventriloqui....These are such
as take upon them to give oracles, to tell where things
lost are become, and finallie to appeach others of mis-
cheefs."

106-108. Th'art . . . me͡/ Cf. Hamlet, I.iv.40-44.
Hamlet questions whether the ghost of his father is "a
spirit of health or goblin damned" as it "com'st in such a
questionable shape." Scot explains that "Plato and his

That from a reverend Fryer has stoln his shape

To abuse me-- Stay-- Art gone? No Hagge I will not.

<u>Exit Ghost</u> beckoning <u>him</u> <u>to</u> <u>follow</u>.

It spake sure, told me <u>Bruce</u> should be my bane,--   109

Cannot-- Shall not. Heaven knows such things onely.

<u>Enter</u> Old Wallace <u>his</u> <u>Ghost</u>.

That eye hath shot me throw, wounds me to death.

I know that face too well, but 'tis so gastly,

I'le rather with my nayles here dig my grave,

Then once more behold thee. Part from me

Vext spirit; my bloud turnes to water!   115

<u>Exit Ghost</u>.

I beseech thee, affright me not-- It's gone!

<u>Enter</u> Peggies <u>Ghost</u>.

<u>Peggie</u>. Alace <u>Scotland</u> to wham salt thou compleyne?

Alace, fra mourning wha sall the refayne?

---

followers hold, that good spirits appeare in their owne
likenesse; but that evill spirits appear and shew themselves
in the forme of other bodies" (p. 418).
    108. Hagge/ Evil spirit.
    111. throw/ through.
    117-123. Alace . . . crawe/ "Alack, Scotland, to whom
shall you complain? Alack, when shall you refrain from
mourning? I beseech you for him /that/ died on the cross,
come not near Bruce, though Bruce shall not hurt you.
Alack, alack! No man can stand against fate. The damp dew
begins to fall from the heaven; I must go to my rest before
the cock crows."

294

I thee beseekand for him dy'd on tree,   119

Come not nere <u>Bruyce</u>, yet <u>Bruyce</u> sall not hurt thee.

Alace, alace, no man can stand 'gainst fate.

The dampe dew fra the heaven does gyn to faw,

I to my rest mim gange ere the Cock crawe.

                          /Exit Peggie's <u>Ghost.</u>/

<u>Wallace</u>. It was my wife. What horror meete I here?

No Armour in the world can hold out feare.   125

                        Enter Grimsby.

<u>Grimsby</u>. We stay for your direction.

<u>Wallace</u>. Whom did you meete?

<u>Grimsby</u>.   No body.

<u>Wallace</u>.   Saw ye nothing?

<u>Grimsby</u>. Not any thing.

117-118. Alace . . . refayne/ Cf. Hary's <u>Wallace</u>:
"Allace, Scotland, to quhom sall thou compleyn? Allace,
fra payn quha sall the now restreyn?" (XII.1109-1110).
Though this is slight evidence, it indicates that the
edition of the <u>Wallace</u> used by J.W. was probably the
Lekpreuik edition of 1570, the only edition to end line
1110 with "refrene," the source for "refayne."
    119. beseekand/ "beseech"; cf. line 96.
          for . . . tree/ Cf. Hary's <u>Wallace</u>: "for him
that deit on tre" (I.236 and elsewhere).
    123. I . . . craw/ The departure of a ghost upon the
cock's crow is traditional; cf. "Sweet William's Ghost," 14
(Child, II, 229) and "The Wife of Usher's Well," 11 (Child,
II, 239). Cf. also Horatio's explanation in <u>Hamlet</u>: "I
have heard The cock, that is the trumpet to the morn, Doth
with his lofty and shrill-sounding throat Awake the god of
day, and at his warning, Whether in sea or fire, in earth
or air, The extravagant and erring spirit hies To his confine" (I.i.149-155).

Wallace.   'Twas my braines weaknesse then.

   I have seene strange sights, that anon I'le tell;

   If <u>Grimsbie</u> we meete never more, farewell.   130

                            <u>Exit</u> ⌊Wallace⌋.

<u>Grimsby</u>. Ha, I am strucke dumbe. Oh mans slippery fate!

   Mischiefes that follow us at our backs we shunne,

   And are strucke downe with those we dreame not on.

---

   129. anon⌋ soon.
   131-133. Oh . . . on⌋ Cotgrave quotes this passage:
"Oh mans slippery fate, Mischiefs that follow us at our
backs we shun, And are struck down by those we thought not
on" (pp. 194-195).

/Actus V. Scena iii/

Enter Mentith, and Coming.

Mentith. I have beside with Wallang sherife of Fife,

Held private conference, who in Longshancks name

Sweares to me we shall have good preferment,

Beside the promist gold.

Enter Wallace.

Coming. Peace, Wallace comes.   5

1. Wallang sherife of Fife/ Wallace sherife of life Q.
2. Sweares/ Who sweares Q.

V.iii. The place of this scene is Glasgow Moor.
1-4. I . . . gold/ The conference between Wallang and
Mentith is reported in Hary's Wallace (XII.798-832). At
this meeting Mentith agrees to betray Wallace in exchange
for £3,000 and an English peerage. However, Wallang swears
that Wallace will only be imprisoned, that he will not be
killed.
    1. Wallang . . . Fife/ Carver (p. 85) discusses Q's
confusing substitution of "Wallace sherife of life" for the
actual name and title of the English official found in
Hary's Wallace: "And Ihon Wallang, was than schirreff off
Fyff" (XII.891). The substitution of Wallace for Wallang
may be explained by the similarity of the names. By Act V,
a compositor would have "Wallace" so imprinted in his mind
that this mistake would be almost inevitable.
    3. Sweares/ Q's "Who sweares" repeats the "who" of
line 2. Abbott provides no paradigm for such a repeated
pronoun. It must be that the compositor subconsciously
cast back for the subject of the clause as he prepared to
set the verb "sweares."

297

Mentith. Is the <u>Bruyce</u> come?

Wallace.   It is not yet his houre.

Mentith. Who came along with you?

Wallace.   My foot-boy onely,

  Who is tying up my horse.

Mentith.   /Aside./ Him must I kill.--

  I'le looke if <u>Bruce</u> be in sight yet--

Wallace.   Do.

                            Exit /Mentith/.

Coming. Y'are sad.   10

Wallace. My minde is shaken, but the storme is o're.

        A <u>cry</u> within: "<u>Helpe</u>, <u>murder</u>!"

  What cry is that?

               /Enter Mentith./

Mentith. Be arm'd! <u>Bruce</u> with a force comes to

           betray thee.

  From some villaines hand thy foot-boy is murdred.

Wallace. Murdred? <u>Bruce</u> shall repent this deed.   15

----

   7. foot-boy/ boy attendant, page.
   8-16. Him . . . him/ The murder of Wallace's man and
his own capture are taken from Hary's <u>Wallace</u> (XII.1013-
1061). In Hary's account, the traitors beset Wallace while
he is asleep, but he throws off his attackers and resists
until he is persuaded to yield by Mentith's promise that
his life will be spared.

Coming. ⎤
        ⎬ So shalt thou! Away with him.
Mentith. ⎦

Enter Souldiers, knocke him downe, hurry him
away in a sound.

                            Exeunt.

16.2. _sound_⁊ swoon, unconscious state.

/Actus V. Scena iv/

Enter Bruce muffled, with a Souldier.

Bruce. Helpe to disguise me Souldier, in exchange

   Take these for thine, and here's some gold to boot.

                    /Gives clothes to Soldier./

Soldier. If I be hang'd my Lord, in all my bravery,

   I care not.   4

Bruce. Phew, I warrant thee, seale up thy lips and eyes;

   Thou neither seest nor canst tell where I am.

Soldier. Not I my Lord.

Bruce. Oh my poore wrong'd countrey. Pardon me heaven,

   And with a feather pluck'd from mercies wing,

8. Bruce/ This speech is attributed to Soldier in Q.

V.iv. The place of this scene is the same. Scarcely
has Wallace been rushed away by the soldiers than Bruce
arrives for the rendezvous.
  0.1. muffled/ cloaked.
  5. Phew/ hushing sound.
  8. Bruce/ This speech is attributed to the Soldier in
Q; however, the subject matter and the rhetorical level
make it clear that it should belong to Bruce. Also, there
is a separate speech-heading for the Soldier in line 12,
which would not be necessary if lines 8-11 were a continua-
tion of his comment in line 7.
  9. mercies wing/ Mercy is here personified as a winged
creature, probably a forgiving angel. Cf. Massinger's The
Renegado: "though repentence Could borrow all the glorious
wings of grace, My mountainous weight of sins would crack
their pinions" (III.ii /Works, p. 110/).

Brush off the purple spots, that else would grow,   10

Like freckles on my soule.

Enter Northumberland and Clifford.

Soldier. My Lord, here comes company.

Bruce. Here quicke, mine own agen, and get thee gone.

/They exchange clothes./

Percy. Sirra Souldier, saw'st thou the Earle of

      Huntington?

Soldier. Huntington?   15

Percy. The Lord Bruce, I meane.

Bruce. Who cals for Bruce?

Percy. Muffled up, and alone, I'le to the King.

Exit /Percy/.

Clifford. Do, sirra be gone.

Bruce. Whither's Percy gone? He ask'd for Bruce.   20

Clifford. There's great enquirie for you.

---

   10. purple spots/ Bruce's sins against Scotland are
here depicted as corrupting spots like the blisters of
smallpox. Cf. The Revenger's Tragedy" "O you heavens,
Take this infectious spot out of my soul" (IV.iv.50-51).
Cf. also Richard II: "their spotted souls" (III.ii.134)
and Hamlet: "Thou turn'st mine eyes into my very soul, And
there I see such black and grainèd spots As will not leave
their tinct" (III.iv.89-91).
   11. freckles/ Freckles were regarded as disgifuring
during the seventeenth century. Shakespeare does not apply
the term to human beings, but describes the monster,
Caliban, as "A freckled whelp, hag-born" (Tempest, I.ii.
283). Cf. Dekker, The Whore of Babylon: "How Truth was
freckled, spotted, nay made leprous" (III.ii.70).

301

Bruce.   By whom?

Clifford. The King has a fresh command for Bruce.

Bruce. For me? He may command his Subjects.

Clifford. True, and Huntington is one.

Bruce.   Is none.

Clifford. No Subject?

Bruce.   None that dare oppose your King.   25

/Aside7 Oh my impostum'd spleene will flie into

      their faces.--

What command has England now?

Clifford.   Fresh powers

Are to be levied, which Bruce of Huntington

Must leade.

Bruce.   'Gainst whom?

Clifford.   'Gainst proud Wallace,

'Gainst the Scots.

Bruce.   I will not. I'm not his Butcher;   30

'Gainst the Scots I will not fight.

   22-24. The King . . . none7 In Hary's Wallace (XI.720-
736), King Edward commands Bruce to drive back the Scots
after Wallace engages at Falkirk. Bruce refuses, asking to
be released from his bond of loyalty to the English King.
Realizing that Bruce is turning against him, Edward strips
Bruce of his Scottish vassals and surrounds him with English
guards. See Introduction, p. 81-82, for a discussion of
J.W.'s intention in his version of this incident.
   26. impostum'd7 abcessed, infected.
      spleene7 the organ, regarded as the seat of anger
and malice, hence those emotions themselves; cf. I.i.9.
   30. Butcher7 Cf. I.ii.35.

Clifford.   How, will not?

Bruce. No, will not <u>Clifford</u>.

Clifford.   Peace.

Bruce.   My Lord, I dare not;

   In this last battell I receiv'd some wounds

   That yet bleed inward. I will no more

   Banquet strangers with my native bloud.   35

Clifford. <u>Bruce</u> speaks not like a subject.

Bruce. <u>English</u> <u>Edward</u> commands not like a King.

   Thrice honour'd <u>Clifford</u>, I'le trust you with my bosome.

Clifford. No, you shall not.

   My virgin honour is so chast, it shall not   40

   Keepe companie with a disquiet bosome,

   Nor talke with discontents.

Bruce.   It shall not.

   I will but--

   33-34. wounds . . . inward/ i.e., Bruce's realization
of guilt.
   38. bosome/ innermost thoughts.
   41. disquiet/ uneasy, disturbed.
   42-46. It . . . Lord/ In Q these lines are telescoped
into a single passage assigned to Bruce. It seems evident,
however, that "Spare me" of line 43 belongs to Clifford,
for it has the same sense as his speech in lines 39-42.
Again, lines 45-46 seem to belong to Clifford for the same
reason. We note that this passage occurs in the same scene
with the only other major speech misattributed in the play,
that of lines 8-11. When these speeches are restored to
Clifford, it is evident that in the present passage Bruce
is seeking a sympathetic confidant in Clifford. Clifford,
reluctant to confront a moral dilemma which would place him
between his loyalty to his king and his love of honor,
refuses to listen.

/Clifford turns away.7

Clifford. Spare me.

Bruce. /Aside7 The ayre hath eares no more.--

       You sent to me--

    /Clifford turns away again. Bruce follows.7

I will but tell bold Clifford--

Clifford.   Not a word!   45

    My thoughts owe as much honour as their Lord.

       /Cries7 within, "Traytor! Traytor!"
       Enter Mentith.

      Enter King, Northumberland, Herefor/d7
        and followers.

King. A mutinie! What noyse is't?

Percy. Mentith, a Knight of Scotland.

Clifford. Keepe him off.

King. What com'st thou for?   50

Mentith. Comyn my countryman and I have brought

    A jewell to your Highnesse, which if 'twere right

    As 'tis known counterfeit, 'twere worth a kingdome.

---

46. owe7 own, possess.
52-53. jewell . . . kingdome7 Cf. William Rowley, The Birth of Merlin: "Oh, Gloster, he's a jewell worth a King-dom" (I.ii.27). Cf. also The White Devil: "such counter-feit jewels Make true ones oft suspected" (III.ii.141-142).
52. right7 genuine.

Wearied with warre, and pittying the deep wounds

Which fainting <u>Scotland</u> beares upon her breast,   55

And knowing that the onely sword which gashes

Her tender sides is grip'd in <u>Wallace</u> hands,

I in my love to peace, and to the safetie

Of two great Nations, am the man that layed

Snares to entrap this monster that devoures   60

So many thousand lives. The Rebells' tane.

<u>King</u>. Where is he?

<u>Mentith</u>. I have brought him to your <u>English</u> Camp.

Force would not doo't, but policie. We struck

The Stagge to the ground, and thought him dead,   65

But heaven put backe the blow of purpose.

Hee's now come to life, from an astonishment

When we thought him dead, to th'end the world

54-57. wounds . . . sides⏖ This speech powerfully
unites images from two highly emotional moments earlier in
the play: "wounds Which fainting <u>Scotland</u> beares upon her
breast" recalls Wallace's complaint to Grimsby of the
"wounds and mortall stabs of that distressed breast (II.i.
8-9), while "sword which gashes Her tender sides" recalls
Bruce's determination not bo be a "goad Pricking thy sides".
(V.i.20-21). Despite the ambiguous intention of Mentith
who is, of course, trying to justify his betrayal of
Wallace, the statement is fundamentally true: it is Wallace
who makes Scotland suffer through his unjust rebellion (see
Introduction, pp. 95-100).
   61. tane⏖ taken.
   66. put . . . purpose⏖ i.e., repelled the blow on
purpose.
   67. astonishment⏖ stupor, insensibility; cf. <u>Paradise
Lost</u>: "If such astonishment as this can seize Eternal
spirits" (John Milton, <u>Complete Poems and Major Prose</u>, ed.
Merritt Y. Hughes ⏗New York: The Odyssey Press, 1957⏖ I.316).

May see the publique shame of an Arch-traytor. 69

King. Mentith hath wonne fame, and honour by this act.

    Fetch in this devill.

                    Exit Mentith.

Clifford. Thou wilt have Englands thanks, but

             Scotlands curse;

    Thou never hast done better, never worse,

    Damn'd Judas to thy Country-man and friend.

          Enter Wallace, Mentith, Coming.

Wallace. Where am I?

Bruce.   Here with Bruce.

Wallace.   Bruce my Soveraigne? 75

    My bloud is sold, this is not Glasco-moore.

    Some villaine hath betray'd me.

Clifford. Speak to your country-men, Comyn and Mentith.

Wallace. Comyn and Mentith?

    Something it was that made the modest night 80

    Looke angry on the world. I this was it,

    And this was it that cleft my fathers grave,

    And rais'd him from his monumentall bed of earth

    To give me gentle warning. This was it

---

76. My . . . sold⌐ Cf. IV.iv.44.
81. I⌐ Aye.
83. monumentall⌐ pertaining to the tomb (monument); cf.
Rowley, All's Lost by Lust: "I will enjoy thy monumentall
bed" (V.v.105).

That made my starre, when all the rest look's pale,   85

Blush like a fiery Meteor. Can Heaven

Winke at this?

Mentith. It can, it doth, and at farre greater mischiefs.

Wallace. Not of thy acting?

Mentith.   Yes of mine.

Wallace.   Not here.

Mentith. Here or in Hell.

Wallace.   Why then goe act them there,   90

Boast of them there. In that black Kingdome tell

That by a true subject a base Rebell fell.

         /Wallace7 kils him with his fist.

King. What's that?

Clifford.   Your Scotch jeweller is slain.

King.   By whom?

Clifford. By Wallace.

Wallace.   Heare me speak King Edward.

Clifford. Good my Liege heare him.

    85-86. That . . . Meteor7 This image refers to Wallace's imminent death. The star guiding his destiny has assumed the color of a meteor, thus, by extension, a change from the normal fixed position of the star to the meteoric fall to destruction. The distinction is referred to in Massinger, The Emperor of the East: "we are falling meteors, And not fix'd stars" (II.i /Works, p. 2467).
    87. Winke7 Blink, ignore. This term may stem from the proverb mentioned in II.iv.9: "Wink at small faults" (Tilley, F123). The meaning of this rhetorical question is "Though Heaven overlooks small faults, it will not fail to revenge one such as this."
    93. jeweller7 Cf. lines 52-53.

King.   Clifford, I have vow'd   95

Neither to heare nor see him. Drag him hence!

Mine eye shall not be so compassionate

To view him, least I pitie him. Hang,

Draw, and quarter him.

Wallace.   First heare me speak.   99

King. Drag him hence, and let that heart, those limbes,

Which were the motives to rebellious warre

Be torn asunder, cast upon that ground,

Which he with unkinde steele so oft did wound.

Away with him!

Wallace. Farewell to all the World.   105

I ha' met death too often to feare him now,

Only it grieves me that I have not freed

Scotland my native soile from tyranny.

Bruce, thou hast a Kingdome, lose it not.

95-99. Clifford . . . him/ The nature of the sentence
and King Edward's insistence on immediate execution without
hearing from Wallace recalls King Edward III's execution of
Mortimer in Marlowe's Edward II (V.vi). Especially close
is Edward's refusal to hear his mother plead for Mortimer:
"Away with her, her words enforce these tears, And I shall
pity her if she speak again" (lines 85-86).
98. least/ lest.
101. motives/ instruments. Schmidt cites Richard II:
"my teeth shall tear The slavish motive of recanting fear"
(I.i.192-193).
102-103. ground . . . wound/ Cf. Richard II: "Dear
earth, I do salute thee with my hand, Though rebels wound
thee with their horses' hoofs" (III.ii.6-7).
103. unkinde/ (1) unnatural, (2) hostile.

<u>King</u>. Stop his throat.   110

<u>Wallace</u>. I go to one, too,

    And on my grave, when death hath there down laid me,

    Be this my Epitaph, mine own betrayes me--

                    Exeunt /Wallace <u>and</u> <u>Souldiers</u>/.

<u>Bruce</u>. Let him have noble triall.

<u>King</u>. He shall have the triall of an Arch-traitour.   115

    <u>Percy</u> and <u>Clifford</u> take hence <u>Bruce</u>.

<u>Bruce</u>.   Me hence?

<u>King</u>. You hence sir; from this houre I sweare

    Never to see thee Earle of <u>Huntington</u>.

    Harke <u>Clifford</u>, and <u>Northumberland</u>, away.

<u>Bruce</u>. What is King <u>Edwards</u> meaning?

<u>King</u>.   Your head shal feel   120

    Our meaning. See it dispatch'd.

<u>Bruce</u>.   You may--

        Exeunt Bruce, Northumberland, <u>and</u> Clifford.

<u>Coming</u>. My honor'd Lord, although untimely death

    Hath taken hence one engine of that work

    That brought that Rebell <u>Wallace</u> to his end,

    Seeing our Countries peace, and <u>Englands</u> good,   125

---

110. Stop . ._. throat/ i.e., Shut him up.
113. betrayes/ Although the play has no other examples
of female rhymes, "betrayed" is probably the proper reading
in order to rhyme with "laid."
123. one engine/ one instrument, i.e., Mentith.

Is by his death made perfect and compleat,

I doubt not but the promised reward

Of full ten thousand Crowns shall now remayn,

To the Survivor.

King.   Comin, I perceive

It was reward, not love that acted it,   130

But you shall have your due; of that anon.

                                        A flourish.

                    Enter all in state.

I told thee Bruce, that thou upon thy head,

Shouldst feele our meaning; and that all the world

May know we value honour above conquest,

Having a power able to turn all Scotland   135

Into a Chaos, here twixt both our Armies,

Give us thy oath of fealty, and weare

Both Crown and title of thine Ancestors.

Bruce. England is full of honour, Bruce doth bend

To thy command.   140

                    They crown him.

King. Give him his oath of fealty;

---

126. made perfect/ completed.
129. To . . . Survivor/ To himself, as the sole remaining captor of Wallace.
130. acted it/ i.e., set the plot into action.
136. Chaos/ Cf. II.i.30.
137. oath . . . fealty/ The oath of fidelity sworn by a feudal tenant or vassal to his lord.

310

With him those Lords which are his Countrymen.

They sweare. Bruce stabs Coming.

Bruce. Stand back, a Serpent shall not with his breath

 fect our Kingly eares. Die slave, for he

That would betray his friend shall nere serve me.   145

King. What hath Bruce done?

Bruce.   A sacrifice

 Of honour and revenge. No traitors hand

 Shall help to lift a Crown up to my head:

 Thou didst betray, then die unpitied.   149

Clifford. Brave Bruce, I'le love thee for this honor'd act;

 Thou hast perform'd a noble piece of justice.

 Now shall the Ghost of Wallace sleepe in peace,

 And perfect love shall twixt these Lands increase.

 He hath his full reward for his foule treason;

 Drag hence the slave, and make him food for Crows. 155

 143-144. Serpent . . . infect/ The breath of a serpent
was traditionally said to be poisoned; cf. A Discourse of A
Strange and Monstrous Serpent (London: John Trundle, 1614),
sigs. B4v, C1, which refers for authority to Lucan, Phar-
salia: "noxia serpentum est admixto sanguine pestis" (IX.
(IX.614).
 144-145. Die . . . me/ Bruce's slaying of Coming had
no connection with the death of Wallace. It was actually
Coming's betrayal of Bruce's intentions to Edward that led
to Bruce's cutting him down in a church. Hary's comments
on the death of Coming appear in XI.1169-1177 and XII.1180-
1190.
 152. Ghost . . . peace/ Cf. I.vi.112.
 154. He/ i.e., Coming.
 155. food . . . Crows/ Cf. I.iv.13.

The Lamp that gave Rebellion light hath spent

The oile that fed it; all our spears are turn'd

To Palmes and Olive branches; all our stars

Are now made whole. Peace is the balme of wars.

/Exeunt./

FINIS.

156-157. Lamp . . . it/ Cf. 1 Henry VI: "These eyes, like lamps whose wasting oil is spent, Wax dim" (II.v.8-9). Closer to the essential idea of a man's life as a lamp is Richard II: "My oil-dried lamp and time-bewated light Shall be extinct with age and endless night" (I.iii.221-222) and Anthony and Cleopatra: "Our lamp is spent, it's out!" (IV.xv.85).

158-159. all . . . branches/ At the base of this image is the Biblical passage from Micah. IV.3: "and they shall beat their swords into plowshares, and their spears into pruninghooks." Here, the spears are turned into palms, the symbol of victory, and into olive branches, the symbol of peace.

158-159. all . . . whole/ i.e., our destinies are now made complete, fulfilled.

159. Peace . . . wars/ Cf. Hary's Wallace: "Warly scho said, 'Thus wysmen has we kend, Ay efftir wer pees is the final end; Quharfor ye suld off your gret malice ces. The end off wer is cheryte and pes" (VIII.1315-1318).

balme/ medical ointment (with perhaps a quibble on the sense of holy oil used to annoint kings at their coronations).

The reading to the left of the square bracket is that of
the present edition. The reading to the right of the
bracket is that of Q. The use of a caret indicates absence
of punctuation. As the twenty copies of The Valiant Scot
collated were examined primarily in reproduction, no
attempt is made to indicate all the minor printing variations (blotted letters, faintly inked letters, etc.) that
do not appear in the copy text (the Trinity College copy).

Dedication

9. Mens⌐ MEns

13. followers⌐ Q (final o, e, s faintly inked in many
          copies).

14. Souldier;⌐ Q (semicolon faint).

16. Play⌐ Q (a partially inked).

17. denied⌐ Q (e uninked).

     acceptance,⌐ Q (comma missing; probably uninked).

     since⌐ Q (n faintly inked).

18. hath⌐ Q (final h partially uninked).

I.i

0.1. S.D. Haslerig⌐ Haslerigge

      S.D. Jeffrey⌐ Jeoffrey

6. Conferred . . . lenity⌐ Q lines: Conferred . . .
          us. / That's . . . lenity

8. Has⌐ Ha's

10. With . . . Ahlas⟧ Q lines: With . . . bitts. / Ahlas

11. mild.⟧ mild,

13. head;⟧ head,

    tyranny_⟧ tyranny,

14. bitt? By⟧ bitt, by

    cleer'd;⟧ cleer'd,

15. fear'd,⟧ fear'd?

18. foes--⟧ foes.

19. th'eares.⟧ th'eares,

20. true:⟧ true,

21. life;⟧ life,

23. it.⟧ it,

24. cause_⟧ cause,

29. meeting_⟧ meeting,

33. up;⟧ up,

35. And . . . seat⟧ Q lines: And . . . Haggards. /
    Selbie . . . seat

40-41. Selbie . . . Edward⟧ Q lines: Selbie . . . doe, /
    And . . . Edward

40. will!⟧ will,

45. did. Reade⟧ did, reade

46. self_⟧ self,

47. Be . . . commands⟧ Q lines: Be . . . Ayre. / To
    . . . commands

49. Both . . . breaks⟧ Q lines: Both . . . Office./
    Which . . . breaks

314

52-58. Your . . . life_] Q lines: Your . . . Lands. / That's . . . Commission. / What . . . surrender, / For . . . own, / Were . . . Ancestors, / And . . . silly / Larke . . . life

54. surrender._] surrender,

56. Ancestors!_] Ancestors,

58. I'le_] Ile

60. neither! Royall_] neither, royall

61. Sits . . . Groom_] Q lines: Sits . . . malice. / Surly Groom

62. subjects:_] subjects,

63. Service._] Service

64. none! That_] none, that

68. feet._] feet,

69. it:_] it,

71. He . . . can_] Q lines: He . . . 'em. / So . . . can

72. sufficient--_] sufficient,

76-77. Both . . . title_] Q lines: Both . . . lawfull. / If . . . title

81.1. S.D. Enter . . . Graham._] Q places stage direction in right margin

83. justice._] justice,

84. dissolutes_∧_] dissolutes!

85. Has_] H'as

87. A forced . . . foole_] Q lines: A forced marriage. / Inconsiderate foole

89. marriage:7 marriage,

90. Her . . . bloud7 Q lines: Her . . . for. / Oh . . . bloud
     'um7 u'm

     hate:7 hate,

92. With . . . thoughts7 Q lines: With . . . Countrey.
         / Rest . . . thoughts

     thoughts.7 thoughts,

93. has her:7 has her,

95. lands.7 lands,

96. Fret . . . Sir, shall7 Q lines: Fret . . . he
         shall. / Shall? / I, Sir shall

     Sir, shall.7 Sir shall,

     I_∧_7 I,

103. Will . . . dower7 Q lines: Will . . . Lands. /
         Inforce . . . dower

     dower!7 dower.

105. Complain . . . alas7 Q lines: Complain . . . King.
         / The King alas

109. Prefer'd7 Prefrr'd

     Lion . He7 Lion, he

112. difference. The7 difference; the

117. Men . . . men7 Q lines: Men . . . souls. / But
         . . . men

118. none. Complaints7 none; complaints

     slaves_∧_7 slaves,

119. graves7 Q (s blotted in most copies).

120. pitied. Heaven7 pitied, heaven
                    316

has] ha's

122. friend:] friend

I.ii

0.1. S.D. Young] yong

1. her! Come] her, come

2. face? My] face, my

3. English feace:] English feace,

4. sweet,] sweet∧

8. flee-flaps! Na] flee-flaps, na

10. her:] her,

now? Fay] now, fay

12. wapins? Whay] wapins, whay

13. me? Am] me, am

16. jalor? What] jalor? what

17. hangman . . . Wha] hangman? senu you? where's hee? wha

19. hangman] Q (m appears partially uninked).

24. luiffe! Fay] luiffe, fay

sike] Q (k faintly inked in all copies).

26. me.] me∧

31-34. Hang . . . gange] Q lines: Hang . . . lowne, /
What . . . understood / My . . . gange

31. lowne!] lowne,

34. gange:] gange

35. toth'] toth∧

38. away! I'le] away, Ile

40.1. S.D. Comming] Coming

317

40.1. S.D. Mentith;_7 Mentith,

  41. Yonder's_7 Yonders

       Wallace_7 Wallace,

  43. luife._7 luife_∧

  45. Selby. Wallace_7 Selby, Wallace

       Jo._7 Jo_∧

  46. I!_7 I.

  49. Slave! Th'art_7 Slave! th'art

  50. brave?_7 brave.

  52. S.P. Coming. ⎫
                     ⎬ _7 Com. Ment.
             Mentith. ⎭

53-54. We . . . Scot_7 Q lines: We . . . dozens. / Back
             . . . Scot

  54. quarrel's mine;_7 quarrels mine,

  55. Proud'st_7 proud'st

  57. Harke_7 Q (ark appears to be uninked).

  59. raiz'd_7 Q (apostrophe uninked in many copies).

  60. storme; too_7 storme, to

  61. shoots_∧_7 shoots,

  63. kindle. Get_7 kindle, get

  64. Take . . . Agreed_7 Q lines: Take . . . taverne. / Agreed

  65. Look_7 Q (k partially inked in all copies).

66-67. Guard . . . words_7 Q prints as prose.

70-71. Is . . . heart_7 Q lines: Is . . . all? / Yes. / I
             . . . cold, / Strike . . . heart

  71. cold_∧_7 cold,

318

72. Is . . . whore_7 Q lines: Is . . . wife? / No. /
     She's . . . whore

75. dewle kens_7 dewlekens
     whither:_7 whither,

76. weare her:_7 weare her,

78. is:_7 is,

80. shalt:_7 shalt,

81. Thou . . . Instantly_7 Q lines: Thou . . . Scot.
     / When? Instantly.

82. time, and_7 Q (comma may be semicolon in all copies).

83-85. This . . . anon_7 Q lines: This Winyard. / This. /
        Our . . . scantling. / Why . . . Surgeons /
        Have . . . anon

85. morrow._7 morrow_∧

86. now? 'Tis_7 now, 'tis

89. gash'd_∧_7 gash'd,

94. beaten:_7 beaten,

95. I . . . death_7 Q lines: I . . . sicknesse. / Yet
     . . . death

96. hotly?_7 hotly.

98. conquest:_7 conquest,

100-101. There . . . infamy_7 Q lines: There . . . part. /
          I'le . . . infamy

101. heart-bloud_7 heart_∧bloud

102. Mercy . . . Away_7 Q lines: Mercy . . . soule. /
      He's slain. / Away
     Away!_7 Away.

319

103. selves:] selves,

I.iii

0.1. S.D. <u>within</u> . . . <u>murder!"</u>] <u>within murder, murder</u>.

0.2. S.D. Old Selby, Thorn<u>e</u>] <u>old</u> Selby, Thorne

Peggi<u>e</u>] Peggy

1. Search! Cal<u>l</u>] Search, call

Surgeons! Follo<u>w</u>] Surgeons, follow

2. me! Lig<u>s</u>] me, ligs

ground?] ground,

3. Le<u>t</u>] Q (L <u>is</u> <u>blotted</u> <u>in</u> <u>all</u> <u>copies</u>, <u>probably</u> <u>because</u>

<u>of</u> <u>damaged</u> <u>type</u>).

4. is'<u>t</u>] ist

6. Ha! M<u>y</u>] Ha' my

9. I'z<u>e</u>] Ize

11. me.] me∧

I.iv

0.1. S.D. King] <u>King</u>

5. <u>France</u> . . . demande<u>d</u>] Q <u>lines</u>: <u>France</u> . . . not. /

Yet . . . does. / 'Twas . . . demanded

<u>France</u>] Q (n <u>lightly</u> <u>inked</u>).

6. Think<u>s</u>] thinks

8. But . . . Percy] Q <u>lines</u>: But . . . command. /

Yes . . . <u>Percy</u>

9. Garison;⟧ Garison.

12. hangman-like⟧ hangman ∧ like

16. What . . . trade⟧ Q lines: What? / Ile . . . it. /
     Cut throat. / 'Tis . . . trade
     I'le⟧ Ile

18-20. A man . . . leane⟧ Q lines: A man . . . as-- / A
     hangman. / A foule blot / Lies . . . throat. /
     Thy Scot. / In . . . wash't. / Grimsby . . .
     leane

20. I'le⟧ Il'e

21. Too⟧ To

24. hazzard;⟧ hazzard,

26. qualitie;⟧ qualitie,

29. No . . . Soveraigne⟧ Q lines: No . . . temper'd. /
     May . . . Soveraigne

30. Confirme . . . Scotland⟧ Q lines: Confirme . . .
     touching-- / The . . . Scotland
     Scotland;⟧ Scotland,

31. time. Grimsby⟧ time, Grimsby (comma lightly inked
     in many copies).

40. begs ∧⟧ begs,

41. pension-- . . . Percy--⟧ pension (. . . Percy)

44. Grimsby;⟧ Grimsby,

46-47. Have . . . hands⟧ Q lines: Have . . . power. / My
     . . . passions. / Then . . . hands

46. power--⟧ power.
     Soveraignes⟧ Q (s faintly inked).
     321

47. hands] Q (s *faintly inked in all copies*).

48. both.] both∧

53. time:] time,

57. Edward!] Edward,

58. warre∧] warre,

61. promise∧] promise,

63. selfe:] selfe,

65. none?] none,

66. more.] more,

66.1. S.D. *Enter* Haslerig.] (*follows* "The news" *in* Q).

67. The news . . . infected] Q *lines*: The news. /
       Dread . . . infected
   news?] news.

68. surfet:] surfet,

69. In . . . Bruce] Q *lines*: In . . . rebellion. /
       This . . . Bruce
   your] Q (y *faintly inked in all copies*).

71-72. Shouldst . . . bred] Q *lines*: Shouldst . . . it, /
       Whose . . . chief? / One . . . bred

71. it:] it,

77. in't-- Warlike] in't, warlike

80. Ruine . . . Edward] Q *lines*: Ruine . . . Nation. /
       Gracious Edward

81. has] ha's

82. Subjects . . . you] Q *lines*: Subjects . . .

vassals. / We . . . you

you;] you,

85. head;] head,

87-88. We . . . along] Q lines: We . . . not. / See . . .

not. / Let . . . along∧

88. along;] along

89. conquer'd∧ 'las,] conquer'd, 'las

95. <u>Grimsby</u>. Should] <u>Grimsby</u>, should

97. subjects. Let] subjects, let

99. I'le . . . sent] Q lines: I'le . . . it. / Let

. . . sent

sent∧] sent,

102. armes;] armes,

103. designes.] designes,

104. has] ha's

107. wars. Observe] wars, observe

Lords;] Lords,

108. policie;] policie.

109. eye;--] eye,

110. Star;] Star,

111. 'um] ∧um

I.v

1. Prethee . . . soule] Q lines: Prethee . . .

<u>Wallace</u>. / Ill . . . soule

323

4-5.   Imprison'd . . . mad] Q lines: Imprison'd Peg. /
       But . . . me. / _Laverck_ . . . brick. / Turn'd
       mad

9-10. Swim't . . . Eg-shell] Q lines: Swim't . . . Eg-
       shell

13-15. Were . . . life] Q lines: Were . . . _Peg_? / Poor
       . . . murtherer. / In . . . weapon / In . . .
       life

17-20. She . . . sonne] Q lines: She . . . made / Him
       . . . oft. / Wher's . . . sonne

17.   has] ha's
       private.] private;

19.1. S.D. Old] _Old_

20.   griefe_^] griefe,

21.   Hang . . . off] Q lines: Hang . . . sences. /
       Shake . . . off

23.   Or . . . that] Q lines: Or . . . dies. / What
       that
       that_^] that?

25.   shoulders? _Peggie_] shoulders, _Peggie_
       dies?] dies,

26.   lies:] lies,

27.   Who . . . breath] Q lines: Who . . . _Nuntio_? /
       His breath
       breath.] breath.

28.   being. _Haslerig's_] being, _Haslerigs_

Haslerig's] (a _faintly_ _inked_ _in_ Q).

30-31. From . . . aire] Q lines: From . . . instant /
But . . . life / Dissolves . . . aire

30. instant,] instant‸
in‸] in,

34. her? Singly] her, singly

37. Castle-gates,] (_comma_ _faintly_ _inked_ _in_ Q).

39. Attempt . . . impossible] Q lines: Attempt . . .
rescue. / 'Tis impossible

40. Impossible! What's] Impossible, what's
England‸] Englands

42. you;] you,

47. with;] with,

50. What's . . . rumour] Q lines: What's . . . rescue?
Much . . . rumour

52. ours;] ours,

56. prisoner;] prisoner,

58. What . . . destinie] Q lines: What . . . _Wallace_? /
Prosper'd destinie
destinie.] destinie,

60. thrive;] thrive,

I.vi

0.1. Sir] _Sir_

2. dies?] dies,

325

3. Cryer_s_] Q (s _blotted_ _in_ _all_ _copies_).

4. 'Ti_s_] T'is

    stirre_;_] stirre

    King_∧_] King,

6. rather_∧_] rather,

7. Wallace_,_] Q (_comma_ _may_ _be_ _full_ _stop_).

15. educatio_n_] Q (io _blotted_).

18. good_;_] good,

    dottrels_∧_] dottrels,

19. alike. He] alike, he

23. Them . . . _Graham_] Q _lines_: Them . . . suspect-

    lesse. / So . . . _Graham_

24. knowledge. You] knowledge, you

25. prisoner_;_] prisoner,

27-28. If . . . produc'_d_] Q _lines_: If . . . traitors /

    And . . . bands? / Let's . . . produc'd

30. ha'_s_] has

31. content. S_o_] content, so

34. And . . . polici_e_] Q _lines_: And . . . thine. /

    Good policie

35. trowe_∧_] trowe,

    Wallas. His] _Wallas_∧ his

36-37. And dowty . . . traitou_r_] Q _lines_: And dowty . . .

    nor / Sike . . . language. / A fowle traitour

37. traitour!] traitour,

42. sa_∧_] sa,

    Wallace] _Wllace_

326

44. ends. Hearing] ends, hearing
     proclaim'd∧—] proclaim'd,

45. on't:] on't,

46. constancy:] constancy,

47. has] ha's

49-50. Wholly . . . gave] Q lines: Wholly . . . me. /
     Hawd . . . give / Him . . . gave

49. there] (t is broken letter).

51. His . . . have] Q lines: His . . . protect? / I
     have

     have:] have,

51.1. S.D. guard,] guard

52. have.] have,

53. No . . . man] Q lines: No . . . Rebell. / Traiter-
     ous man

54. love? These] love? these

58-59. Thou . . . Snakes] Q lines: Thou . . . eyes. / May
     Snakes

58. not. Thy] not∧ thy
     eyes∧—] eyes,

59. as soon] assoon
     mine:] mine,

61. first.] first,

62. sentence?] sentence.

63-64. Here . . . daughter] Q lines: Here . . . service, /
     We . . . daughter

63. service⟧ service,

65-66. A milde . . . restore⟧ Q lines: A milde exchange, /
              Angels . . . it. / Next . . . restore

65. exchange:⟧ exchange,

67. And what . . . thoughts⟧ Q lines: And what . . .
              Wallace? / Race . . . thoughts

68-69. Rac'd . . . shrude⟧ Q lines: Rac'd . . . the /
              Whayte . . . it. / Hence. / Dear . . . shrude

70. wee's⟧ wees

72. pulchritude.⟧ pulchritude,

73. gate⟧ gate,

74. wee'se⟧ weese

75. resolution:⟧ resolution,

78. flesh:⟧ flesh,

79-82. Then . . . one⟧ Q lines: Then . . . voyage. /
              'Tis . . . forwards. / Raise . . . high, / ye
              . . . way. / All's one

81. high. Ye⟧ high, ye
    water:⟧ water,

82. one:⟧ one,

83. fire:⟧ fire,

84. heaven.⟧ heaven,

86. heart.⟧ heart,

88-89. Find . . . know⟧ Q lines: Find . . . welcome. /
              Stay . . . know

89. Warrant⟧ Warrant,

93. With . . . worst] *Q lines:* With . . . torture. /
I . . . worst

worst!] worst,

96-97. 'Tis . . . care] *Q lines:* 'Tis . . . hud-winckt, /
Then . . . care

96. else. First] else, first

98. Bear . . . service] *Q lines:* Bear . . . love. /
My service.

102. rise;] rise,

105. clouds. So] clouds, so

secure,] secure.

107. followers;] followers,

112. bloud's] blouds

rest--] rest.

113. quiet. Wher's] quiet, wher's

114. Commission;] Commission,

116. mutinies. Search] mutinies, search

117. door. Sir] door, Sir

118. bels;] bels,

119. 'um] u'm

120. proud] prond

122. purse;] purse,

0.1. S.D. Grimsby⟧ Grimsbie

   1. Conscience? Th'art⟧ Conscience? th'art

   5. What . . . cause⟧ Q lines: What . . . conquest? /
       Then . . . cause

   6. mine? Respected⟧ mine? respected
       Country-man⟧ Q (hyphen unclear in most copies).

   8. deserves. Look⟧ deserves, look

  10. slaves.⟧ (comma blotted in Q).

  12. to:⟧ to,

  15. Traitour.⟧ Traitour,

16-17. Whither . . . worst⟧ Q lines: Whither . . . me? /
       To Northumberland / And Beaumont. / Butchers
       . . . worst

       worst:⟧ worst,

  19. an arme⟧ a narme

  20. As . . . waife.⟧ Q lines: As . . . wert. / Thy
       Father. / And . . . waife.

       wert--⟧ wert.

       S.D. Old⟧ Old

       Father--⟧ Father.

  22. Speake:⟧ Speake,

  23. neither? Tell⟧ neither? tell

  25. Fryer-- What⟧ Fryer, what

26. sences. Deerest_7 sences, deerest

    friends._7 friends_∧

30. Chaos._7 Chaos_∧

31. dimensions._7 dimensions,

33. And make . . . prayer_s_7 Q lines: And make . . .

             blush. / May luive. / Our prayers

    luive--_7 luive.

    prayers--_7 prayers.

35. Stand . . . hand_s_7 Q lines: Stand . . . danger. /

             All . . . hands

    him_∧_7 him,

    hands:_7 hands,

38. _Jove;_7 _Jove,_

40. house. Thi_s_7 house, this

43. Or . . . shiel_d_7 Q lines: Or . . . bloud. /

             Heaven shield

    shield!_7 shield

45. stoope. Hee_d_7 stoope, heed

    Gertrid sawe:_7 **Gentrid** sawe_∧

46. shal_l_7 Q (a partially inked in all copies).

    aw_∧_7 aw,

47. folk. Man_y_7 folk, many

    man_y_7 Q (a partially inked in many copies).

48. barns_∧ er_e_7 barns, e're

    flie:_7 flie,

50. clouds. Til_l_7 clouds, till

331

bloud∧_7 bloud,

bloud7 Q (letters separated: bl o u d).

52. false?7 false,

56-58. The town . . . mirth7 Q lines: The town . . .
        pride / And overjoyed . . . mirth

58. surpriz,7 surpriz∧

     mirth.7 mirth,

61. advantage! Put7 advantage, put

62. lives. This7 lives, this

65. way∧_7 way,

66. To . . . wheane/ Q lines: To . . . doom. / Nea
      . . . wheane

     wheane:7 wheane,

69. Thou'se7 Thouse

     wrang:7 wrang

70. Thou'se7 Thouse

     feare∧_7 feare,

71. I'se7 Ise

     meare.7 meare,

72. Sier,7 Sier

     crave:7 crave,

73. grave.7 grave,

76. kisse. Thilke7 kisse, thilke

79. has7 ha's

332

0.1. S.D. way;⟧ way,

0.2. S.D. and⟧ and

0.3. S.D. Old⟧ old

1-2. Whom . . . Wallace⟧ Q lines: Whom . . . there? /
      Seeking . . . shelter, / See . . . us. /
      Treacherous Wallace

4. Rebellion. Now⟧ Rebellion, now

5. feast;⟧ feast,

6. musick_⟧ musick,
    dint_⟧ dint,

7. Smiles . . . wae⟧ Q lines: Smiles . . . cheeks. /
    Alas . . . wae

8. Fewde? What⟧ Iewde? what

9-10. To . . . age⟧ Q lines: To . . . fatherlesse, /
       And murder . . . widdower. / Oh . . . age

11. Pitie . . . religion⟧ Q lines: Pitie . . . beauty.
     / My religion
     beauty--⟧ beauty.

13. I'le⟧ ile

14. pitie,⟧ pitie
     pitilesse_⟧ pitilesse,

17. I'le⟧ Ile

21.1. S.D. Exit.⟧ Exit Haslerig.

25. Revenge . . . Religion⟧ Q lines: Revenge . . .
     waif. / Revenge Religion

25.1. S.D. "Wallace and Conquest!"⟧ Wallace and

Conquest.

25.2. S.D. Haslerig] Hasslerigg

26. throats!] throats,

27-28. The slave's . . . selves] Q lines: The slaves . . .

infinite, / And moves . . . once, / Shift . . .

selves

28. once.] once,

29. Lavercke] Lavercke

31. slaughter. The] slaughter, the

32. limbes:] limbes,

33. death^_] death,

flight.] flight,

34. company!] company,

36. Wee'le] Weele

II.iii

1. I-- Salvation] I, salvation

me!] me.

2. Fryer] Fryer

3. sweat?] sweat,

4. Father. Fellon] Father, fellon

5-6. Tha'st . . . excuse] Q lines: Tha'st . . .

father. / Wallace. / No excuse

6. my-- Father!] my father.

7. Ay,] Ay^

8. both,] both.

9. robbery.] robbery,

10. then,] then∧

    (mercy, fate!).] (mercy∧ fate,)∧

12. abilitie.] abilitie,

14. 'gainst] ∧gainst

19-20. Torture . . . awake] Q lines: Torture . . .
      indurance, / King . . . vision. / Wallace . . .
      awake

19. indurance!] indurance,

24. murderers.] murderers,

25. Peggie,] Q (comma uninked in most copies).
    where,] where∧

28-30. I'le . . . hangmen] Q lines: I'le . . . how, /
      Selby . . . blood-hounds / Whae . . . death. /
      Are . . . hangmen

28. how:] how,

31-33. Religious . . . death] Q lines: Religious . . .
      well-awayes / Could . . . favour, / Wallas
      . . . death

33. favour.] favour,

34. breath--] breath.

35. And house . . . eye] Q lines: And house . . .
      here. / Where's . . . eye
    Wallas? Never] Wallas? never

36. Saw . . . Grimsby] Q lines: Saw . . . massacre. /
      Yes Grimsby

38. Thine . . . strange] Q lines: Thine . . . may-

game. / Terrible . . . stragne

39. this? Then] this? then

41. heaven.] heaven,

42. thunder∧] thunder,

43. senceles:] senceles,

44. Whose . . . act's] Q lines: Whose . . . this? /
The bloody acts

act's] acts

46. Who . . . English] Q lines: Who . . . authors? /
Judge . . . English

47. Dialect.] Dialect,

50.1. S.D. Messenger] Mess∧

52. welcome. Let] welcome, let

57. King:] King,

59. thefts∧] thefts,

61. There's . . . English] Q lines: There's . . .
life. / Still . . . English

62. 'Tis] ∧Tis

sure:] sure,

64. This] Q (blot appears in position of comma or full
stop).

69-70. Hang'd . . . begin] Q lines: Hang'd . . .
villaine. / This . . . spoke? / We have. /
Then . . . begin

69. English:] English,

71. subject:] subject,

76. life. Thi_s_7 Life, this

     deny_,_7 deny_∧_

80. Of . . . ma_n_7 Q <u>lines</u>: Of . . . himselfe / Now

     . . . man

81. Would . . . spleen_e_7 Q <u>lines</u>: Would . . . Olympus.

     / Calme . . . spleene

82. mercy_:_7 mercy,

85. Punish't . . . Englis_h_7 Q <u>lines</u>: Punish't . . .

     deservers. / This . . . English

87. What . . . m_e_7 Q <u>lines</u>: What . . . <u>Wallace</u>. /

     First . . . me

91. father_∧_7 father,

     wife_._7 wife,

95. sacrifice_:_7 sacrifice,

98. This . . . Edwar_d_7 Q <u>lines</u>: This . . . act. / Yet

     <u>Edward</u>

99. commission. O_h_7 commission, oh

     'twa_s_7 t'was

     Plac'_d_7 (a <u>blotted in</u> Q).

102. Good . . . Edwar_d_7 Q <u>lines</u>: Good gentlemen. / But

     . . . <u>Edward</u>

     gentleman--7 gentleman.

116. Of . . . i_t_7 Q <u>lines</u>: Of . . . commission? /

     <u>Wallace</u> . . . it

118-119. One . . . headsma_n_7 Q <u>lines</u>: One . . . followers. /

     Good . . . inserted, / One . . . headsman

119. inserted.⟧ inserted,

121. And nephew . . . King⟧ Q lines: And nephew . . .
                   Queene. / Wer't . . . King
    Wert⟧ Wer't

123. head. Goe⟧ head, goe

125-128. Thrust . . . cries⟧ Q lines: Thrust . . . sword. /
                   Wallace . . . milde. / Wallace . . . just /
                   Then . . . disgrac'd. / Sound . . . cries

128. disgrac'd.⟧ disgrac'd∧

129.1. S.D. again⟧ Agen

130. stage.⟧ stage,

131. sight∧⟧ sight,

134. wee'd⟧ weed

135. Nephew. You⟧ Nephew, you

136. mute∧⟧ mute,

137. messenger:⟧ messenger,

138. delivery. Make⟧ delivery, make

139. you. Share⟧ you, share

140. tongue.⟧ tongue,

143. This . . . Grimsby⟧ Q lines: This . . . English. /
                   Honor'd Grimsby

145. anger. You⟧ anger, you

146. inhum'd:⟧ inhum'd
    disguis'd∧⟧ disguis'd,

148. And see . . . danger⟧ Q lines: And see . . .
                   usage. / 'Twill . . . danger

338

149. it;] it,

151. danger. Disswade] danger, disswade

152. bent;] bent,

153. spent] (s faintly inked in Q).

154. be. Honour'd] be, honour'd

156. earth;] earth,

157. deaths. Mentith] deaths, Mentith

158. oath∧] oath,

159. us. Hark! How] us, hark∧ how

160. Chide . . . welcome] Q lines: Chide . . .
      loytring. / Honor'd . . . welcome

162. Not∧] Not,
     more∧] more,

163. Could . . . welcome] Q lines: Could . . . supply. /
      The better welcome
     welcome;] welcome,

164. wealthy∧] wealthy,

165. companions. Wher's] companions, wher's

166. The hopefull . . . death] Q lines: The hopefull
      Wallace? / Gone . . . death

167. fate. 'Cause] fate, 'cause
     'Cause] Q (apostrophe damaged and faint in all
      copies).

170. deserves∧] deserves,
     Generall∧] Generall,

174. charge. His] charge, his

176. feed 'em:⏋ feed 'em,

II.iv

1. man? Till⏋ man? till
    you?⏋ you,

2. Gad⏋ gad

3. westward:⏋ westward,

6. Ha'⏋ ha'

7. tongue:⏋ tongue,

9. then. Make⏋ then, make

15. sawle. A⏋ sawle, a

16. liegeman:⏋ liegeman,

17-18 Countryman. What⏋ Countryman, what

21. 'Tis⏋ ₍Tis
    murder'd⏋ murderd

22. man! A⏋ man! a
    scalpe? I⏋ scalpe, I

24. gudenes:⏋ gudenes,
    is't⏋ ist

28-31.Walas . . . farder.⏋ Q prints as verse: Walas . . .
        him, / Sawe . . . too, / Ized . . . Campe / Or
        . . . farder

28. him.⏋ him,

29. too; I'zed⏋ too, Ized

30. English⏋ Q (n damaged and faint in all copies).

340

neere7 (_final_ e _partially blotted in_ Q).

32. 'Twol_d_7 ∧Twold

33-36. And you . . . clampers7 Q _prints as verse_: And
you . . . Wallace / Cut . . . him / To . . .
weare / Na . . . clampers

33-34. man. Wallace7 man, Wallace

34. 'caus_e_7 ∧cause

35. Prince. Hark_e_7 Prince, harke

39-42. Gang . . . shoulders7 Q _prints as verse_: Gang
. . . head / I . . . lawe / And sae . . .
shoulders

39. man.7 man∧
'ti_s_7 ∧tis
now. _A_7 now, a

40. head--7 head∧
gangan_d_7 gaugand∧

44. marry? Na7 marry? na
cruell? Fay7 cruell? fay

47. begging. H_e_7 begging, he

48. off:7 off,

49. mynded.7 mynded∧

50. judg_e_7 (e _blotted in_ Q).

54. lawyer? How7 lawyer? how

55. how:7 how,

57. o'th'7 o∧th∧
tyles. Th_e_7 tyles, the

60. cryed.7 cryed∧

341

hawd.] hawd_∧
61. lowne.] lowne_∧
   hawd! As] hawd, as
63. thee. Stay] thee, stay
65. Stand.] Stand_∧
   voula! Spyes] voula, spyes
66-68. And see . . . are you?] Q prints as verse: And
       see . . . sirra, / You . . . hood, / What are
       you?
66-67. downe. Sirra] downe sirra
70-71. What . . . word] Q prints as verse: What . . .
       Tongue / In . . . word.
70. thee? Hast] thee? hast
71. head? Give] head? give
72. Tongue] tongue
73-75. Two . . . so] Q prints as verse: Two . . . you? /
       That . . . so
73. tongue? What] tongue, what
   you_∧] you?
75. so?] so,
76. indeed.] indeed,
78. How, Lords? Are] How_∧ Lords, are
81-82. 'em? What] 'em, what
81. 'em] (apostrophe faint in Q).
82. sirra? Come] sirra? come
   not;] not,

let's*s*7 lets

84. I'z*e*7 Ize

86-88. A <u>Scotch</u> . . . you7 Q <u>prints as verse</u>: A Scotch
　　　 . . . sir? / Your . . . scull, / Where's . . . you

86-87. are sir,7 are sir?

87. scull?7 scull,

90. is;7 is,

91. stumps. Guid*e*7 stumps, guide

92. men,7 men˄

95-97. I . . . mawegu*t*7 Q <u>prints as verse</u>: I . . .
　　　 Elbows) / To . . . match / Made . . . mawegut

98-99. By matc*h*7 Q <u>prints as verse</u>: By . . . come/
　　　 To'th . . . match

98. sir,7 sir˄
　　　 toth'7 to'th

100-102. Here's . . . touch-hol*e*7 Q <u>prints as verse</u>:
　　　 Here's . . . so, / Thou . . . touch-hole

100. so.7 so,

102.1. S.D. Queen Elino*r*7 <u>Queene Elenor</u>

104-105. Every . . . roague*s*7 Q <u>prints as verse</u>: Every
　　　 . . . parrapet, / To . . . roagues

104. parrapet!7 parrapet,

105. tatter'*d*7 tatterd

106. It's*s*7 Its

107-109. Cry . . . frien*d*7 Q <u>prints as verse</u>: Cry . . .
　　　 mercy, / This . . . see, / Whither . . . friend

108. see.7 see,

343

113. money. Hence] money, hence
114.1. S.D. Bolt∧ and Souldiers.] Bolt. and Sould.
115. these? I] these, I
116. unheard.] unheard,
117. Sebastian,] Sebastian
    Queene,] Queene∧
120. Embassie,] Embassie∧
    disguis'd,] disguis'd∧
122. Mountford!] Mountford.
123. Who . . . told] Q lines: Who . . . villany? / Our
    . . . told
127. Hye,] Hye∧
    violent (in] violent, In
129. ∧Tho] (Tho
    Herald-like] Herald∧like
130. spies;] spies,
132. this;] this,
    these. Trusse] these, trusse
133.1. S.D. Mountford . . . Glascot] Moun. . . . Glas.
136. thus? Hang] thus? hang
137. mercy. I'le] mercy, I'le
138. barnes.] barnes,
139. Fire] fire
    houses! Hang] houses, hang
140. 'um] um
142. charrity? I'ze] charrity, I'ze
144. feight and] feightand

144-145. Prince. Ah] Prince, ah

145. men:] men,

147. far. For] far‸ for

148. giffe] Q (e partially uninked in all copies;
      probably damaged).

151. Out . . . Clifford] Q lines: Out . . . men. / So
      . . . Clifford

152. sirra:] sirra,

156. Wallace:] Wallace,

158. wife‸] wife,

161. Forget . . . death] Q lines: Forget . . . duty. /
      But . . . death

162. Embassadours?] Embassadours.

164. companies‸] companies,

166. sawle.] sawle‸

167-168. No . . . word] Q lines: No . . . Wolfe? / How
      . . . fo? / Sure . . . word

173. it. Dispatch] it, dispatch

179-180. Insnare . . . rest] Q lines: Insnare . . . feare,
      / That . . . rest

182. do.] do‸
      'em--] 'em.

183. 'em! 'Sdeath.] 'em, sdeath‸

186. And waking... No] Q lines: And waking... him. / No.

189-190. I'le . . . guide] Q lines: I'le . . . Rebell. /
      Do . . . guide

189. Beaumont.] Beaumont,

345

191-192. But . . . for't7 Q lines: But . . . yee /
                Y'are . . . for't

193. yee:7 yee,

194. mee. Cum7 mee, cum
     Joe. I7 Joe, I

195. Campe. They'le7 Campe, th'yle

196. I'se7 Ise
     I'ze7 Ize

199. I. Luke7 I, luke
     I'se7 Ise

201.1. S.D. Exeunt . . . Wallace7 Exeunt Beaum. and Wal.
                                   (precedes line 201 in Q)
203. be.7 be?

206. him?7 him,

207. Rebell. His7 Rebell, his

208. Gentry:7 Gentry,

209. Wer't7 Wert

212. honour∧7 houour

213. alike. But7 alike, but

214. betray'd. He7 betray'd, he
     not!7 not,

215. first.7 first∧
     not!--7 not,

218. plots.7 plots,

219-220. Call . . . traitor7 Q lines: Call . . . back. /
                Is . . . mad? / No . . . traitor

219. No.7 No∧

346

220. lunatick;] lunatick,

223. Beare? Goe] Beare? goe

225-226. The news . . . token/ Q lines: The news. / News
. . . tents, / Wallace . . . token

225. it? Let] it, let

226. tents.] tents,

227. Ha . . . traitor] Q lines: Ha . . . Wallace. /
Was . . . traitor

Wallace?] Wallace.

228. Warrior!] Warrior,

232. spoke.] spoke,

233. need_∧_] need.

234. own;] own,

235-238. And . . . stay] Q lines: And . . . it, / If . . .
field. / Base . . . here? / None . . . stay

238. stay;] stay,

239. 'Twas] ∧Twas

240. sends_∧_] sends,
wish:] wish,

241. life_∧_] life,

245. payed.] payed,

247. succour;] succour,

248. me.] me,

250. Armes. What] Armes, what

235. tels. Here] tels, here

347

4. _Jeffry_. Bu_t_7 _Jeffry_, but

5. this. I_s_7 this, is

6. Si_r_7 sir

J _Jeffery_? You_r_7 _Jeffery_? your

7. la_w_7 Q (w _misaligned_ _in_ _some_ _cases_).

9. split_:_7 split,

12. ha_s_7 ha's

18. us. Di_d_7 us, did

20. Si_r_7 sir

22. a'7 a_∧_

26-27. Didst . . . spli_t_7 Q _prints_ _as_ _verse_: Didst . . .
       made, / When . . . split

35. hee'_s_7 hees

41. too. Bot_h_7 too, both

42. away_:_7 away,
    Si_r_7 sir

48. stomach_:_7 stomach,

49. 'ti_s_7 _∧_tis

51. that_:_7 that,

53. sea_:_7 sea,

57. Westhod. A_s_7 Westhod, as

58. bad there_:_7 bad there,

59. gulls there_:_7 gulls there,

60. men_,_7 men:

67. quarrell_:_7 quarrell,

71. Knights_:_7 Knights,

79. Si<u>r</u>7 sir

  Justices<u>;</u>7 Justices,

86. too't. The<u>n</u>7 too't, then

88. Baud<u>s</u>7 Q (s <u>faintly inked; missing in some copies</u>).

92. ha<u>s</u>7 ha's

93. swarme<u>;</u>7 swarme,

98. you<u>.</u>7 you

  Si<u>r</u>7 sir

100. Faulconer'<u>s</u>7 Faulconers

  pricksong<u>.</u>7 pricksong,

104. ho ho<u>.</u>7 ho ho,

108-109. Answer . . . ou<u>t</u>7 Q <u>prints as verse</u>: Answer . . .
  master / For . . . out

112-113. Do . . . ano<u>n</u>7 Q <u>prints as verse</u>: Do . . . Rat-
  catcher, / Youle . . . anon

112. Si<u>r</u>7 sir

  Rat-catcher<u>?</u>7 Rat-catcher,

113. You'l<u>e</u>7 Youle

114-115. Pox . . . meat<u>e</u>7 Q <u>prints as verse</u>: Pox . . .
  shipwrack't, / Give . . . meate

114. shipwrack't<u>.</u>7 shipwrack't,

116. <u>Mittimus</u>? H<u>e</u>7 <u>Mittimus</u>? he

117. ha<u>'</u>7 ha_∧

  match. <u>Neptune</u>7 match, <u>Neptune</u>

118. masterie<u>;</u>7 masterie,

121. he's . . . spea<u>k</u>7 Q <u>lines</u>: He's drunk. / Yet
  . . . speak

speak:] speak,

124. <u>Scot</u>. Giv<u>e</u>] <u>Scot</u>, give
victuals,] victuals

129. Bolt. I<u>n</u>] Bolt_∧ in

130. thee:] thee,
earn bread:] earn bread,

131. house. Tho<u>u</u>] house, thou

133. fire. Up,] fire, up

135. Na<u>y</u>] nay

138. sir? O<u>n</u>] sir, on
Si<u>r</u>] sir

140. slip.] slip,

146. Knave? Wh<u>y</u>] Knave? why

147-148. Because . . . nam<u>e</u>] Q <u>prints as verse</u>: Because
. . . half-hang'd, / And your . . . name

147. ha<u>s</u>] ha's

148. an<u>d</u>] And

156. Greedi-gut. Plum-porridg<u>e</u>] Greedi-gut, Plum-
porridge

162-164. Hunger . . . firs<u>t</u>] Q <u>prints as verse</u>: Hunger
. . . good, / But . . . first

165. Hold,] Hold_∧

168. back:] back,
I's<u>e</u>] Ise

169. weele. I<u>f</u>] weele, if

173. ha<u>s</u>] ha's

175. S.P. Jeffrey. ⎫ _/_ Both:
          Bolt.   ⎭

Wallace!_/_ Wallace.
176. Si_r_/_ sir
Jeffrey!_/_ Jeffrey.
178. D'y_e_/_ D'e ye
grumble? Rai_se_/_ grumble? raise
179. victuals._/_ victuals,
180. wals_:_/_ wals,
182. bar'd_._/_ bar'd,
183. Victual_s_/_ --victuals
too-_-_/_ too,--
184. thus. _O_/_ thus, o
185.1. S.D. _poore,_/_ _poore._
Selby_._/_ Selby_ʌ_
186. carver_:_/_ carver,
188. enter? Ye_s_/_ enter? yes
189. doo't. I_s_/_ doo't, is
191. him? Ugl_y_/_ him, ugly
194. want_s_/_ Wants
197. wives. M_y_/_ wives, my
198. ha_s_/_ ha's
199. yeares_:_/_ yeares,
on't_._/_ on't_ʌ_
205. Earth. Ho_w_/_ Earth, how

351

206. together? It's_s] together, It's

212. hunger;] hunger,

216. Th'Antipodes_s] th' Antipodes

217. thee;] thee,

218. drowne.] drowne,

219. downe.] downe,

221. it. How] it, how

224. life. How] life, how

226. Sea;] Sea,

228. 'em. I] 'em, I

229. done;] done,

232. heaven. I] heaven, I

236. tyrant.] tyrant,

239. showme.] (full stop in Q may be slightly blotted
      comma).

241. dyes.] dyes,

244. waves;] waves,

245. saves.] saves,

251. Idle] idle

252. it.-- Sit.] it, sit

253. last.-- Sit] last, sit
      rise.--] rise,

254. wine. Drinke] wine, drinke

255. I am . . . sticks] Q lines: I am . . . cold. / I'le
      . . . sticks

260. power] Q (e partially inked in all copies).

265. hand_˄] hand,

267. what.] what,

269-270. I'le . . . man] Q lines: i_˄le . . . fire./ I
        I thanke . . . man

269. ye. If] ye, if

270. man.] man,

272. I. Eate] I, eate
      fire.] fire,

274. it:] it,

275. it.] it,

277. me.] me,

278. nothing:] nothing,

279. debter:] debter,

280. thee.] thee,

282.1. S.D. th'other,] th' other

283. Selby!] Selby,

285-286. And . . . Selby] Q lines: And . . . Selby

285. misery.--] misery--

286. Selby!] Selby?

293. paring. What] paring, what

295. thee:] thee,

296. Lawyer.] Lawyer,

303. end:] end,

305. And I'le . . . off] Q lines: And ile . . . this--
      / Hands off

off!] off_˄

307. thee:7 thee,

    two∧7 two,

308. woes. Heaven7 woes, heaven

    both. Adue7 both, adue

309. Fount∧7 Fount,

310. fatall.7 fatall,

    Selby∧7 Selby,

311. has7 ha's

312. has7 ha's

    defac'd:7 defac'd,

313. own. I7 own, I

314. overthrew.7 overthrew,

315. care:7 care

316. share.7 share,

318. Oke.7 Oke,

319. I'le7 i'le

320.1. S.D. Sir7 Sir

322. a7 A

328. skin. He's7 skin, he's

332. traitor. Sir7 traitor, Sir

333. down?7 down.

338.1. S.D. Bolt7 Bolt

339. damn'd! Both7 damn'd∧ both

344. detest.7 detest,

344. sprawles. Stay.7 sprawles, stay

    him:7 him,

345. shal<u>l</u>7 Shall

346. Mastive. Th<u>e</u>7 Mastive, the

347. King'<u>s</u>7 Kings

   let<u>s</u>7 Lets

   him. <u>Bolt</u>7 him, <u>Bolt</u>

348. selfe_∧_7 selfe,

349. manl<u>y</u>7 (n <u>blotted in</u> <u>Q</u>).

   deed. A<u>s</u>7 deed, as

                    III.ii

 1. man-- Ha<u>'</u>7 man, ha'

 2. be? Th<u>e</u>7 be? the

 3. he! Jus<u>t</u>7 he, just

 4. other<u>;</u>7 other,

 5. hand. Howeve<u>r</u>7 hand, however

 6. lie<u>;</u>7 lie,

 .8. grave<u>;</u>7 grave,

10. <u>Philomell.</u>7 <u>Philomell</u>,

13. shall. M<u>y</u>7 shall, my

   adue<u>.</u>7 adue,

14. swim<u>.</u>7 swim_∧

   calme<u>.</u>7 calme_∧

15. Venture<u>:</u>7 Venture,

0.2.   S.D. Scotland͹ Scotland

  1.   night:͹ night,

  2.   pillow. Here͹ pillow, here

  3.   S.P. Omnes.͹ Men. Om.

  3.   words.͹ words,

  6.   sits:͹ sits,

  7.   Generall). Up͹ Generall)⌃ up

        tents.͹ tents⌃

 12.   Pikes. Their͹ Pikes, their

 13.   middles:͹ middles,

        feight.͹ feight,

 14.   hands:͹ hands,

 16.   himself. Be͹ himself, be

        slaves;/ slaves,

17.1-17.2. S.D. within . . . Wallace!"͹ Within. A Wallace,

        A Wallace, A Wallace! (Q prints without

        spacing directly beneath line 17).

17.3.   S.D. Ruge-crosse,͹ Rugcrusse (c may be e in Q).

 18.   Rugcrosse . . . Army͹ Q lines: Rugcrosse . . .

        . . . this? / Of . . . Army

        Rugcrosse͹ (c may be e in Q).

26.1.   S.D. within . . . Wallace!"/ Within. A Wallace,

        A Wallace. (Q prints without spacing

        directly beneath line 26).

27.1.   S.D. Souldiers.͹ Souldiers,

28. march? The*y*] march? they

32. is'*t*] ist

best*.*] best∧

their marc*h*] Q (e *and* a *partially* *inked* *in* *most* *copies*).

33. Or . . . Stan*d*] Q *lines*: Or . . . Plaine / Stand

'em*?*] 'em.

38. ne're] Q (e *partially* *inked*, *perhaps* *damaged* *in* *all* *copies*).

44. back? Not I. Deat*h*] back? not I, death

part*;*] part,

45. here's] heres

46. falls*.*] falls∧

47. Funerals∧] Funerals,

48. Coronations*;*] Coronations,

wound∧] wound,

49. crown'd*.*] crown'd,

50-53. Where . . . Rear*e*] Q *lines*: Where . . . you? / In . . . *Grimsby*. / Is . . . infantry / By . . . you / Shall . . . Reare

50. battaile*.*] battaile,

51. Horse*;*] Horse,

52. *Comming*] comming

commanded*;*] commanded,

54-55. The Reare . . . choos*e*] Q *lines*: The Reare. / Yes. / No, sir. / Let . . . not. / He . . .

357

choose

Mentith;7 Mentith,

60. him. Let7 him, let

62. indignation.7 indignation,

64. lag.7 lag,

66-67. Then . . . dishonour'd7 Q lines: Then . . . plac'd,
/ And . . . So, dishonour'd

66. none. You7 none, you
all;7 all,

68. sake:7 sake,

70. Well,7 Well
Reare. See7 Reare, see
hill?7 hill,

71. I'le7 i'le
Butchers,_7 Butchers,

73. Till . . . On7 Q lines: Till . . . selve. / Your
. . . on
pleasure. On!7 pleasure, on

IV.ii

0.1. S.D. King7 King

0.2. S.D. Sir7 Sir

3. King.7 King,

6. sir:7 sir,

8. him? Hand7 him? hand

358

9. dogs;⟧ dogs,

12. did;⟧ did,

    fell'd⟧ felld

14. borne. My⟧ borne, my

18. Sir⟧ sir

21. Sir⟧ sir

26. money.⟧ money,

28. charge!⟧ charge.

30-34. The daring . . . 'um⟧ Q lines: The daring . . .
           strength / Stand . . . battell. / Throw . . .
           Heralds / Northumberland . . . 'um

33. Northumberland⟧ Northumberland

    thine.⟧ thine,

35. steele;⟧ steele,

37. has⟧ ha's

38. breasts;⟧ breasts,

    Upon . . . shall⟧ Q lines: Upon . . . this. / I
           shall

39-40. Where's . . . too⟧ Q lines: Where's . . . Bruce? /
           Here. / I . . . too

40. 'tis⟧ ʌtis

    too;⟧ too,

41-43. The Herald . . . reare⟧ Q lines: The Herald . . .
           his / Spite . . . great / As . . . reare

41. ye;⟧ he,

45. sir;⟧ sir,

46. to stand . . . gallows.] Q prints as one line of
       verse.

47. kept:] kept,

49. i_f_] If
       kept_∧_] kept,

50. 100_∧_ pounds. Wip_e_] 100. li. wipe

52-53. That . . . to day] Q prints as prose.

52. lives. Let] lives, let

62-64. What's . . . Coward] Q lines: Whats . . . off? /
          Sure . . . brand, / Kindles . . . Wallace? /
          What . . . Coward

63. brand_∧_] brand,

64. Wallace.] Wallace?
       What? Turn'_d_] What turn'd

68-69. To . . . brav_e_] Q lines: To . . . him / Charge
          . . . brave

68. strong!] strong,

                    IV.iii

0.1. S.D. Generall,] Generall

0.3. S.D. A cry . . . flie!] A cry within. They flye,
          they flie. (Q prints this stage direction
          lined up without spacing as part of the verse.)

1-2. The English . . . offe_r_] Q lines: The English . . .
          nerves / And fasten . . . offer

                    360

1. shrink!] shrink,

3. footing:] footing,
   stir.] stir,

4-5. Stirr . . . backe] Q lines: Stirre . . . tempest. /
   I . . . on. / And I. / So . . . (begins a
   section of prose).

5-7. So . . . strong] Q prints as prose.

5. I.. This] I, this

6. dust_] dust,

10-11. For . . . last] Q lines: For . . . farre? / We
   . . . fight / So . . . last

16-17. And now . . . wound] Q lines: And now . . . lyme-
   twigs? / Keepe . . . ground. / If . . .
   bravely. / Wound . . . wound

17.1. S.D. King] King

18-21. Take . . . toyle] Q prints as prose.

18. breath. I] breath, I

19. spirits. Poast] spirits, poast

21. toyle:] toyle,

23.2. S.D. A cry . . . Charge!"] Q prints the single
   word Charge near left margin.

24. For . . . Countrey] Q lines: For . . . thy /
   Countrey

25. Whose . . . rescue] Q lines: Whose . . . day? /
   Tis . . . rescue
   'Tis] _Tis
   Edwards. Come] Edwards, come

26. Our . . . Who?7 Q lines: Our . . . Grimsby. / Who?

27. enclos'd7 enclosd

28. steele. Come7 steele, come

29. Or . . . lost7 Q lines: Or . . . lost. / Is . . .
      lost? / Lost, lost

31-32. 'Tis . . . againe7 Q lines: Tis . . . lost. / Why
      . . . lost? / Yes. / Then . . . againe

31. 'Tis7 ∧Tis
      amaine.7 amaine,

32. 'tis7 ∧tis

33. How . . . traytor7 Q lines: How now? / The King. . .traytor

34. That . . . day7 Q lines: That . . . kill. / Charge . . . day
      them! Blacke7 them∧ blacke

35.2. English∧7 English,

37-39. Why . . . thee7 Q lines: Why . . . farewell, /
      I'le . . . thee, / Bruce . . . thee, / Dares thee

37. farewell;7 farewell,

38. thee.7 thee,
      here.7 here,

39. thee--7 thee.

40. lure!7 lure,

41. thine;7 thine,

45. Ye . . . traytor7 Q lines: Ye . . . full. / I . . . traytor
      full;7 full,

47. You . . . King7 Q lines: You . . . not. / Tell . . . King
      so.7 so∧

49. lives. Bruce7 lives, Bruce
      362

Soveraigne:] Soveraigne,

50. borne.] borne,

54. foe:] foe,

58. note∧] note,

    scorne∧] scorne,

59. The English . . . try] Q lines: The English . . .
        merit. / This . . . try

62. Thou . . . hand] Q lines: Thou . . . me? / Here's . . . hand

63. Innocence. Had] innocence, had

64. thee:] thee,

66. The time . . . untie] Q lines: The time. / Some
        . . . hence. / There . . . untie

IV.iv

 1. We . . . hunting] Q lines: We . . . day. / Twas . . . hunting
    'Twas] ∧Twas

1.1. S.D. King] king

2-3. Sit . . . this] Q lines: Sit . . . wine / Away
        . . . this

 2. wine.] wine∧
    fellows!] fellows,

 4. 'tis] ∧tis

 5. Away! Why] Away, why

 8. heele. Th'art] heele, th'art

9-10. My . . . come] Q lines: My . . . England. / Let
        . . . come

9.   companion._7 companion,

12-13. No . . . lye_7 Q prints as verse: No . . . so, /
          As . . . lye

12.   so._7 so,

17.   I'th'_7 I'th‸

23.   Two_7 Q (T partially uninked or broken letter).
     heads._7 heads‸

24-25. head. It_7 head, it

30.   has_7 ha's
     pin'd_7 pind

32-33. Sirra . . . dead_7 Q prints as prose.

35.   I'le_7 i'le

37.   How . . . Bravely_7 Q lines: How . . . English? /
        Bravely

39.   throwes._7 throwes

41.   shipwrack, sweet‸_7 shipwrack‸ sweet,
     taste._7 taste,

42.   heart:_7 heart,

43.   as much_7 asmuch

46.   command‸_7 command,

48.   say._7 say,

51.   thee:_7 thee,

52.   not. So_7 not, so

57.   would. No_7 would, no

58-60. Percy . . . give_7 Q lines: Percy . . . buy / That
     . . . money. / I . . . give

62. arme--] arme,

63-64. But . . . straw] Q prints as single line.

64. I'th'] i'th_∧

   hand. Not] hand, not

66. passe.] passe,

68-71. I saw . . . Gules] Q lines: I saw . . . day, / I
   did . . . sword / Like . . . Scots. / Here
   comes. / Brave Gules

68. day.] day,

71. Gules.] Gules,

72-73. Where . . . length?] Q lines: Where . . . Bruce? /
   Following . . . held / Three . . . length

74-76. Give . . . come] Q lines: Give . . . thirsty? /
   Yes . . . have / Enough . . . health. / Let
   come

74. wine. Art] wine, art

75. on't.] on't,

80. What's . . . jest] Q lines: What's . . . at? /
   Nothing . . . jest

81-83. Nay . . . words] Q lines: Nay . . . me. / An . . .
   Bruce. / No . . . much. / Wallace . . .
   parlee. / How . . . words

81. jest:] jest,

82. much.] much,

83. How,] How_∧

84. prater:] prater,

swords.] swords,

85. Your . . . no] Q lines: Your . . . me? / Sir, no

86. <u>Bruce</u> . . . si<u>r</u>] Q lines: <u>Bruce</u> . . . quarrell, /
        I . . . sir

    quarrell.] quarrell,

    ha'] ha_ʌ

87. Peace . . . sur<u>e</u>] Q lines: Peace . . . that? /
       From . . . sure

    Peace. Wha<u>t</u>] Peace, what

88.1. S.D. Ruge-cross<u>e</u>] Rugecrosse

89. I . . . hi<u>m</u>] Q lines: I . . . <u>Wallace</u>. / So . . . him

90. speaks:] speaks,

91-94. He . . . decid<u>e</u>] Q lines: He . . . sunne, / Army
       . . . challenges, / Or . . . decide

91. battaile.] battaile,

93. challenges:] challenges,

94. fifty_ʌ] fifty,

95. Or . . . traito<u>r</u>] Q lines: Or . . . one. / A
       Herald . . . traitor

96. speak:] speak,

    steele_ʌ] steele,

98. vassall. Bid] vassall, bid

100-104. His . . . Arm<u>e</u>] Q lines: His . . . head, / To
       . . . minutes, / Wee'le . . . ruine, / Go
       . . . Arme

100. ruine. Charg<u>e</u>] ruine, charge

103. ruine.⫧ ruine,

gon.⫧ gon,

104. Arme!⫧ Arme.

105. Arme, Arme!⫧ Arme, Arme.

1. Noble,⁊ noble∧

3. A book . . . cannot⁊ Q lines: A book . . .
   graveld. / Perhaps . . . cannot
   gravel'd⁊ graveld

4. Yes . . . dares⁊ Q lines: Yes . . . can. / Dare
   . . . dares

8-11. I care . . . bloud⁊ Q lines: I care . . . in / My
   . . . lip. / Behold . . . Scot, / Drinks . . .
   bloud

9. enemy. The⁊ enemy, the

10. lip,⁊ lip.
   one,⁊ one∧

11. Scot∧⁊ Scot,

12-13. Yon . . . me⁊ Q lines: You . . . Scot? / Best
   . . . Oracle. / Who . . . me

14.1. S.D. Clifford,⁊ Cli∧

15. here. Oh⁊ here, oh

16. now:⁊ now,

17. English∧ witchcraft. Drinks⁊ English, witchcraft∧
   bloud!⁊ bloud,

18. curse:⁊ curse,

19. bowles. Oh⁊ bowles, oh

20. goad∧⁊ goad,

24-26. My . . . so⁊ Q lines: My Generall / Charg'd . . .

these. / Thanks . . . say? / Nothing . . . so

25. <u>Clifford;</u>⌉ <u>Clifford</u>,

27. ner<u>e</u>⌉ Q (e <u>blotted</u> <u>in</u> <u>most</u> <u>copies</u>).
    runaway!⌉ runaway,

28. pence! O<u>h</u>⌉ pence, oh
    Judas_∧⌉ Judas,

31. die<u>;</u>⌉ die,

32. pence. Sterling⌉ pence, sterling

33. Scotland. Spur<u>s</u>⌉ Scotland, spurs
    flight--⌉ flight,

34. I'l<u>e</u>⌉ i'le

V.ii

0.1-0.2. S.D. English . . . Ruge-cross<u>e</u>⌉ <u>English</u> <u>Herald</u>,
    and <u>Rouge-crosse</u>

2. Generall<u>.</u>⌉ Generall,

4. so<u>;</u>⌉ so,

5. Let . . . agree<u>d</u>⌉ Q <u>lines</u>: Let . . . pleasure. /
    Come agreed

    Come<u>;</u>⌉ Come

7-13. At . . . no<u>t</u>⌉ Q <u>lines</u>: At . . . Gauntlet. /
    Gauntlet . . . <u>English</u> / Fight . . . swaggerers,
    / A fray . . . so, / The man . . . cut, / Is
    . . . Nation, / Thei'le . . . not

7. Gauntlet? No<u>,</u>⌉ Gauntlet, no_∧

369

8. together;] together,

11. cut‸_] cut,
    brother.] brother,

12. they'le] Thei'le

13. Spaniels. Will] Spaniels, will

14. And that's . . . commonly] Q lines: And that's
    . . . not. / Commonly . . . are
    is't] ist

15-21. When . . . gilded] Q prints as prose.

15. too] (t blotted in Q).

18. has] ha's
    ever.] ever,

21. Smoothly . . . sir] Q lines: smoothly gilded. /
    He . . . sir

22-23. I . . . friend] Q prints as prose.

25. gallants. He] gallants, he

27. His . . . already] Q lines: His . . . Minion. /
    Hee . . . 'tis

27-31. Hee . . . head] Q prints as prose.

31. so] Q (s partially uninked in all copies).

32.1. S.D. Ruge-crosse] Ruge‸

37-41. Ten . . . massie] Q lines: Ten . . . Crowns. / I
    . . . too, / Some . . . friends, / Should . . .
    not, / I . . . oreaway / Your . . . massie

38. so. Here] so, here

39. friends:] friends,

conference$_\wedge$_7 conference,

40. not:_7 not,

42. Mentith;_7 Mentith,

45-46. My . . . comes_7 Q lines: My hand. / They . . .
dead. / No . . . comes

45. ours:_7 ours,

46.1. S.D. Grimsby, Herald_7 Grimsbie, Herald

47. tyrant:_7 tyrant,

49. tree._7 tree,

53. gold._7 gold:

55. bonnets. We'le_7 bonnets, we'le

56. Souldiers:_7 Souldiers,

57. slaves._7 slaves,

59. You'le . . . defiance_7 Q lines: Youle . . . mad. /
A brave defiance

60. Defiance!_7 Defiance,

61. more. They_7 more, they
night._7 night,

62. drum. Let_7 drum, let

63. Army_7 Q (A missing in many copies).

64. dislodg'd:_7 dislodg'd,

65. body_7 Q (y partially uninked in most copies).
body. Some_7 body, some

67. Drum! Call_7 Drum, call

67.1. S.D. Grimsby_7 Grimsbie

68. Sir_7 sir

Ice‸] Ice,

71. S.P. Coming. / Mentith. }] Ment. Com.

75. all. I'm] all, I'm

77-78. How . . . seal'd] Q lines: How . . . him? / As . . . any. / Our . . . seal'd

77. am;] am,

alone.] alone,

80. No . . . foot] Q lines: No . . . ride. / Wee'le . . . foot

81. face‸] face,

82. Longshancks] Longshancks

84-87. What . . . there] Q lines: What . . . sure. / Oh . . . him. / For . . . hand, / I . . . there

84. face? He'le] face? he'le

86. part‸] part,

88. For . . . come] Q lines: For . . . sweare. / Time . . . come

90. Hence. Hye] Hence, hye

wood.] wood,

92. S.P. Coming. / Mentith. }] Both.

92.2. Friar's] Fryers

93-94. Ha . . . terror] Q lines: He . . . speake, / I . . . terror

94. Speake.] speake,

96. What's . . . lang] Q lines: What's . . . thee? /
        Thouse . . . lang

    Thou'se] Thouse

97. bluide. By] bluide, by

98. mine;] mine,

99. Thou . . . bane] Q lines: Thou . . . spirit. /
        Bruce . . . bane

    bane;] bane,

100. againe.] againe,

103. Stay! If] Stay, if

104. am. Let] am, let

105. sound.] sound:

106. me! Th'art] me, th'art

108. me-- Stay-- Art] me--stay--art

    gone? No] gone? no

109-110. It . . . onely] Q prints as prose.

110. Cannot . . . Heaven] cannot--shall not, heaven

110.1. S.D. Old] old

111. death.] death,

114-115. Then . . . water] Q lines: Then . . . thee. /
        Part . . . water

115. spirit;] spirit,

    water!] water,

116. thee,] thee

    It's gone!] it's gone.

117. compleyne?] compleyne,

120. thee.] thee,

124. wife. What] wife, what

125.1. S.D. Grimsby] Grimsbie

127. Whom . . . nothing] Q lines: Whom . . . meete? /
No body. / Saw . . . nothing

128. Not . . . then] Q lines: Not . . . thing. / Twas
. . . then

'Twas] ∧Twas

then.] then,

131. dumbe. Oh] dumbe, oh

V.iii

0.1. S.D. Coming] Comyne

2. name∧] name,

6. Is . . . houre] Q lines: Is . . . come? / It
. . . houre

is] Q (s faintly inked).

7-8. Who . . . kill] Q lines: Who . . . you? / My
. . . horse. / Him . . . kill

8. kill.--] kill.

9. I'le . . . Do] Q lines: I'le . . . yet-- / Do.

9.1. S.D. Exit] (follows "yet--" /line 9/ in Q).

11. o're.] o're,

12.1. S.D. A cry . . . murder!"] A cry, helpe, murder
within.

13. arm'd! Bruce] arm'd, Bruce

374

13. thee.7 thee,

16. S.P. $\left.\begin{array}{l}\underline{Coming.}\\ \underline{Mentith.}\end{array}\right\}$ 7 <u>Both</u>.

   thou! Away7 thou, away

V.iv

5-6. Phew . . . am7 Q <u>lines</u>: Phew . . . thee, / Seale
   . . . seest / Nor . . . am

5. eyes:7 eyes,

8. countrey. Pardon7 countrey, pardon

11.1. Northumberland7 North∧

13. quicke,7 quicke∧

18. alone. I'le7 alone, I'le

20. gone? He7 gone? he

21. There's . . . whom7 Q <u>lines</u>: There's . . . you, /
   By whom

23. me? He7 me? he

24. True . . . none7 Q <u>lines</u>: True . . . one. / Is
   none

25-30. No . . . Butcher7 Q <u>lines</u>: No Subject? / None
   . . . spleene, / Will . . . command / Has . . .
   now? / Fresh . . . levied, / Which . . . leade.
   / 'Gainst . . . whom? / Gainst . . . <u>Scots</u>. /
   I will . . . Butcher

25. Subject7 Q (b <u>and</u> e <u>faintly</u> <u>inked</u>).

King.] King,

26. spleene_∧] spleene,

faces--] faces,

29. 'Gainst] ∧Gainst

Wallace,] Q (_comma faintly inked_).

30. not. I'_m_] not, I'm

Butcher:] Butcher,

31. 'Gainst . . . no_t_] Q _lines:_ ∧Gainst . . . fight.
/ How . . . not

32. No . . . no_t_] Q _lines:_ No . . . **Clifford**. / Peace.
My . . . not

not:] not,

34-35. That . . . blou_d_] Q _lines:_ That . . . strangers /
With . . . bloud

34. inward. _I_] inward, I

35. bloud.] bloud_∧ (_full stop faint in some copies_).

37. King.] King,

38. I'le] Q (_apostrophe uninked in most copies_).

42-45. Nor . . . wor_d_] Q _lines:_ Nor . . . discontents. /
It . . . but, / Spare . . . more, / You . . .
Clifford / Not . . . word

42. not.] not,

43. but--] but,

me.] me,

44. more.--] more,

me--] me,

45. Clifford--] Clifford
     word!] word,

46.1. S.D. within . . . Traytor!"] Within traytor,
       traytor. (Q prints without spacing directly
       beneath line 46).

46.3. S.D. King . . . Hereford] King, North, Herefor∧

 47. mutinie! What] mutinie, what
      noyse] Q (y faintly inked in many copies).

 49. off.] Q (full stop faintly inked).

 50. com'st] Q (apostrophe faintly inked in most copies).

 53. kingdome.] kingdome,

 57. sides∧] sides,

 60. this] Q (s faintly inked).
      monster∧] monster,

 61. lives. The] lives, the

 63. Camp.] Camp,

64-69. Force . . . Arch-traytor] Q lines: Force . . .
        Stagge / To . . . backe / The . . . life, /
        From . . . dead, / To . . . shame / Of . . .
        Arch-traytor

 64. policie. We] policie, we

 66. purpose./ purpose,

70-71. Mentith . . . devill] Q lines: Mentith . . . fame,
        / And . . . devill

 70. act.] act,

71.1. S.D. Exit Mentith] Exit Ment.

377

72. curse:7 curse,

74.1. S.D. Coming7 Comyn

75. Where . . . Soveraigne7 Q lines: Where . . . I? /
      Here . . . Bruce. / Bruce . . . Soveraigne

76. Glasco-moore.7 Glasco-moore,

81. world. I7 world, I

84. warning. This7 warning, this
      it ⌃7 it,

86-87. Blush . . . this?7 one line in Q.

86. Meteor. Can7 Meteor, can

89. Not . . . here7 Q lines: Not . . . acting? / Yes
      . . . mine. / Not here

90. Here . . . there7 Q lines: Here . . . Hell. / Why
      . . . there

91. there. In7 there, in

93. What's . . . whom7 Q lines: Whats that? / Your .
      . . . slain. / By whom
      slain.7 slain,

94. By . . . Edward7 Q lines: By Wallace. / Heare
      . . . Edward

95. Good . . . you'd7 Q lines: Good . . . him, /
      Clif. . . . vow'd
      him.7 him,
      Clifford,7 Clif.
      vow'd ⌃7 vow'd,
      him. Drag7 him, drag

378

hence!7 hence,

98-99. To . . . speak7 Q lines: To . . . quarter / him.
          / First . . . speak

98. him. Hang7 him: hang

99. speak.7 speak,

103. wound.7 wound,

104. him!7 him.

105. Farewell⌃7 Farewell,
     World.7 World,

106. ha!7 ha⌃

104. tyranny.7 tyranny,

111. one.7 one

113.1. S.D. Exeunt7 Exit

115. Arch-traitour.7 Arch-traitour,

116. Percy . . . hence7 Q lines: Percy . . . Bruce. /
       Me hence

117. sir:7 sir,
     sweare⌃7 sweare,

118. Huntingdon.7 Huntingdon,

119. away.7 Q (y missing in some copies).

120-121. What . . . may7 Q lines: What . . . meaning? /
       Your . . . dispatch'd. / You may

121. meaning. See7 meaning, see

121.1. S.D. Northumberland7 North

122. death⌃7 death,

123. work⌃7 work,

379

124. end,] end.

129. To . . . perceive] Q lines: To . . . Survivor. /
      Comin . . . perceive

131. due;] due,

133. meaning;] meaning,
      world_] world;

141. fealty;] fealty,

142.1. S.D. sweare. Bruce] sweare, Bruce
       S.D. Coming] Comin

144. eares. Die] eares, die
      slave] Q (a partly inked in many copies).

146-147. What . . . hand] Q lines: What . . . done? / A
         sacrifice . . . hand
      done] Q (one blurred).

147. honour] Q (r faint).
     revenge. No] revenge, no

148. head;] head,

150. act;] act,

151. justice.] justice;

154. treason;] treason,

156. light_] light,

157. it;] it,

158. branches;] branches,

159. whole. Peace] whole, peace

380

GLOSSORIAL INDEX TO THE COMMENTARY

bloud, I.i.90

bloud is sold, V.iv.76

bloudy, I.i.112

bolt, I.v.5

bosome, V.iv.38

bought, IV.iv.45

brake the jest, V.i.13

brave, IV.iv.1

braves, V.ii.58

braving, V.i.17

Breake forth, V.ii.91

brest, I.iv.104

bully <u>Joe</u>, II.iv.194

but, I.v.30

butchers, I.ii.35

butter, III.i.80

by head and shoulders, II.iv.
41-42

Cans, IV.i.11

Casheer'd, I.iv.61

Cast, I.i.116

Cave, III.ii.7

capring, V.ii.25

cease, II.i.62

Cedar, II.i.36

certifie, V.ii.2

Chaire of State, II.iii.97

Chaos, II.i.30

<u>Character</u>, Ded. letter, line 17

Charter, I.i.63

Checkt, II.iii.67

chinks, III.i.41

Christians, I.iv.56

City, IV.ii.36

clampers, II.iv.36

cleer'd, I.i.14

close, V.ii.90

close feight, IV.i.13

Close with advantage, II.i.61

cobs, III.i.66

cocke sure, III.i.35

cold words, I.ii.58

commends, II.iv.240

commendations, II.iv.252

comment, V.i.34

compleate, II.iv.228

conceit, I.iv.82

conjure, V.i.2

consent, II.iv.188

court it, II.iv.229

coxcombe, IV.ii.55

Crabs, III.i.80

crackt the Ice, V.ii.68

384

Make time, I.ii.82

man, IV.iv.43

manacles of griefe, I.v.20

manag'd, I.i.9

marry, II.i.66

Maske her, I.ii.1

master painter abuife, I.ii.9

mawegut, II.iv.97

may-game, I.ii.13

measled, I.ii.31

mercies wing, V.iv.9

Minion, V.ii.27

Mittimus, III.i.116

monumentall, V.iv.83

motives, V.iv.101

moulded, II.i.28

muffled, V.iv.0.1

naked, I.i.77

native, I.iv.48

needs, I.i.13

nightcap, III.i.21

Nothing but so, V.i.26

Nuntio, I.v.27

oath of fealty, V.iv.137

Of force, II.iii.40

offer, II.iv.59

office, III.ii.3

old Palace, III.i.351

one, I.ii.94

one engine, V.iv.123

our bosome, I.iv.75

out at Elbows, II.iv.95

out at heeles, II.iv.91

out worn souldier, I.iv.40

Over head and eares, III.i.142

owe, V.iv.46

Oysters, III.i.87

Palme and Olive branches, V.iv.158

paring, III.i.293

parly, IV.iii.44

parrapet, II.iv.104

part of, III.i.277

passing, III.i.81

peece, II.iv.96; II.iv.204

perriwinckles, III.i.76

Pettifoggers, III.i.93

Phew, V.iv.5

Philomell, III.ii.10

pin'd the foole, IV.iv.30

place, I.i.42; IV.ii.16

Play not the Tyrant, II.iii.11

playeand at bo-peep, II.iv.140-141

Plum-porridge, III.i.156

points, III.i.7

pole, I.i.57

policy, I.i.23

post, III.i.347

poverty of Gentry, II.iv.207

powers, II.iii.173

practis'd, I.v.17

prater, IV.iv.84

pregnant, I.i.26

present charge, II.iii.174

present execution, II.iv.202

prest, II.iv.69

Prethee, I.v.1

pricksong, III.i.100

principall, I.ii.90

project for bloud, I.iv.10

purple spots, V.iv.10

put backe, V.iv.66

que voula, II.iv.65

quick lightning, I.ii.61

quicke, III.i.274

quick-sets, IV.iii.28

quittant with owe none, I.iv.65

rais'd the storme, II.iii.90

raise the Country, III.i.177

rampant Lion, IV.iv.71

rampier, II.ii.26

rank, II.iv.3

rate, IV.ii.23

Ravens, III.i.225

reck, I.iii.11

Recognizance, III.i.334

recollect, V.ii.64

red, III.i.41

reckand, I.ii.23

reeking, II.iii.95

reele to hell, III.i.254

refayne, V.ii.118

remembrances, II.iii.101

resolves, II.i.21

right, V.iv.52

right of Armes, II.iii.142

Robin-redbrest, III.ii.13

roll of men, II.iv.151

rope, III.i.175.2

rough winds, I.ii.59

rouse, II.iv.234

rowz'd, IV.i.61

Ruge-crosse, IV.i.17.3

Ruine, I.iv.80; II.iii.107

ruines, II.iii.90

Saint <u>Thomas</u> onyons, III.i. 31-32

salt eyes, III.i.33

satisfaction, I.i.68

sawle, II.iv.166

scandall, II.iv.207

scantling, I.ii.84

Scholership of war, IV.i.10

score, III.i.342

Scotch Jigge, I.iv.55

Screech-owles, III.i.225

scull, II.iv.87

'Sdeath, II.iv.183

sea of purple teares, II.iii. 23

sea time, IV.i.73

sen, II.iv.134

Senu, I.ii.17

Serpent breath, V.iv.143

Service, I.i.63

set upon, III.i.324-325

shamoys, I.iv.10

sharer, III.i.281

sheep-biter, IV.ii.4

sheets, III.i.205

Shift, II.ii.28

schoola-groate, II.iv.5

shrimps, III.i.75

Sier, II.i.72

sifting, II.iv.111

silly, I.i.58

single, IV.iii.41

Singly, I.v.34

slop, II.iv.90

slow the minutes, IV.iv.102

smelt out, III.i.109

soft mercy, I.iv.98

sound, V.ii.105; V.iii.16.2

Southern, I.ii.43

spend, IV.i.74

spheare, I.i.3

spheares, II.iii.40

spirit, IV.ii.42

spirits, IV.ii.58

spit defiance, II.i.18

spleene, I.i.9; II.iii.81

Stand, II.iv.65; II.iv.237

stand the braves, IV.iv.97

standing cups, V.ii.53

stars, I.iv.42

state, I.i.95

states, I.iv.96

stay, II.iii.40

Sterling, V.i.32

BIBLIOGRAPHY

Abbott, E. A. <u>A Shakespearian Grammar</u>. 3rd ed., 1870;
    rprt. New York: Dover, 1966.

Apperson, G. L. <u>English Proverbs and Proverbial Phrases</u>.
    London & Toronto: J. M. Dent, 1929.

Beaumont, Francis and John Fletcher. <u>The Dramatic Works in
    the Beaumont and Fletcher Canon</u>. Gen. ed. Fredson
    Bowers. 2 vols. Cambridge: Cambridge Univ. Press,
    1966-1970.
    This critical edition is used for those plays edited
    in these first two volumes. Plays not contained herein
    are consulted in the Waller and Glover edition and so
    indicated in the footnotes.

_____. <u>The Works of Francis Beaumont and John Fletcher</u>.
    Ed. A. R. Waller and A. Glover. 10 vols. Cambridge:
    Cambridge Univ. Press, 1905-1912.

Bentley, Gerald E. <u>The Jacobean and Caroline Stage</u>. 7
    vols. Oxford: Clarendon Press, 1941-1968.

Carver, John Linton. "<u>The Valiant Scot</u>, by J. W." <u>Studies
    in English Drama</u>, 1st series. Ed. Allison Gaw. Univ.
    of Pennsylvania Series in Philology and Literature,
    14. Philadelphia: Univ. of Pennsylvania, 1917, 75-
    104.

Cotgrave, John. <u>English Treasury of Wit and Language</u>.
    London: Humphrey Mosely, 1655.

Dent, Robert W. <u>John Webster's Borrowing</u>. Berkeley:
    Univ. of California Press, 1960.

<u>The English and Scottish Popular Ballads</u>. Ed. Francis
    James Child. 5 vols. 1883-1884; New York: The
    Folklore Press, 1956.

<u>The English Dialect Dictionary</u>. Ed. Joseph Wright. 6 vols.
    London: Henry Frowde, 1898-1905.

<u>Fergusson's Scottish Proverbs</u>. Ed. Erskine Beveridge.
    Scottish Text Society, New Series, 15. Edinburgh and
    London: William Blackwood and Sons, 1924.

Ford, John. The Broken Heart. Ed. Donald K. Anderson, Jr. Regents Renaissance Drama Series. Lincoln: Univ. of Nebraska Press, 1968.

_____. Perkin Warbeck. Ed. Donald K. Anderson, Jr. Regents Renaissance Drama Series. Lincoln: Univ. of Nebraska Press, 1965.

Gardiner, Samuel R. History of England from the Accession of James I to the Outbreak of the Civil War 1603-1642. 10 vols. London: Longmans, Green and Co., 1886.

Greg, W. W. A Bibliography of the English Printed Drama to the Restoration. 4 vols. Illustrated Monographs of The Bibliographical Society, 24. London: The Bibliographical Society, 1939-1959.

Hary's Wallace: (Nobilissimi Defensoris Scotie Wilelmi Wallace Militis). Ed. Matthew B. McDiarmid. 2 vols. Scottish Text Society Publications. 4th ser., 4 and 5. Edinburgh and London: William Blackwood, 1968 and 1969.

Heywood, Thomas. The Dramatic Works of Thomas Heywood. Ed. John Pearson. 6 vols. 1874: rpt. New York: Russell & Russell, 1964.

Holinshed, Raphael. The Chronicles of England, Scotlande, and Irelande. 2 vols. London: George Bishop, 1577.

The Holy Bible: Authorized King James Version. New York: Hawthorn Books, 1956.

Howarth, R. G. "The Valiant Scot as a Play by John Webster," Bulletin of the English Association, South African Branch, 9 (1965), 3-8.

Hoy, Cyrus. "The Shares of Fletcher and his Collaborators in the Beaumont and Fletcher Canon," Studies in Bibliography, 7 (1956), 129-146; 9 (1957), 143-162; 11 (1958) 85-107; 12 (1959), 91-116; 13 (1960), 77-108; 14 (1961) 45-67; 15 (1962), 71-90.

Huch, Friedrich. Ueber das Drama The Valiant Scot. Hamburg: M. Lekmann, 1901.

Jonson, Ben. Ben Jonson. Ed. C. H. Herford and Percy Simpson. 11 vols. 1925-52; rpt. Oxford: The Clarendon Press, 1965.

Marlowe, Christopher. Edward II. Ed. H. B. Charlton and
R. D. Waller. In The Life and Works of Christopher
Marlowe, gen. ed. R. H. Case. London: Methuen, 1933.

_____. The Jew of Malta. Ed. R. W. Van Fossen. Regents
Renaissance Drama Series. Lincoln: Univ. of Nebraska
Press, 1964.

Marston, John. Antonio and Mellida, Part I. Ed. G. K.
Hunter. Regents Renaissance Drama Series. Lincoln:
Univ. of Nebraska Press, 1965.

_____. The Plays of John Marston. Ed. H. Harvey Wood.
3 vols. Edinburgh and London: Oliver and Row, 1938.

Massinger, Philip. The City-Madam. Ed. T. W. Craik. The
New Mermaid Series. London: Ernest Benn, 1964.

_____. The Maid of Honour. Ed. Eva A. W. Byrne.
London: Byrn Mawr College, 1927.

_____. A New Way to Pay Old Debts. Ed. T. W. Craik.
The New Mermaid Series. London: Ernest Benn, 1964.

_____ and John Ford. The Dramatic Works of Massinger
and Ford. Intro. by Hartley Coleridge. London:
Edward Moxon, 1851.
The text of Massinger's plays followed in this edition
is the standard edition edited by W. Gifford in 1805.
This edition is used for those plays not available in
modern versions.

McKerrow, Ronald B. An Introduction to Bibliography for
Literary Students. 1927; rpt. Oxford: The Clarendon
Press, 1960.

Middleton, Thomas and William Rowley. The Changeling. Ed.
N. W. Bawcutt. The Revels Plays. London: Methuen,
1958.

The Oxford English Dictionary. Ed. Sir James A. H. Murray
et al. 13 vols. Oxford: The Clarendon Press, 1933.

Partridge, Eric. Shakespeare's Bawdy. 2nd ed., 1955; rpt.
London: Routledge & Kegan Paul, 1956.

Plomer, Henry R. A Dictionary of the Booksellers and
Printers Who Were at Work in England, Scotland and
Ireland from 1641 to 1667. London: The Bibliographical
Society, 1907.

Prosser, Eleanor. _Hamlet and Revenge_. Stanford: Stanford Univ. Press, 1967.

Ribner, Irving. _The English History Play in the Age of Shakespeare_. 1957; London: Methuen, 1965.

Rowley, William. _All's Lost by Lust_. With Thomas Middleton, _The Spanish Gypsy_. Ed. Edgar C. Morris. Belles-lettres Series. Boston and London: D. C. Heath, 1908.

_____. _The Birth of Merlin_. In _Pseudo-Shakespearian Plays_. Ed. Karl Warnke and Ludwig Proescholt. Halle: Max Niemeyer, 1887.

_____. _A Merrie and Pleasant Comedy, Called A Shoo-Maker a Gentleman_. London: J. Okes, 1637.

Shakespeare, William. _The Complete Works of Shakespeare_. Ed. G. B. Harrison. New York: Harcourt, Brace, and Co., 1952.

Schoenbaum, Samuel. _Internal Evidence and Elizabethan Dramatic Authorship_. Evanston: Northwestern Univ. Press, 1966.

Schmidt, Alexander. _A Shakespeare-Lexicon_. 2 vols. 3rd ed. 1901; rpt. New York: Benjamin Blom, 1968.

Spenser, Edmund. _The Works of Edmund Spenser: A Variorum Edition_. Ed. Edwin Greenlaw et al. 10 vols. 1932-1949; Baltimore: John Hopkins Press, 1958.

The Telltale. Ed. R. A. Foakes and J. C. Gibson. The Malone Society Reprints 1959. Oxford: The Malone Society, 1960.

Tilley, Morris P. _A Dictionary of the Proverbs in England in the Sixteenth and Seventeenth Centuries: A Collection of the Proverbs Found in English Literature and the Dictionaries of the Period_. Ann Arbor: Univ. of Michigan Press, 1950.

Tourneur, Cyril. _The Atheist's Tragedy_. Ed. Irving Ribner. The Revels Plays. Cambridge, Mass.: Harvard Univ. Press, 1966.

_____. _The Revenger's Tragedy_. Ed. R. A. Foakes. The Revels Plays. Cambridge, Mass.: Harvard Univ. Press, 1964.

Webster, John. The Complete Works of John Webster. Ed. F.
     L. Lucas. 4 vols. 1927; rpt. New York: Gordian
     Press, 1966.
     This edition is used for all Webster's works except
     for The White Devil and The Duchess of Malfi, which
     are consulted in the Revels Plays editions.

_____. The Duchess of Malfi. Ed. John Russell Brown.
     The Revels Plays. Cambridge, Mass.: Harvard Univ.
     Press, 1964.

_____. The White Devil. Ed. John Russell Brown. The
     Revels Plays. Cambridge, Mass.: Harvard Univ. Press,
     1960.